FACE TO FACE
WITH ANIMALS

I0125821

FACE TO FACE WITH ANIMALS

Levinas and the Animal Question

Edited by

PETER ATTERTON

and

TAMRA WRIGHT

SUNY PRESS

Published by State University of New York Press, Albany

© 2019 State University of New York

All rights reserved

No part of this book may be used or reproduced in any manner whatsoever
without written permission. No part of this book may be stored in a retrieval
system or transmitted in any form or by any means including electronic,
electrostatic, magnetic tape, mechanical, photocopying, recording, or otherwise
without the prior permission in writing of the publisher.

For information, contact State University of New York Press, Albany, NY
www.sunypress.edu

Library of Congress Cataloging-in-Publication Data

Names: Atterton, Peter, editor. | Wright, Tamra, editor.
Title: Face to face with animals : Levinas and the animal question / edited
    by Peter Atterton and Tamra Wright, State University of New York.
Description: Albany : State University of New York Press, [2019] | Includes
    bibliographical references and index.
Identifiers: LCCN 2018027993 | ISBN 9781438474090 (hardcover : alk. paper) |
    ISBN 9781438474083 (pbk. : alk. paper) | ISBN 9781438474106 (ebook)
Subjects: LCSH: Animal welfare. | Animal rights. | Lévinas, Emmanuel.
Classification: LCC HV4701 .F34 2019 | DDC 179/.3—dc23
LC record available at https://lccn.loc.gov/2018027993

10 9 8 7 6 5 4 3 2 1

For John Llewelyn,
who asked about Bobby

Contents

Part III: Responsibility toward Animals

Part IV: Traditions: Greek/Hebrew/Asian

Acknowledgments

We are grateful to everyone who made the original 1986 interview with Emmanuel Levinas and its subsequent publication possible: Andrew Benjamin, who first proposed the idea; David Wood and Robert Bernasconi, who published it under the title "The Paradox of Morality: An Interview with Emmanuel Levinas" in their collection *The Provocation of Levinas: Rethinking the Other* (Routledge, 1988); the Association of Commonwealth Universities, who provided a travel grant for Tamra; and, of course, Emmanuel Levinas himself, who was gracious and welcoming, both in correspondence before and after the interview, and in the way he responded to the interviewers' questions.

More recently, Stewart Brookes's help with digitizing the audio recording was invaluable; Sophia Efstathiou made several important contributions to the new translation of "The Animal Interview"; Matthew Calarco helped with the Introduction; Norm Guthartz did an excellent job of proofreading an early draft of the manuscript of this book; and Agnes Erdos did an admirable, painstaking job preparing the index.

We are grateful to the London School of Jewish Studies, the College of Arts and Letters at San Diego State University, and an anonymous donor for help with some of the costs related to preparing this volume for publication.

The team at SUNY Press has been a pleasure to work with.

Peter Atterton,
San Diego, California

Tamra Wright,
London, England

September 2018

Editors' Introduction

Extending the Boundaries of "The Ethical"

> I also think that quite clearly, even if it is not as simple as that, even if animals are not considered as human beings, the ethical extends to living beings. I really think so.
>
> —Emmanuel Levinas, "The Animal Interview"

Since the topic of Levinas and animals has by now received rather a lot of attention, the reader may be wondering why we felt compelled to compile this volume of essays. The short answer is that though Levinas's neglect of animals in his philosophical work has already been subject to repeated criticism,[1] the majority of commentators and critics still write as though Levinas's "profound anthropocentrism and humanism"[2] rather than a serious flaw in need of remedy, were entirely justified. Most take it for granted that it is not possible for the Other to be anything other than human. Only posterity knows whether this will ever change, though it looks unlikely that it will. This is not due to any deficiencies in the arguments for including animals within the scope of Levinas's ethics. It is probably because the force behind the conviction that humans are the center of the moral universe is more affective than philosophical, and wells from the same source as what Freud called "the universal narcissism of men." But even if a single collection of essays like this one is unlikely to make much of a difference here, it behooves us as academics to keep reminding ourselves that the animal question is a live one and as long as an ethics like Levinas's does not take the question into account, then so much the worse for it philosophically.

In order to contextualize Levinas's approach to animal ethics, we present below a brief synopsis of approaches to animal ethics in Western philosophy. However, before turning to that discussion, we begin with an introduction to a new digitized transcription and English translation of the most relevant text in Levinas's corpus: "The Animal Interview" (see chapter 1).

The Animal Interview:
New Digitized Transcription and English Translation

In the summer of 1986, three MA students at the University of Warwick, in the UK, traveled to Paris to interview Levinas at his home at rue Michel-Ange in the sixteenth arrondissement. Alison Ainley, Peter Hughes, and Tamra Wright were members of a graduate reading group that had been meeting on a regular basis throughout the academic year, focusing on *Totality and Infinity*. The interview had originally been planned as an informal discussion, but at the suggestion of David Wood, who was at the time in the process of editing, with Robert Bernasconi, *The Provocation of Levinas*, the students decided to record and transcribe the interview, with the hope of its appearance in that volume of essays. The team collected questions from members of the *Totality and Infinity* reading group, and from other faculty and students in the Department of Philosophy at Warwick.

Much to the surprise of everyone involved in the project at the time, the interview, which was published by Routledge under the title "The Paradox of Morality: An Interview with Emmanuel Levinas" (*PM*), attracted a wide readership and has become an important resource for researchers; indeed, it has recently been cited by one scholar as Levinas's "famous interview with students at the University of Warwick in 1986."[3] Much of the interest in the article can be attributed to the fact that it is one of the very few places where Levinas discusses responsibility for nonhuman animals at some length.

Given the scholarly interest in this interview, particularly the animal sections, *and the fact that it was only ever published in translation*, we decided that the time is ripe for a full transcription and new translation of those parts of the interview that relate to animals. In the process of retranscribing and translating this material, we have discovered various errors in the original version. The original recording was made without the benefit of any specialist equipment (the interview was recorded on a household cassette recorder!), making transcription itself challenging, and this was further complicated by Levinas's habit of jumping from one question to another in his responses, and occasionally leaving sentences unfinished. Additionally, unaware that scholars would eventually want to weigh every nuance of Levinas's answers to the questions about animal ethics, the translators, Andrew Benjamin and Tamra Wright, opted for avoiding a full, literal translation of those sections of the interview, and attempted instead to convey Levinas's thoughts in a more coherent and accessible way.

The cassette recording was encoded as an MP3 and digitally remastered by Dr. Stewart Brookes, a medieval scholar and specialist in digital humanities (as well as a committed vegetarian) at King's College London, using Audacity open-source software. Unfortunately, even after the application of multiple filters to remove background noise, there remained a few moments in the interview when it was not possible to make out what was being said. This may be due to degradation of the original cassette tape, but it could also be because of the low quality of the original recording equipment, and the fact that Levinas from time to time spoke very softly or turned his head too far away from the microphone. Nevertheless, we ended up overall with a very accurate and scholar-friendly transcript to work from in producing the translation that is included in this volume, and has been referred to by the contributors.

Interviews are a good way to try to make philosophical ideas available to a more general audience, though inevitably they give rise to oversimplification.[4] Notwithstanding that the questions in the interview were translated into French and sent to Levinas in advance, it is probably safe to say Levinas relied on certain impromptu formulations rather than giving detailed elaboration and careful expression to what he wanted to say. Perhaps the most poignant illustration of this is the claim that is likely to leave some readers of Levinas scratching their heads: ". . . the ethical extends to living beings."

Levinas does not specify whether he is referring to the aggregate of "living beings" (*vivants*) or only a subset. If the former, then this would suggest that we have obligations not only to animals, but also to plants, fungi, bacteria, and perhaps even viruses! While there may indeed be Levinasian grounds for expanding the moral circle beyond sentient life to encompass the nonhuman world in general, laying the foundations for a robust environmental ethics,[5] judging from the context it seems more likely that Levinas meant to restrict the claim to animals that are sentient or capable of suffering. Thus, he is saying that we have obligations to animals that can suffer. This would explain his dismissal of the idea that a flea has what he calls a face (a remark that was omitted from the original interview), presumably because insects are not generally considered to be sentient.

One of the more infelicitous errors that crept into the original translation of the interview was the insertion of the adjective "all" in the above ("the ethical extends to all living beings" [*PM*, 172]). Several other key changes from the original version of the interview are as follows: "One cannot entirely refuse a dog the face" (in place of "One cannot entirely refuse the face of an animal" [*PM*, 169]); "What an insuperable line!" [*Quel trait noir!*] (not included in original version); "Not in the flea, for example. The flea! It's an insect, which jumps, eh?" [*laughter*] (not included in original version); "One always loves in the animal, the wolf, the memory of the wolf, the memory of the lion, the dog, I don't know.

In any case, there is there the possibility of a specific phenomenological analysis, which cannot be used when things are understood from the beginning. There are some forms of animal. . . . There are certainly, I don't know, vegetarians—those who [are in] the animal protection league; that exists. Clearly, one [approach to] ethics is the transference of the idea of suffering to an animal, certainly" (not included in original version); "Because there are people who will tell you, on the contrary, that it is in life that there is a certain sympathy regarding our life and that ethical morality is a development of a purely biological phenomenon—that's it" (not included in original version); "It is a widespread thesis saying ultimately the human is but the culmination of the animal" (in place of "The widespread thesis that ultimately the ethical is biological amounts to saying that, ultimately, the human is only the last stage of the evolution of the animal" [*PM*, 172]); "I am telling you that because to say that saintliness begins with animals implies that animals have already heard the word of God—which makes no difference to me. But, in any case, there is something other than pure Being that persists in being" (not included in original version).

While we believe the new transcription/translation more accurately repre-sents Levinas's views on animals than the one that was done thirty years ago, it nevertheless should be kept in mind that the complete translation of the *original* interview was sent to Levinas for his approval prior to publication, as had been agreed with him beforehand. At the very least we can say that the interview merits reading as a work of fresh philosophical importance, even today, for the views on animals expressed there are not to be found anywhere in Levinas's major works. It would be a gross mistake to consider Levinas's remarks on animals as mere *orbiter dicta*, or exotic remarks that can easily be ignored. The reason why the interview needs to be read is for the critical challenge it presents to Levinas's "humanism of the other man," especially when taken in conjunc-tion with Levinas's remarks about the unknowability and inscrutability of the Other. It certainly doesn't answer every question that a philosopher interested in the moral status of animals would want answered. Nor does it constitute anything like a complete (or even fully coherent) train of philosophical thought. However, the editors' suspicions are (1) that many of the views on animals expressed in the interview serve as an important counterweight to Levinas's almost exclusive focus on human beings in such works as *Totality and Infinity* and *Otherwise Than Being*; (2) that any philosophical discrepancies that emerge between what Levinas says in the interview about animals and what he says in his major works are in fact evidence of a real (rather than merely apparent) tension between Levinas's unquestionable (and perhaps unquestioned) human-ism and the wider implications of his ethical theory; and (3) that Levinas's ethics is arguably the best placed among ethical theories, with the exception of

Benthamite utilitarianism, to accommodate the interests and moral consideration of various nonhuman animals.

Brief History of the Status of Animals in Philosophy

For the majority of Western history, philosophers have excluded nonhuman animals from the moral community. The first philosopher to argue that justice does not apply to animals was Aristotle (383–322 BCE). According to Aristotle, nature is organized hierarchically, with humans at the top of the pyramid due to their possession of reason (*logos*). Nonhuman animals, entirely lacking in reason, and thus incapable of ruling themselves, are naturally inferior to humans and subordinate to human interests. Animals are not our equals, they cannot be our friends, and no relations of justice exist between them and us. On the contrary, they are natural slaves.

When Saint Thomas Aquinas (1225–1274) set out to synthesize the philosophy of Aristotle and the teachings of the Roman Church, he had no difficulty showing how the argument purporting to establish the inferiority of animals was entirely consonant with the Judeo-Christian viewpoint that man is made in the image of God, and granted "dominion over the fish of the sea, and over the fowl of the air, and over every living thing that moveth upon the earth" (Genesis 1:28). According to Aquinas, God is an absolutely perfect being who is also an absolutely rational being. We therefore have moral duties to God and to any other terrestrial beings that are sufficiently like him. Only human beings are sufficiently like God because only human beings possess reason. Thus, human beings have duties only to God and each other, to the exclusion of other animals that lack reason.

These ideas continued through the Renaissance and the European Enlightenment. The father of modern philosophy, René Descartes (1596–1650), not only asserted that animals are not rational; he denied that they are even conscious, relegating them to the rank of mere automata, or machines. Since animals do not have souls or the capacity to feel pain, there is no reason why we should not do with them as we please. This was just what the Enlightenment scientists wanted to hear at a time (ca. 1600) when anatomy was starting to play an important role in medicine and research. From now on, dogs would be vivisected in anatomy lessons, sometimes having their vocal cords severed to silence the shrieks of the animal-machine.

While the description of the animal as a machine provided scientifically minded Cartesians with a clear conscience when it came to experimenting on animals, it also presented a serious philosophical problem. If the animal is only a machine, one whose behavior can be explained mechanistically, why not also characterize human beings as machines and explain their behavior the same way? The leading German Enlightenment philosopher, Immanuel Kant (1724–1804), provided a solution of sorts. For Kant, animals are like us to the extent that they are conscious and feel pain, but unlike us to the extent that they are not rational and free. Inasmuch as animals are not rational and free, they are excluded from the moral community, which, according to Kant, is populated only by beings (God, angels, and human beings) that are capable of moral agency. Unlike Descartes, however, Kant did not argue that we are morally entitled to do anything we want to other animals. On the contrary, to the extent that animals, as sentient beings, are capable of feeling pain, then we ought to treat them, if not with respect ("respect always applies to persons only"), then at least with some moral consideration. But this obligation is only a duty *regarding* animals (i.e., one that affects animals), not a duty *to* animals. Kant calls it an "indirect" duty to humans, since its performance is said to make it more likely that we will perform our duty to each other. If we treat animals badly, then we are prone to become indifferent to human suffering as well.

It was only when Charles Darwin (1809–1882), in the middle of the nineteenth century, produced incontrovertible evidence of the evolutionary descent of human beings from ape-like ancestors that philosophers and scientists were forced to take seriously the idea that human beings are much closer to other animals than had hitherto been believed. Darwin, of course, was not the first to speak of a kinship between humans and nonhuman animals. Pythagoras (ca. 570–ca. 490 BCE), Empedocles (ca. 495–ca. 435 BCE), Theophrastus (ca. 371–ca. 286 BCE), Porphyry (ca. 232–ca. 304), Michel de Montaigne (1533–1592), David Hume (1711–1776), Jeremy Bentham (1748–1832), and Arthur Schopenhauer (1788–1860) had all maintained that humans have something significantly in common with animals. Indeed, many of them (e.g., Pythagoras and Bentham) even suggested that this was a reason to include animals in the moral community. But it was Darwin who put the idea of the human-as-animal on a firm scientific basis and showed the philosophical inadequacy of excluding animals from the moral community based on a dogmatic appeal to the metaphysics of antiquity, Scriptural authority, or Cartesianism. Of course, this did not stop philosophers retreating to the traditional view that humans are superior to other animals because only humans possess reason, despite Darwin's insistence that the differences between the mental capacities of humans and those of apes are not as decisive as was once thought. (As Darwin stated in *The Descent of Man*, "Nevertheless the difference in mind between man and the higher animals, great as it is, certainly is one of degree and not of kind.") Indeed, even the great nineteenth-century thinkers who welcomed aspects of Darwinian theory for the scientific backing that it gave their own viewpoints—Karl Marx (1818–1883),

Friedrich Nietzsche (1844–1900), and Sigmund Freud (1856–1939)—showed little or no interest in invoking our biological kinship with animals as a reason for including them in the moral community. Until fairly recently, the overwhelming scientific evidence that humans are animals would seem to have had little impact on the traditional tendency of philosophers to view themselves as belonging to a moral class all their own to the exclusion of other animals.

Twentieth-Century Animal Ethics

Utilitarianism

It is only since the publication of Peter Singer's book, *Animal Liberation*, in 1975,[6] that contemporary philosophers have begun to take seriously the idea of extending moral consideration to animals. Singer, a utilitarian, defends the thesis that we are obligated to extend moral consideration to animals that are capable of feeling pain. Drawing an analogy between "speciesism," understood as a bias in favor of the members of one's own species, and traditional racism and sexism, Singer claims that the refusal to consider the interests of those animals that can suffer is wrong for the same reasons that discrimination against blacks or women is wrong, namely, that it constitutes a violation of the fundamental moral *principle of equal consideration of interests*. That an animal has interests is shown by the fact that it is sentient, which Singer defines as the capacity to feel pain (or pleasure). Animals that are capable of feeling pain clearly have an interest in not being put in pain, and thus it morally behooves us to consider such an interest when deciding how to act. Anything less constitutes an act of discrimination that is no more defensible than discrimination against human beings on the basis of the possession of some morally irrelevant feature, such as skin color or gender. An appeal to the principle of equal consideration of interests, however, does not constitute an absolute guarantee that human interests will *never* override the interests of an animal, but it does rule out ignoring or overriding the interests of other animals for trivial reasons. Thus, while it may be possible to justify experimenting on an animal in the case where thousands of human lives might be saved, it is not possible to justify injuring an animal for shallow or trivial human interests, such as the enjoyment of meat or non-crucial animal research.

Deontology

Eight years after Singer's landmark book appeared, Tom Regan published *The Case for Animal Rights*[7] (1983), a deontological defense of animal ethics. In it,

Regan calls for the complete abolition of the use of animals in science, commercial farming, commercial and sport hunting, and trapping. Regan argues that the majority of animals involved in such practices are like us: conscious beings whose welfare is not a matter of indifference to them. Thus, "they too must be viewed as experiencing subjects of a life, with inherent value of their own." To have inherent value, according to Regan, is to have a fundamental right *not* to be treated merely as a means to an end. Regan rejects the argument that animals have less inherent value than humans do because they lack the requisite reason, intelligence, or autonomy. If such an argument were valid then, by parity of reasoning, we should grant less inherent value to *human beings* who are deficient in these attributes, such as the severely mentally impaired, something few critics would be willing to concede. Indeed, it is our very reason that compels us to recognize that humans and animals that are subjects of a life have equal inherent value, and therefore equal rights. Insofar as animals have equal rights, then we as humans have correlative obligations to do them no harm, no matter how beneficial the expected results might be for *us*. This entails that animal experimentation be categorically abolished. "Lab animals are not our tasters; we are not their kings." A similar conclusion is drawn with respect to commercial animal agriculture.

Contractarianism

The following decade witnessed an explosion in the field of animal ethics. It is impossible to mention all the pioneering work that was done, though especial mention should be made of Mark Rowlands's essay "Contractarianism and Animal Rights"[8] (1997), which attempts to counter the theory that has been most hostile to the idea of animal liberation, namely, the view that moral rights are the product of a social agreement or contract. The assumption behind this theory (called "contractarianism") is that because the parties to the contract are necessarily rational agents, then the direct *beneficiaries* of the moral contract are necessarily rational agents too. Rowlands makes a case for why we should view the capacity for rational agency as a "morally arbitrary property" in our attempt to establish just moral principles. Using the work of the well-known political and moral philosopher John Rawls, Rowlands argues that in order to arrive at fair and equal moral principles for regulating actions, we should reason as though we were behind a "veil of ignorance" by ignoring any socioeconomic, intellectual, or natural advantages that might bias us toward adopting unjust moral principles. Rowlands's thesis is that this contractarian approach to arriving at moral principles cannot be used to exclude the interests of nonhuman animals *in principle*. In fact, when properly understood, contractarianism *must* include such interests if it is to be truly impartial when developing just moral principles. Rowlands's adoption of contractarianism to defend a robust conception of animal rights is noteworthy for the fact that it turns the tables on contractarianism, a theory that is extremely popular among philosophers and political theorists, and which is often assumed to include only rational human beings within its scope, to the exclusion of nonhuman animals. If Rowlands is correct, and contractarianism actually *entails* strong rights for animals, then much of the work done in moral philosophy—work which is chiefly human-centered and grounded on a rejection of strong animal rights—calls for radical revision.

Human and Animal Rights

Paola Cavalieri, an Italian philosopher who has written extensively on animal ethics, is best known for her work with the Great Ape Project, an organization dedicated to securing basic rights (such as the right to life, individual liberty, and protection from torture) for all of the great apes (including humans). Her chief philosophical contribution to the animal ethics debate is found in her book *The Animal Question: Why Nonhuman Animals Deserve Human Rights*[7] (2002). Much like Singer, Regan, and Rowlands, Cavalieri is determined to find a compelling case for granting animals strong moral consideration. But in order to make such a case, she argues, we should make use of a normative theory that has intuitive and widespread appeal, not just among philosophers, but also among the public. Cavalieri believes the normative theory that fits these criteria is *the universal doctrine of human rights*. Cavalieri is aware of the obvious irony of using a theory of *human* rights to protect *non*human animals. She believes, however, that a rigorous analysis of human rights doctrine shows that it cannot be limited to human beings by the force of its own logic. In order to make her case, Cavalieri examines what is required for one to be a rights-bearer. Following philosopher Alan Gewirth, Cavalieri shows that to be a rights-bearer one needs to have "the capacity to enjoy freedom and welfare, as well as life which is a precondition for them, both directly and as prerequisites for action." This classical criterion is intentionally broad to cover all members of the human species, regardless of inequalities and differences between them. However, drawing the criterion for moral consideration this widely necessarily brings within its scope many nonhuman animals, which are also "intentional agents," and have a stake in their own "freedom and welfare," too. This leads Cavalieri to conclude that the very doctrine that establishes human rights also establishes *non*human rights. The upshot of this argument, according to Cavalieri, is that we ought to understand ourselves as having direct duties to animals that are similar to the ones we have toward human beings under human rights doctrine. In brief, animals are owed basic rights of noninterference and the right to be treated as legal *subjects* rather than as mere property.

The Feminist Care Tradition in Animal Ethics

Since the early nineties, the traditional reliance on the normative ethical theories of utilitarianism, contractarianism, and natural rights doctrine in philosophical discussions of the treatment of animals has come under critical attack by feminists working within a theory known as "the ethics of care." This moral theory, which emerged in the mid-eighties with the publication of Nel Noddings's *Caring: A Feminine Approach to Ethics and Moral Education* (1984),[10] called into question the "masculine" bias within the Western tradition in which morality is essentially conceived of as a method of arbitrating between my own interests and those of others. Feminists argued that such an approach overvalued importance of rationality at the expense of relationality (between persons), justice at the expense of caring for the needs of individuals, universal obligations at the expense of "feeling with" the other. In two edited volumes of essays, *Beyond Animal Rights* (1996)[11] and *The Feminist Care Tradition in Animal Ethics* (2007),[12] feminists Josephine Donovan and Carol J. Adams organized a debate that sought to apply these insights beyond the provincial human-to-human relation and extend them to the issue of animal well-being. Arguing for ethical attentiveness and sympathy in our relationships with animals, while also proposing a link between the continuing domination of women by men and the human domination of nature, this approach by feminists does not argue for abandoning wholesale universal principles, the need to justify or condemn ratiocinatively the way we treat others, principles based on respect for life, sentience, or rights, but reminds us of the legitimate role of the natural human feeling of sympathy and compassion in morality. This feminist care tradition in animal ethics emphasizes the importance of *relations* above all else grounded in our essential connectedness with each other—people *and animals*—rather than seeing ourselves as isolated Donnian islands *in abstracto*.

Some Facts and Figures

What is the net result of the historical exclusion of nonhuman animals from the moral community? A brief look at the current meat-eating industry and animal experimentation, two paradigm examples, shows just how detrimental to the welfare of animals the refusal to attribute them moral status has become. According to the United States Department of Agriculture, nearly 10 billion animals were killed for food in 2015 in the United States alone; the United Nations Food and Agriculture Association puts the worldwide number of animals slaughtered at 56 billion. As staggering as these numbers are, they do not provide a complete picture, inasmuch as the deaths of aquatic animals and animals that die prior to slaughter are not counted by either organization. Large numbers of animals are also used for experimentation purposes. The USDA's Animal and Plant Health Inspection Service estimates that in 2004, three quarters of a million animals were used for research purposes, and that half of those animals were involved in painful, including distressful, experiments. This number is highly misleading, however, as the Animal and Plant Health Inspection Service does not include rats, mice, and some other species, which are excluded under the Animal Welfare Act, even though these constitute the vast majority of animals used for experimentation purposes. When these other animals are included, the most conservative estimates put the number of animals used in experiments at about 100 million

The intensive raising and slaughtering of animals for food and the high numbers of animals used for experimentation purposes are, however, only the tip of the iceberg. Animals suffer routine abuse and death in other industries and practices. Animals are trapped, hunted, and used for any number of entertainment purposes (e.g., bullfighting, cockfighting, rodeos, zoos, and circuses), as well as being killed for their fur and other byproducts. It is hoped that this volume will help to make the Levinasian case for stopping, reforming, or curbing unethical practices such as these.

Thematic Overview of Essays

In the first original essay in this collection, "Levinas and the Other Animals: Phenomenological Analysis of Obligation," Alphonso Lingis presents a critical discussion of Levinas's phenomenological account of the encounter with a human being who faces me. Although Lingis acknowledges the originality and importance of Levinas's work, he finds deficiencies and distortions in Levinas's account of the experience of being faced by another human being. For example, whereas Levinas's account of this encounter focuses on the vulnerability and neediness of the other, Lingis's own analysis suggests that this vulnerability is secondary to the "positive plenitude of a life," which calls for my attention and respect independently of any needs of the other that I may be called on to fulfill. For Lingis, to be faced by another and perceive this positive plenitude is to find myself called on "to respect its space, to let it flourish, to care about it and care for it." More generally, Lingis argues that the obligation that arises from the face-to-face encounter differs from and can conflict with the rules and maxims that govern behavior in the economic, social, and political order, which, according to Levinas, would derive from this experience. Turning to the phenomenology of encounters with nonhuman animals, Lingis argues that there is also an experience of finding oneself under obligation in the empirical encounters with individuals of other species. We respond to their needs, but similarly to his analysis of the encounter with another person, Lingis insists that this need is perceived within the context of "the antecedent positivity of the fullness of an organism that is there." Like the obligations that issue in the face-to-face encounter with other human beings, this kind of obligation can conflict with the principles and maxims of ethical and legal theories of animal welfare and rights. In the concluding section of his essay, Lingis considers the phenomenology of interspecies community. Drawing on Bentham and Nussbaum, he argues that the general principles that determine obligation in ethical and legal systems refer back to the ways in which we experience obligation in empirical encounters with nonhuman animals. He looks at two very different types of experience, namely instinctual revulsion against cruelty, on the one hand, and a sense of wonder, on the other. Contra Levinas, he reiterates that ethical experience does not begin with the perception of the other's neediness and vulnerability. Rather, a phenomenology of interspecies community should take as its starting point the fact that we share this world with a vast array of "nonhuman companions—5,000 species of mammals, 10,500 species of birds, 17,000 species of reptiles and amphibians, 33,000 species of fish." The wonder that we feel in contemplating them is not an irrational feeling, but issues in a quest for knowledge about them, and in active respect for them.

Bob Plant's essay, "Vulnerable Lives: Levinas, Wittgenstein and 'Animals,'" tackles the anthropocentrism at the heart of Levinas's ethics. Plant argues that Levinas's hyperbolic emphasis on the radical alterity of the other is inconsistent with his view that only human beings qualify as others, and that his highly metaphorical and sometimes "overtly spiritualized" language detracts attention from his account of the "mundane corporeality of intersubjective life." He sees in Levinas's thought a valuable corrective to the abstractions of moral philosophers, insofar as Levinas reminds us that both self and other are embodied creatures, and that our finitude and vulnerability are not merely contingent facts, but constitute "the mundane conditions of possibility for ethical life." While acknowledging the anthropocentrism that underlies a number of Levinas's remarks about animals in general, Plant is encouraged by Levinas's confession in the "The Animal Interview" that he doesn't know whether or not specific types of animals can be said to have a face. Drawing on the later Wittgenstein, he explores the relational possibilities between humans and different forms of animal life, focusing on what

Wittgenstein refers to as "an attitude towards a soul." Admittedly, Wittgenstein himself uses the phrase explicitly in the context of interhuman relations, but Plant argues that the responsiveness to the other—particularly to the other's pain and suffering, which is a key component of having an attitude toward a soul—is also a feature of human relations with at least some types of animals. Although Wittgenstein's work is anthropocentric, in that he asserts that we are more hesitant to attribute pain to the animals that least resemble humans, Plant argues that this is an anthropocentrism that is at least more hospitable than Levinas's, insofar as Wittgenstein suggests that we may be able to talk of "pain" in a meaningful way, even with reference to a fly. However, Wittgenstein's emphasis on pain, Plant argues, is potentially misleading; an investigation of the neurology of the common housefly might lead us to conclude that we would be mistaken in attributing pain to it. Plant therefore turns instead to the notion of vulnerability, and argues that we can have "an attitude towards a soul" of an animal, even if it doesn't have the neurological capacity to experience pain because, like that animal, we humans "are creatures of flesh and blood who are born, require nurturing and protection, grow old, suffer illness and die."

In his essay "Dog and Philosophy: Does Bobby Have What It Takes to Be Moral?" Peter Atterton focuses on the question as to whether animals are capable of Levinasian responsibility for the Other. The essay begins with a close reading of the short essay "Name of a Dog or Natural Right," appearing in the second edition of *Difficult Freedom* (1976),[13] and which is best known for the story of Bobby, the stray dog who befriended Levinas and the other Jewish prisoners during their internment in a POW camp in Germany during World War II. Although Atterton's interest in the essay is primarily philosophical, his reading of the text is also attentive to its literary qualities and structure. It also provides helpful background from the Jewish tradition regarding the first part of the essay, in which Levinas offers a commentary on the biblical injunction not to eat meat from an animal that has been killed by beasts in the field, but rather to "cast it to the dogs" (Exodus 22:31). According to rabbinic tradition, the dogs' entitlement to this meat is a reward for their silence (Exodus 11:7) during the tenth and final plague (the death of all firstborn humans and animals) in the story of the Exodus, on the eve of the Israelites' redemption from slavery in Egypt. For Levinas, this transition point is no less than "the supreme hour of humanity's institution," as the Israelites' redemption institutes their freedom to "follow the most high Voice"; they will celebrate their freedom by remembering their servitude "in solidarity with all those who are subjugated"; and the silence of the dogs at this ethically charged moment "will attest to the dignity of the person." Levinas sees in this evidence of "a transcendence in the animal." Atterton points out that there is no literal possibility that dogs would not bark during such an upheaval, and that Levinas himself seems to acknowledge this. In the second part of the essay, Levinas turns from biblical exegesis and recounts the now well-known story of Bobby, the wandering dog who welcomed Levinas and the other prisoners. Levinas, Atterton says, clearly sees this autobiographical story as isomorphic with the biblical tale of silent dogs. As mentioned above, Atterton sees the essay as evincing two apparently contradictory ideas in Levinas's thought: the view of animals as morally inferior beings compared with humans, and the view of (at least some) animals as moral subjects. Much of the argument hinges on the interpretation of Levinas's description of Bobby as the "last Kantian in Nazi Germany, not having the brain needed to universalize the maxims of its drives." Whereas Derrida and others critique Levinas for complimenting Bobby and then immediately undermining his praise of the dog's putative moral behavior, Atterton argues that this is based on a flawed understanding of Levinas's intention in invoking Kantian ethics. The compliment "last Kantian" refers to the second formulation of the categorical imperative, which calls for respecting the other, rather than the first formulation, which calls for the adoption of universalizable maxims. Atterton elaborates on this by distinguishing between respect as *observentia*, which is acting on the basis of an impersonal reason (something that Bobby would appear to be incapable of), and respect as *reverentia*, which is a feeling aroused by the Other. He argues that it is the capacity that the Other has to awaken respect in the latter sense that unites Levinas's ethics with Kant's, and enables us to recognize the morally significant behavior of animals.

Michael L. Morgan's contribution, "Animals, Levinas, and Moral Imagination," opens with an analysis of Levinas's ethics that distinguishes between the "ground" of our moral world in the face-to-face or ethical relation, and "our moral world" itself, which he defines as "the complexity of decisions, actions, norms, and other considerations that make up our everyday lives in the light of this dimension." In exploring the extent of this moral world, Morgan draws on the thought of Martin Buber as a comparison case. Buber, like Levinas, offered a dialogical, first-person account of human existence, and presented interpersonal relations as paradigmatic of ethical and moral normativity. Yet Buber, as is well known, explicitly referred to a much wider range of potential types of Other who could be encountered as my "thou," including natural objects like trees and animals, as well as cultural objects and works of art. Morgan suggests that Levinas may have been similarly open to including such beings in our moral world, but the challenge he, and we, face is the intellectual or philosophical task of accounting for our sense of responsibility in these relations. Morgan cites the work of Alice Crary to develop his argument that no morally neutral, scientific information can determine for us whether or not we should regard animals as having "faces" in the Levinasian sense. On his reading of Levinas's later work in particular, we can discern the idea that "there is nothing and no one that could not in principle make a claim upon any one of us, at any time and in any circumstances." In a move that has some similarities with Bob Plant's discussion of vulnerability and our "attitude toward a soul" of a nonhuman animal, Morgan argues that "if we can imagine being drawn by the pain and suffering of a creature before us," then we can understand Levinas's philosophy as teaching that we "encounter that creature face-to-face." Morgan acknowledges the anthropocentrism that is evident in a number of Levinas's texts, but also develops a reading of "The Name of a Dog" to present an understanding of Levinasian ethics that is not limited to interhuman relations.

In his essay "Small Justice: The Rights of the Other Animal," Jonathan Crowe explores two common objections to using the language of duties and rights to talk about human responsibility for animals. The first objection is the claim that animals should not be considered bearers of rights, because they are not capable of showing moral concern for others, and are therefore not members of the moral community. The second, related objection is based on what is assumed to be a strict demarcation between the realm of ethics and that of justice. Crowe argues that these objections to talking about the rights of animals and the duties of humans toward them rest on the mistake of thinking that "ethical and institutional questions can and should be separated." After considering two radically different views of the potential for a human "economy of kindness"—contrasting Nietzsche's pessimistic views on the limits of human compassion with the utopianism of Jesus—he turns to Levinasian ethics, focusing on the often neglected "temporally extended character of the ethical moment." Crowe emphasizes that for Levinas each face-to-face encounter "includes traces of prior ethical experiences," such that "the alterity of each face increases and deepens ever more profoundly" (*TI*, 283). The individual subject's passive synthesis of these repeated ethical encounters, argues Crowe, produces an attitude toward social life that "contains the beginnings of an ethical attitude that can, in turn, prepare the ground for legal and political discourse." In other words, Levinas's philosophy undermines the stark demarcation between the realms of ethics and justice, and therefore calls into question the grounds for one of the objections to using the language of rights and duties vis-à-vis animal ethics. However, rather simply undermining this objection, Crowe extends his analysis even further. A key feature of Levinasian ethics is its asymmetry and rejection of the reciprocity of obligations, whereas Crowe argues that moral discourse introduces a form of symmetry altogether unknown in the ethical encounter. In moral discourse, or the realm of justice, I am the potential holder of both duties and rights, thus leading to the risk of ethical avoidance on my part.

But this same risk does not exist in animal rights because, as Crowe suggests, animals cannot engage in ethical avoidance. In a conclusion that the casual reader of the "The Animal Interview" might find surprising, Crowe proposes that "the rights of the other animal might therefore properly be regarded as a model for human rights." For it is in the realm of animal ethics that we can see "the economy of the pure ethical gift, without exchange or consideration."

In his essay "*Ecce Animot*: Levinas, Derrida, and the Other Animal," Matthew Calarco provides an important critical overview of Derrida's engagement with Levinas and animals, particularly in his posthumous book *The Animal That Therefore I Am* (1997). Calarco argues that key elements of Derrida's criticism of Levinas in that work were already present, if not fully developed, in Derrida's highly influential 1964 essay "Violence and Metaphysics," in which Derrida suggested that Levinas ran the risk of reproducing a kind of classical humanism and anthropocentrism. Similar points were also raised by Derrida in the 1987 interview "'Eating Well,' or the Calculation of the Subject." Although Derrida recognized in Levinas's ethics an original and important resource for challenging traditional notions of subjectivity, he also argued that, in Calarco's words, "Levinas's anthropocentric tendencies carry a sort of intellectual baggage that keeps his ethics firmly lodged within the metaphysical tradition that gave rise to the classical notion of human subjectivity." Derrida credits Levinas's notion of subjectivity as partially posthumanist because it calls into question the idea that ethics has its ultimate origin in the autonomous self. On Levinas's account, ethics originates in the call of the Other. However, according to Derrida, by limiting the ethical call to human sources, Levinas effectively allows the epistemology of presence to reassert itself, and, like many other philosophers in the Western tradition, opens up a zone that allows for the killing, with impunity, of nonhuman others. Calarco's analysis of Derrida's approach distinguishes between Levinas's humanism ("his efforts to determine in advance that radical alterity will arrive only from the human") and his anthropocentrism (his unwillingness to include animals in the realm of ethics), but argues that the former is a "logically necessary, concomitant implication" of the latter. Calarco then suggests that Derrida's entire discussion of the question of animals amounts to an attempt to lead scholars in this field "beyond the critique of humanism towards a critique of anthropocentrism." Calarco proceeds to offer a detailed and critical analysis of *The Animal That Therefore I Am*, beginning with a consideration of whether Derrida revised in any way his judgement of Levinas's humanism and anthropocentrism subsequent to the original publication of the "Animal Interview." He notes that Derrida did not seem to have access to "The Paradox of Morality," but instead was reading it at a remove through excerpts quoted by John Llewelyn in *The Middle Voice of Ecological Conscience*, and that Derrida sometimes confused

Llewelyn's questions with questions in the published interview. Derrida picked up on the ambivalence expressed in the interview, observing, in Calarco's phrase, "that Levinas grants a certain face to the animal with one hand while taking the face away with the other"; however, according to Derrida, it is the second move that dominates in Levinas's thought. Nevertheless, both Derrida and Calarco find Levinas's remarks about not knowing whether or not the snake has a face, and not knowing "at what moment one has a face," a promising starting point for undermining the humanist and anthropocentric thrust of Levinas's own work. Calarco concludes the essay with reflections and suggestions for how to think "with and beyond" Levinas in view of doing justice to animals beyond the limitations of humanism and anthropocentrism.

Sophia Efstathiou's essay "Facing Animal Research: Levinas and Technologies of Effacement" builds on Emmanuel Levinas's concept of the face to analyze encounters between humans and animals in research. Efstathiou identifies key normative challenges in animal research as indicating a tension between facing and effacing animals and humans. Efstathiou follows Levinas in understanding a face as a sensible surface that can communicate an inner depth: the being of the Other. This extends an ordinary idea of the face as a "head-face" to include other types of embodied expression that can "hit" one, like the front of a storm, and that speak of the inner being of an Other. These may include, for instance, smells, touching, voices, and bodily noises or movements. Efstathiou considers Levinas's account of his experience as a prisoner of war in Nazi Germany to argue that the face, as a capacity, is not sufficient for facing. So, what conditions encountering the Other through his or her face? The central claim in the essay is that doing animal research involves a process of effacement happening to both animals and humans. Effacement can facilitate some types of objectification (happening to animals) and distancing (happening to researchers), but it is, Efstathiou argues, a more basic process. Effacing an Other happens by conditioning encounters with his or her face. Efstathiou identifies five types of technologies of effacement that operate to structure such encounters: (1) built architectures; (2) entering and exiting procedures; (3) protective garments and equipment; (4) identification and labeling techniques; and (5) experimental protocols. Such technologies can block animal and human face (while often adding a new one): they help transform looks, auditory, tactile, smell or other sense-scapes that structure encounters in the lab, and they help participants perform their expected professional roles. However, effacement is never complete. Animal research vacillates between conceiving animals as "faceless," laboratory equipment, made, bought, quality checked, and discarded once used, and conceiving them as beings researchers must "face," and whose behaviors, pains, and bodies the researchers can and should relate to their own. What

Efstathiou calls "humanimal" research ethics stresses the difficulty of divorcing animal and human suffering in the lab, and the importance of considering how these relationships can be mutually transformative and ethically relevant. It is standard for ethical assessments to take the form of harm-benefit analyses, which recognize costs as borne by animals (only) and benefits by people, despite the loss of face that both may suffer in the lab.

Katharine Loevy, in an essay titled "*Homo Homini Lupus*: Levinas and the Animal Within," explores the implications of Levinas's identification of the human as both animal and not-animal. On the one hand, in the "Animal Interview," Levinas insists that humanity, identified here with ethicality, is "a new phenomenon" in relation to the animal. Yet Loevy points out that Levinas also uses the figure of the animal "to identify a part of the human that must be suspended or overcome in order for the humanity of the human to be manifest," and that this double-positioning of the figure of the animal has been relatively common in the history of philosophy. Drawing on Derrida, she notes a "pernicious ambiguity" in Aristotle's famous characterization of the human being as a "political animal." At the same time as asserting human superiority over nonhuman animals, Aristotle portrays the human project as that of overcoming our own animality. Another common definition of "human being" in Western philosophy is that of the "rational animal"; Loevy traces a similar ambivalence in this conception, and argues that it too has largely derisive implications for nonhuman animals. Levinas's work evinces a similar pattern: the evils of human history threaten to show that humans are no better than animals, and the ethical interruption of egoism is portrayed in such a way that violence is associated with animality. In interviews from the 1980s, including the "Animal Interview," Levinas reformulates the traditional definition of the human being and suggests that "man is an unreasonable animal" (*AI*, 5); the ethical moment, in which the life of the other appears more important than my own life, is "unreasonable." Levinas subverts the traditional association of humanity with rationality, positioning rationality as part of the self-interested, animal aspect of human nature that is in tension with human ethicality. Unlike Machiavelli, who argued that human beings should strive to integrate the human and animal aspects of their nature, Levinas portrays human beings as the site of a "perpetual struggle between animality and humanness." Loevy explores the ways in which Levinas's rendering of the human/animal binary is related to a series of other binary oppositions in his thought: totality/infinity, same/other, said/saying, and Greek/Hebrew. Drawing on both the "The Animal Interview" and "The Name of a Dog," she argues that "the animal is the site of a complex and contradictory mix of identification and rejection on Levinas's terms." Although Levinas's account of ethics is oriented to the alterity of the concrete other, his anthropocentrism and his deployment of the human/animal binary limit the potential of his thought to accommodate responsibility for nonhuman animals. Nevertheless, Loevy concludes by proposing that Levinas's corpus contains resources for interrupting this discourse about the human/animal binary and provoking a rethinking of its terms. Such a rethinking might amount to "the mobilization of Levinas's best insights against one of his more prominent shortcomings."

Brian Shūdō Schroeder's contribution, "What Is the Trace of the Original Face? Levinas, Buddhism, and the Mystery of Animality," draws on Zen Buddhism's approach to mystery in its search for an animal ethics that avoids the anthropocentrism of Levinas's thought. The essay begins with a discussion of the relation between the face of the animal and Buddha-nature. According to Schroeder, Buddha-nature is not something that can be cognitively known; rather it must be "transmitted between two beings fully present and aware of each other in the moment of transmission." One of the features of Zen that distinguishes it from other forms of Buddhism is the idea that "awakening is a simultaneously occurring activity between the one who attains realization and the one who acknowledges it." Although this is more usually seen in the context of the relationship between the disciple and the master, Schroeder contends that it can also occur in the relationship between humans and animals. Turning to the literature on Levinas and animal ethics, Schroeder argues that scholars who aim to construct a Levinasian account of responsibility for nonhuman animals tend to do so by attempting to "paganize his distinctively Jewish-based philosophy." Secular interpreters of Levinas often consider the face without reference to the trace, though in so doing, Schroeder argues, "the ethical is stripped of its very force." The challenge that is posed to these commentators is to explain why the notion of the trace "can or should be ignored or transformed." More importantly still, Schroeder asks what would supply "the content to the formalism of the ethical relation between the self and the Other." The trace refers back to the themes of radical alterity and asymmetry in the ethical relation, and Schroeder wonders whether it is possible to "retain a sense of ethical transcendence that is not predicated on a radical asymmetry." He draws on the work of David Wood, a thinker whose work centers on immanence, and that of Jean-Luc Nancy, to explore an ethics that includes both symmetry and asymmetry, and relates these ideas to the Buddhist notion of dependent origination. In the concluding section of the essay, Schroeder considers Levinas's rejection of mystery and paganism, and proposes that mystery may actually be constitutive for an ethical relationship to the environment and, in particular, to nonhuman animals. As he puts it: "The view that all sentient and non-sentient beings are Buddha-nature calls the individual self and its freedom into question in just as powerful a way as does the Levinasian Other."

Tamra Wright's essay, "'Now We're Talking Pedagogy': Levinas, Animal Ethics, and Jewish Education," brings both Levinas's confessional writings and the wider context of animal ethics in the Jewish tradition into dialogue with his responses to questions about ethical responsibility for nonhuman animals in the "Animal Interview." Wright opens with a discussion of an important passage from *Nine Talmudic Readings* that has so far received little consideration from commentators who write about Levinas and animals. In "And God Created Woman," Levinas's commentary on Berachot 61a (which is itself a commentary on the creation narrative in Genesis), he presents a way of understanding the distinction between humans and other animals, going beyond the assertion in the "The Animal Interview" that humanity is marked by the ability to prioritize the life of the Other above one's own. Using language that is very similar to that of *Otherwise Than Being*, Levinas draws on the rabbinic texts to suggest that humanity is defined not by freedom and consciousness, but by a responsibility that is prior to the subject's freedom or initiative; to be human is to be "a hostage to the universe." Wright endeavors to show how this conception of subjectivity can inform an approach to animal ethics that is grounded in both Jewish tradition and the spirit of Levinas's philosophy. She argues, on the one hand, that the anthropocentrism and other key factors of Levinas's thought are consistent with the Jewish tradition, and, on the other hand, that there are ample resources within Judaism to shape an increasingly compassionate animal ethics, inspired by Levinas's ethics, but not encumbered with its shortcomings.

Face to Face with Animals is the first book-length discussion of Levinas and animals to appear in print, though hopefully not the last. Even if there is still much more that is original to say on this subject, we hope at least that the essays compiled here have the distinction of being the happy circumstance in which the animal question has finally entered into "orthodox" Levinasian criticism. The question not only suggests a rich set of new ethical concerns for Levinasians to address but also calls for an appropriate ethical response on behalf of the Other who is *other than human*.

Notes

1. See: John Llewelyn, "Am I Obsessed by Bobby? (Humanism of the Other Animal)," *The Middle Voice of Ecological Conscience: A Chiasmic Reading of Responsibility in the Neighborhood of Levinas, Heidegger and Others* (New York: St. Martin's Press, 1991), 49–67; David Clark, "On Being 'The Last Kantian in Nazi Germany': Dwelling with Animals after Levinas," in *Animal Acts: Configuring the Human in Western History*, eds. Jennifer Ham and Matthew Senior (New York: Routledge, 1997), 165–98; Jacques

Derrida, *The Animal That Therefore I Am*, ed. Marie-Louis Mallet, trans. David Wills (New York: Fordham University Press, 2008); Lisa Guenther, "Le flair animal: Levinas and the possibility of animal friendship," PhaenEx: Journal of Existential and Phenomenological Theory and Culture 2, no. 2 (2007), 216–38; Matthew Calarco, *Zoographies* (New York: Columbia University Press, 2008), 55–77; Bob Plant, "Welcoming Dogs: Levinas and 'the Animal' Question," *Philosophy and Social Criticism* 3, no. 1 (2011): 49–71; Peter Atterton, "Levinas and Our Moral Responsibility toward Animals," *Inquiry* 54, no. 6 (2011): 633–49.

2. Jacques Derrida, *The Animal That Therefore I Am*, ed. Marie-Louise Mallet, trans. David Wills (New York: Fordham University Press, 2008), 113.

3. Hava Tirosh-Samuelson, "Jewish Environmental Ethics: The Imperative of Responsibility," in *The Wiley Blackwell Companion to Religion and Ecology*, ed. John Hart (London: John Wiley & Sons, 2017), 179–94 (190).

4. As Levinas himself wrote in *Totality and Infinity*: "Philosophical research in any case does not answer questions like an interview, an oracle, or wisdom" (*TI*, 29).

5. See *Facing Nature: Levinas and Environmental Thought*, eds. William Edelglass, James Hatley and Christian Diehm (Pittsburgh, PA: Duquesne University Press, 2012).

6. Peter Singer, *Animal Liberation* (New York: Avon Books, 1975).

7. Tom Regan, *The Case for Animal Rights* (Berkeley: University of California Press, 1983).

8. Mark Rowlands, "Contractarianism and Animal Rights," *Journal of Applied Philosophy* 14, no. 3 (1997): 235–47.

9. Paola Cavalieri, *The Animal Question: Why Nonhuman Animals Deserve Human Rights*, trans. Catherine Woollard (Oxford, UK: Oxford University Press, 2004).

10. Nel Noddings, *Caring: A Feminine Approach to Ethics and Moral Education* (Berkeley: University of California Press, 1984).

11. Josephine Donovan and Carol J. Adams, *Beyond Animal Rights: A Feminist Caring Ethic for the Treatment of Animals* (New York: Continuum, 1996).

12. Josephine Donovan and Carol J. Adams, *The Feminist Care Tradition in Animal Ethics* (New York: Columbia University Press, 2007).

13. See *DF*, 151–53/*DL*, 213–16.

Abbreviations

AI   Emmanuel Levinas. "The Animal Interview." Trans. Peter Atterton, Nicholas Chambers, and Tamra Wright, this book, chap. 1.

AT   Emmanuel Levinas. *Alterity and Transcendence.* Trans. Michael B. Smith. London: Athlone Press, 1999.

BPW   Emmanuel Levinas. *Basic Philosophical Writings.* Eds. Adrian Peperzak, Simon Critchley, and Robert Bernasconi. Bloomington and Indianapolis: Indiana University Press, 1996.

BV   Emmanuel Levinas. *Beyond the Verse: Talmudic Readings and Lectures.* Trans. Gary D. Mole. London: Athlone, 1994.

CPP   Emmanuel Levinas. *Collected Philosophical Papers.* Trans. Alphonso Lingis. Pittsburgh, PA: Duquesne University Press, 1998.

DCC   Emmanuel Levinas. "Ethics of the Infinite." In *Dialogues with Contemporary Continental Thinkers: The Phenomenological Heritage.* Ed. Richard Kearney. Manchester, UK: Manchester University Press, 1984, 47–69.

DF   Emmanuel Levinas. *Difficult Freedom: Essays on Judaism.* Trans. Seán Hand. Baltimore, MD: Johns Hopkins University Press, 1990.

DL   Emmanuel Levinas. *Difficile Liberté: Essais sur le judaïsme.* Paris: Albin Michel, 1976.

EE   Emmanuel Levinas. *Existence and Existents.* Trans. Alphonso Lingis. Pittsburgh, PA: Duquesne University Press, 2001.

EI   Emmanuel Levinas. *Ethics and Infinity: Conversations with Philippe Nemo.* Trans. Richard A. Cohen. Pittsburgh, PA: Duquesne University Press, 1992.

EN   Emmanuel Levinas. *Entre Nous: Thinking-of-the-Other.* Trans. Michael B. Smith and Barbara Harshav. New York: Columbia University Press, 1998.

IR   Jill Robbins. Ed. *Is It Righteous to Be? Interviews with Emmanuel Levinas.* Stanford, CA: Stanford University Press, 2001.

LR   Emmanuel Levinas. *The Levinas Reader*. Ed. Seàn Hand. Oxford, UK: Blackwell, 1989.

NTR   Emmanuel Levinas. *Nine Talmudic Readings*. Trans. Annette Aronowicz. Bloomington: Indiana University Press, 1994.

OB   Emmanuel Levinas. *Otherwise Than Being or Beyond Essence*. Trans. Alphonso Lingis. Pittsburgh, PA: Duquesne University Press, 1998.

OGM   Emmanuel Levinas. *Of God Who Comes to Mind*. Trans. Bettina Bergo. Stanford, CA: Stanford University Press, 1998.

OS   Emmanuel Levinas. *Outside the Subject*. Trans. Michael B. Smith. Stanford, CA: Stanford University Press, 1993.

PM   Emmanuel Levinas, "The Paradox of Morality: An Interview with Emmanuel Levinas," trans. Andrew Benjamin and Tamra Wright. In *The Provocation of Levinas: Rethinking the Other*. Eds. Robert Bernasconi and David Wood (London: Routledge, 1988), 168–80.

PN   Emmanuel Levinas. *Proper Names*. Trans. Michael B. Smith. Stanford, CA: Stanford University Press, 1996.

TI   Emmanuel Levinas. *Totality and Infinity*. Trans. Alphonso Lingis. Pittsburgh, PA: Duquesne University Press, 1969.

TO   Emmanuel Levinas. *Time and the Other*. Trans. Richard A. Cohen. Pittsburgh, PA: Duquesne University Press, 1987.

PART I

LEVINAS ON ANIMALS

CHAPTER 1

"The Animal Interview" (1986)

EMMANUEL LEVINAS

TRANSLATION BY
PETER ATTERTON AND TAMRA WRIGHT

In August 1986, three graduate students in philosophy from the University of Warwick interviewed Levinas at his home in Paris. Levinas had been sent the questions in advance and began the discussion by addressing a number of the students' questions about what he means by "the face." In Totality and Infinity, *the face is always understood to be a* human *face, but the students wanted to know if Levinas was prepared to extend the notion to include animal faces, and if not, why not.*

Q: *If animals do not have faces in the ethical sense, do we nevertheless have obligations toward them? And if so, where do they come from?*

E.L.: One cannot entirely refuse a dog the face. It is in terms of the face [that one understands] the dog. . . . It is not in the dog that the phenomenon of the face is in its purity.

You can become a vegetarian . . . not at all because of respect for the life of something resembling a fellow [human being], as though you don't eat man. . . . You are not a cannibal when you eat meat. The parentage of this phenomenon of the face is not at all in the dog. . . . It is not because you recognize the human face that you see the face of the dog. The wisdom of the face does not begin with the dog. There are some who prefer the dog to men. On the contrary, in the dog, in the animal, there are other phenomena.

3

For example, that force of nature—it is pure vitality. That which characterizes above all the dog [is] its vitality—yet there is also a face.

Q: Can the face of an animal be considered also as the other who must be welcomed? Or is the possibility of speech necessary in order to be a "face" in the ethical sense?

E.L.: I don't know. I cannot tell you at what moment you have the right to be called "face." What an insuperable line! The human face is an altogether different thing, and we rediscover [only] afterward the face in the animal. I do not know whether one finds it in the snake! [*laughter*] I do not know how to answer that question, since more specific analyses are needed. Not in the flea, for example. The flea! It's an insect, which jumps, eh? [*laughter*] But, with respect to what you were saying earlier, there is [something] in our attraction, in a complex regard, in regard to an animal, an animal that is beautiful—myself, I don't have much to do with animals—but, there are those who love the dog, for example, and what they love in the dog is perhaps its childlike character. As though it were strong, cheerful, powerful, full of life, but [also] because it doesn't know everything. And, consequently, on the other hand, there is certainly there in regard to the animal, pity, is that not so? A wolf that does not bite—it is like that. One always loves in the animal, the wolf, the memory of the wolf, the memory of the lion, the dog, I don't know. In any case, there is there the possibility of a specific phenomenological analysis, which cannot be used when things are understood from the beginning. There are some forms of animal. . . . A child is often loved for its animality, no? It is not suspicious of anything; it jumps, walks, runs, bites. It's delightful. I also think that quite clearly, even if it is not as simple as that, even if animals are not considered as human beings, the ethical extends to living beings. I really think so. . . . We do not want to make an animal suffer needlessly, etcetera. But the prototype of this is human ethics. [Even] if animals do not have a face in the ethical sense, we have an obligation toward them. . . . There are certainly, I don't know, vegetarians—those who [are in] the animal protection league; that exists. Clearly, one [approach to] ethics is the transference of the idea of suffering to an animal, certainly. The animal suffers. It is because we as men know what suffering is that we can also have this obligation.

Why do these problems especially interest us? Because there are people who will tell you, on the contrary, that it is in life that there is a certain sympathy regarding our life and that ethical morality is a development of a purely biological phenomenon—that's it. I would turn the matter around completely. It is a widespread thesis saying ultimately the human is but the culmination of the animal. I myself say, on the contrary, that in relation to the animal, humanity is a new phenomenon. And this leads me already to the question you asked me: *At what moment does one become a face?* I do not know at what moment the human appears, but what I am going to underline is that the human breaks with pure being, which is always a persistence in being. That is my principal thesis. A being is something that is attached to being, to its being. That is the idea of Darwin. The animal being is a struggle for life, a struggle for life without ethics. Is that not true? It is a question of might, no? Darwinian morality. When I began reading Heidegger, you know, when Heidegger says at the beginning of *Sein und Zeit* that Dasein is a being that in its being is concerned for this very being. . . . Do you know this Heideggerian formula? *Das Dasein ist ein Seiendes*—Do you know a little German?—*dem es in seinem Sein um dieses Sein selbst geht*. Dasein is a "being" [English in the original] that in its being—in its "to be" [English in the original]—is concerned for this very "to be" [English in the original]. The only aim of Being is to be. Do you know this formula? This is the beginning of *Sein und Zeit*, this formula, well, no matter, you know what Dasein is. Now that is the idea of Darwin: the living being struggles for life. The aim of life is life itself. However, with the appearance of the human—here is my entire philosophy—that is, with man, there is something more important than my life, and that is the life of the other. That is unreasonable. Man is an unreasonable animal. [*laughter*] Most of the time my life is closer [than that of the other], most of the time one is preoccupied with oneself. But we cannot not admire saintliness, understood? Not the sacred! Not the sacred! Saintliness. What is saintliness? It is someone who in his being prefers—not prefers!—*is* attached more to the being of the other than to his own. He tries to do that. And so, for me it is in saintliness that the human begins. No, not in the accomplishment of saintliness. It is the first value, an incontestable value. Even when someone speaks badly of saintliness, it is in the name of saintliness that he says it. That is obvious. I am telling you that because to say that saintliness begins with animals implies that animals have already heard the word of God—which makes no difference to me. But, in any case, there is something other there than pure Being that persists in being.

"The Animal Interview" (1986)

Emmanuel Levinas

Transcription by
Peter Atterton, Nicholas Chambers, and Tamra Wright

Q: Si les animaux n'ont pas de visage au sens éthique, avons-nous néanmoins des obligations envers eux? Et si nous en avons, d'où viennent-ils?

E.L.: Le chien, on ne peut pas refuser entièrement le visage. C'est en fonction du visage [qu'on comprend] le chien. . . . Ce n'est pas dans le chien que le phénomène du visage est dans sa pureté.

Vous pouvez devenir végétarien . . . parce que pas de tout [du] respect de la vie de quelque chose de semblable [de humain], comme si tu manges pas de l'homme. . . . Tu n'es pas cannibale quand on mange la viande. La parenté de ce phénomène du visage, c'est pas de tout dans le chien. . . . C'est pas parce que vous connaissez le visage humain que vous voyez le visage du chien. La sagesse du visage ne commence pas par le chien. Il y en a qui préfère le chien aux hommes. Au contraire, dans le chien, dans l'animal, il y a d'autres phénomènes. Par exemple, cette force de nature: C'est la vitalité pure. Ce qui caractérise davantage le chien, sa vitalité, mais il y a aussi un visage.

Q: Peut-on considérer le visage d'un animal aussi comme l'autre qu'il faut accueillir? Ou faut-il la possibilité de parler pour être un visage dans le sens éthique?

E.L.: Je ne sais pas. Je ne peux pas vous dire à quel moment vous avez le droit à être appelé « visage. » Quel trait noir! C'est tout autre chose le visage

7

humain, et nous retrouvons après coup le visage chez l'animal. Je ne sais pas si en le retrouve chez le serpent! [*rire*] Je ne sais pas vous répondre à cette question là, sachons des analyses particulières, puisque c'est nécessaire. Pas chez le poux, par exemple. Le poux! C'est un insecte, qui saute, hein! [*rire*] Mais, dans ce que vous dites tout à l'heure, il y a dans notre attrait à l'égard complexe, à l'égard d'un animal, un animal qui est bel—moi, je n'ai pas beaucoup à avoir avec des animaux—mais, il y en a qui aime le chien, par exemple, et dans le chien ce que ils aiment, en lui, c'est peut-être son caractère d'enfantillage. Comme s'il était fort, gai, puissant, plein de vie, mais parce qu'il sait pas tout. Et, par conséquent, d'autre part, il y a certainement là, à l'égard de l'animal la pitié, n'est-ce pas? Un loup qui ne mord pas, c'est comme ça. On aime toujours dans l'animal, le loup, le souvenir du loup, le souvenir du lion, le chien, je sais pas. En tout cas, il y a là la possibilité d'une analyse phénoménologique particulière qu'on ne peut pas utiliser quand on comprend des choses par le commencement. Il y a quelques formes d'animal de. . . . On aime souvent un enfant par son animalité, non? Il se doute de rien, il saute, il marche, il court, il mord. C'est charmant. Je pense aussi que de manière tout à fait claire que même si ce n'est pas si simple, même si on ne considère pas que les animaux sont des êtres humains, que l'éthique se prolonge à l'égard des vivants? Je pense bien. . . . Nous ne voulons pas faire souffrir l'animal pour rien, etcetera. Mais le prototype de cela est l'éthique humaine. Si les animaux n'ont pas de visage dans le sens de l'éthique, nous avons une obligation envers eux. . . . Il y a certainement, je ne sais pas, les végétariens, ceux qui, société protectrice des animaux, ça existe. Nettement, une éthique, c'est certainement le transfert de l'idée de souffrance sur un animal, certainement. L'animal souffre. C'est parce que nous comme hommes nous savons ce que c'est la souffrance que nous pouvons aussi avoir cette obligation.

Pourquoi ces problèmes nous intéressent spécialement? Parce que, il y a des gens qui vous direz au contraire que c'est dans la vie qu'il y a une certaine sympathie à l'égard de notre vie et que la morale éthique est un développement d'un phénomène purement biologique, c'est ça. Je retournerais la chose absolument. C'est une thèse répandue disant finalement que l'humain n'est que l'aboutissement de l'animal. Moi, je dis au contraire que l'humanité à l'égard de l'animal est un phénomène nouveau. Et ça m'amène déjà à la question que vous me demandez, parce que, maintenant à partir de quel moment on devient visage. Ça, je ne sais pas à quel moment apparait l'humain, mais ce que je vais souligner, c'est que l'humain tranche sur l'être pur, qui est toujours une persistance dans l'être. Ça, c'est ma thèse principale. L'être est quelque chose qui est attaché à l'être, à son être. Là, c'est l'idée du Darwin. L'être animal est une lutte pour la vie, une lutte pour la vie sans éthique. Pas vrai? Question de force, non? Morale darwinien.

Moi, quand je commençais à lire Heidegger, vous savez, quand Heidegger dit au début *Sein und Zeit*, que le Dasein est un être chez qui dans son être il y va de cet être même. Connaissez-vous ce formule heideggérien? *Das Dasein ist ein Seiendes*—connaissez-vous l'Allemand, un peu?—*dem es in seinem Sein um dieses Sein selbst geht*. Dasein est un « being » qui dans son être—dans son « to be »—il y va de son « to be » même. Le seul but d'être, c'est d'être. Connaissez-vous pas ce formule? Ça c'est le début de *Sein und Zeit*, ce formule, peu importe, le Dasein, vous connaissez. Ça, c'est l'idée de Darwin. Le vivant lutte pour la vie. Le but de la vie est la vie même. Et alors, l'apparition humaine—c'est la toute ma philosophie là-dedans—c'est que avec l'homme, il y a quelque chose qui est plus important que ma vie, c'est la vie de l'autre. C'est déraisonnable, ça. L'homme est un animal déraisonnable. [*rire*] La plupart du temps ma vie est plus proche, la plupart du temps on s'occupe de soi-même. Mais, nous ne pouvons pas ne pas admirer la sainteté, entendu? Pas le sacré! pas le sacré! La sainteté. Qu'est-ce que c'est la sainteté? C'est celui qui dans son être préfère—pas préfère!—*est* attaché davantage à l'être de l'autre qu'à le sien. Il essaie de le faire. Et alors, pour moi, c'est dans la sainteté que commence l'humain. Non pas dans l'accomplissement de la sainteté. C'est la première valeur, une valeur incontestable. Même quand quelqu'un dit du mal de la sainteté, c'est au nom de la sainteté qu'il le dit. Ça, c'est évident. Je vous dis ça parce que la manière qui consiste à dire que la sainteté commence chez les animaux, parce que là, les animaux ont déjà entendu la parole de Dieu, cela m'est égal. Mais en tout cas il y a quelque chose d'autre que le pur être qui persiste dans l'être.

PART II

PHENOMENOLOGY

CHAPTER 2

Levinas and the Other Animals

Phenomenological Analysis of Obligation

ALPHONSO LINGIS

Philosophers have located ethical obligation in the cosmic order to which humans are destined to conform, in the rational imperative for the universal and the necessary found weighing on thought, or in principles of justice in force in the human community. Emmanuel Levinas elaborates a phenomenological analysis of the original experience of obligation. He finds it in the empirical encounter with a human being who faces one. His phenomenological analysis of the move with which someone faces me and of my recognition of appeal and demand is an original and important contribution to philosophical understanding.

The phenomenology that shows the original locus of the ethical imperative should supply imperative force to the ethical maxims and regulations elaborated for the human community. But, we shall see, Levinas's analysis of responsibility in the fundamental ethical experience is in conflict with our responsibilities in a community and its institutions.

Levinas restricts obligation to the relations between humans. We shall argue that the essential findings of his phenomenology extend to our empirical encounters with other species. We will describe the experience of appeal and demand in these encounters.

The phenomenological approach conflicts with philosophies that derive their reasonings from universal principles about sentience or personhood in other species. Can the phenomenological account resolve the intellectual and practical difficulties that the philosophies of animal welfare and rights have encountered?

The Phenomenological Account of Being Faced

When I look at other people in the office or the shopping mall, or at dogs, horses, goats, giraffes, ostriches, turkeys, I take them to see the environment that I see. They stand before, approach, and manipulate things that I see I could approach and manipulate; they advance down paths and avoid obstacles that I see I would avoid. In their bodies I see their postural axis, their inner diagram of movement, adjusted to the objects, implements, and obstacles of the environment.

Edmund Husserl, Martin Heidegger, and Maurice Merleau-Ponty had explained that my grasp of the sense of another's movements is not just a hypothetical construction on my part. I perceive their bodies as paired up with my sensory-motor body, Husserl said. My body picks up diagrams of movement from others and passes them on to others, as it picks up and passes on patterns of speech and emotional responses, Heidegger said. I perceive myself and other bodies in an intercorporeality, Merleau-Ponty said.

The experience of being looked at breaks with this experience of parallel perception. The other's look is not something perceived; instead, Jean-Paul Sartre said, I feel, am affected by a modification of my sense of myself. In a sense now of my bulk, I feel myself to be seen by another, to be an object of another's look. I feel the environment about me to be exposed to an alien gaze, and myself in the midst of other objects. I sense that the other surveys the environment about me; the paths, objectives, implements, and obstacles that my gaze had apprehended are now available to him or her. He or she can invalidate my objectives and behaviors and can block my paths, thwart my freedom.

The other's gaze is a visual assessment, a judgment. He sees me reaching for, manipulating objects—perhaps greedily, perhaps illicitly. Her look makes me feel impatient, impolite, timidly conventional, rude, or strong and bold; it makes me feel inarticulate, my words sound ignorant, brazen, or eloquent.

I find myself judged as an inanimate object would be assessed and judged. But, Emmanuel Levinas points out, when someone approaches me and faces me, I am held to respond. When someone faces me, singling me out with his or her eyes, he or she calls on me, asks something of me, asks at least for my attention, and also orders me, requiring that I respond. The other's appeal and demand are formulated for me in words that designate what he lacks and requires and ask for directions, explanations, guidance, support, or sustenance. In this way someone does not simply appear as an alter ego, a variant of me, parallel to me, but as other, situated at a distance, exterior to me, a force, an agency on his or her own. Inasmuch as he or she calls on me, appeals to me, he or she appears as destitute and needy; inasmuch as he or she orders me to respond, he or she appears with authority over me. When I respond, I recognize his or her rights over me, his or her right to question me. There is no reciprocity, which would presuppose a prior, more original, outside point of view before which I and the other would figure as equivalent.

Appeals and demands are formulated in vocative and imperative grammatical forms of language. But when someone faces me, everything he or she says addresses me, calls on me and requires me to respond. What gives this vocative and imperative force to utterances in the indicative, informative form is the presence of someone who moves to face me.

I can, to be sure, refuse to respond, refuse to acknowledge his or her presence and authority, but in my refusal I already acknowledge that in facing me the other appeals to me and orders me.

But do I have to respond to everything another who faces me says? To trivial, frivolous appeals, delusional, exorbitant, extortionate, cruel demands? Levinas eludes this question by specifying that it is the facing itself, rather than the content of the words, that appeals for attention and demands a response. The facing exposes needs, nakedness, and destitution.

Someone faces me with his or her eyes that single me out and hold me. The eyes, ceaselessly in movement, are unclothed and unprotected, naked with a nakedness from which that of the face and the body derive. The eyes do not shine, Levinas says, they speak: in their nakedness they appeal. In their movements they direct and order.

Someone faces me with his or her voice. In putting aside his arms and his forces, in coming to me only in his voice, which hardly stirs the air, which I can resist without doing anything at all, just by doing whatever I was doing, the other presents himself in frailty and weakness. This way of coming, just to speak with me, calling to me to present myself, is the disarmed and disarming way of approaching.

The movements with which someone faces me—facial expressions, gestures of her hands, dispositions of her posture—are not prehensions, not movements that move for-her; they are movements that take hold of nothing, and move for-another. Hands that take hold of nothing and form themselves with the emptiness speak. With such moves, empty-handed, the other solicits me.

There is an essential insubstantiality of the skin, where expressions form and deform in moving ridges, reliefs, and contours and vanish without leaving a trace. I see that the light, the heat, the wind, and also my words affect it, produce eddies of pleasure and pain on it. In its pallor, its contractions, its tremors I perceive hunger and thirst and sickness. I see mortality in the wrinkles and scars that the harsh edges of things have left on it (*OB*, 85, 88). The skin is a surface of sensibility and sensitivity, susceptible to insults and wounds.

The vulnerability and mortality of the other affect me immediately, weigh on me, afflict me. I do not observe the pain in her body, it afflicts, troubles my gaze; the spasms of pleasure and pain on her exposed flesh torment my hand and touch.

The perception of need and suffering awakens and calls on powers in me to respond to another's needs. As the surveying perception that recognizes a hammer is, Merleau-Ponty explained, already in us the outline of a motor diagram of hammering in our hands and posture, so the perception of another's faltering steps and stumbling is already in me the outline of a movement of offering support.

At the same time the perception of another's vulnerability and mortality awakens in me a sense of my power to manipulate, subjugate, or kill him or her (*TI*, 232–36).

Speaking begins a dialectic that continues without end: my response is addressed to the one who faces me for his or her judgment, his or her assent or rebuttal, which requires my response in turn. Eric Weil had elaborated this dialectic in discourse[1]; Levinas materializes the dialectic: the other's question is a quest for a vital need; my response is nourishment and shelter.

I give food to the hungry, and tomorrow they will be hungry again. Levinas affirms that the appeals and demands someone who faces me puts on me are unending. Every need that I satisfy empowers a life that will have more needs. When someone faces me and I respond, I find I have to respond to his response, and also respond to his very irresponsibility, indefinitely. And I have to respond to those who face him and put demands on him; I have to answer for his failings before others (*OB*, 109, 111, 117). The needs that the other exposes to me open on an unending succession of needs, a dimension of unendingness, *infinition*. In this infinition, the other eludes my apprehension and appropriation.

The need with which the other approaches, appeals, and demands is not just the negativity of lack and absence. The move of facing me requires me, puts demands on me. His or her needs are negative as lacks but positive as orders. But negative and positive would neutralize; Levinas argues that the otherness revealed in the need of the one who faces is an alterity irreducible to negative and positive, a third ontological category.

Levinas will then designate this dimension of infinition that opens in the alterity that faces me as God. Not the sacred, he specifies, but God, the monotheist God (*TI*, 214). God is not to be conceived as pure positivity, as absolute substance or Being. He is revealed only in the dimension of infinition that opens in the face of another. God would be the dimension or the movement by which another facing me commences an unlimited contestation and judgment on me and on the course of the world.

But does not this monotheist God, "Wholly Other," eliminate the particularity of the other? As other, the other is no longer individual. In making the alterity of the monotheist God constitutive of the otherness of the one who faces me, Levinas reduces the otherness between one who faces me and another who also faces me to difference—difference in time and place where the dimension of unendingness opens.

Phenomenological Critique of Levinas's Account

We find deficiencies and distortions in the phenomenological account Levinas gives of the experience of being faced by someone.

1. For Levinas, another human whom I perceive is a sensible form that is given, apprehended and understood, appropriated by me. It is inasmuch as someone in facing, exposing his or her needs, nakedness, and destitution, appeals to me and orders me, that he or she appear as other, other than me and other than the object in the environment that I perceive. The otherness of the other is an absence from the representation I have of him or her, a lack in the plenitude of the environment spread about me.

But, we object, it is the presence of a being whose cohesion and coherence I grasp that makes it possible for me to perceive a lack in that being. I perceive someone in whom life has achieved movement, strength, excess energies, and beauty; in whom his or her agency has achieved knowledge and skills, has contracted honesty and loyalty. Because I first see the positivity of a life in another, his or her vulnerability and suffering can be supported or succored, healed or comforted.

This positive plenitude of a life calls for my attention and respect prior to and apart from needs that may or may not address my powers. A being who lives on his or her own, in whom life is an accomplishment, calls for my attention and orders my thoughts and my actions. I find myself called on to let this life be, to respect its space, to let it flourish, to care about it and to care for it.

2. Levinas says that when someone of our own kind faces us, the appeal is displaced and renewed whenever it is satisfied. The fundamental relation between humans would be dependence.

But a human, like any living organism, generates energies, energies in excess of what he or she requires to satisfy his or her needs. Needs are superficial; they are not the core essence of life, and they are limited, satisfiable. As a parent, I care for the needs of my child so that she can grow in knowledge, strength, and skill and be able to, as she will want to, care for her own needs. Refugees appeal for food, shelter, and medicine until they can return to their land and live without dependence on others for their needs. An artist may well need material support from others and access to great teachers to attain fulfillment, but it is from her own resources that the fulfillment will come.

3. When someone faces me, Levinas declares, I have to answer for her needs and answer, too, to those who face her and put demands on her. The more responsible I am, the more guilty I find myself to be (*OB*, 112).

But here a phenomenology of effective action is wanting, as is an examination of the function or harmfulness of a hyperbolic guilt. Effective action assesses the limits of one's resources and capabilities, and assesses the timing and tact that may be required to help someone. Every initiative we undertake involves triage, distinguishing which needs are important, urgent, and immediate. What has to be done has to be done by me if, and because I am the one who is there and has the resources.

4. Levinas locates the appeal made to me, the demand put on me, in the move of someone facing me, and not in his or her expressed intentions. Though the other may be too proud or too shy to ask anything of me, his or her face itself, by facing, addresses an appeal to me, puts demands on me. When facing me is not a deliberate move by someone, his or her vulnerability and suffering are only observed by me and not addressed singularly to my powers and resources. How is it then that I am all the more concerned when the bleeding accident victim is no longer able to turn to me and ask for help? Is it not the importance, urgency, and immediacy of her wounds that determine what has to be done, and does not the fact that I am there and have the resources determine what I have to do?

5. Levinas located the original experience of obligation in a face-to-face encounter. But this empirical experience gives rise to conceptual extension. Once we recognize ourselves to be required to respond to the needs exposed to us when someone faces us, we understand that there are needy and destitute people we have not encountered but could encounter, and needy and destitute people at remote distances who require resources we may have at our disposal. There cannot be an essential difference between perceiving the vulnerability and suffering on the face whose eyes single me out and those who do not or cannot.

6. Sartre and then Levinas make a radical distinction between the face one looks at, the surface of an organism, and the look directed at me or the face

that faces me. The look hides the eyes, Sartre wrote. The face that faces me is abstract, Levinas says, not a signifier of a significant entity but a trace of an absence. But Levinas supplies only a partial account of the face that faces me.

In our environment, the things—envisioned practically as paths, objectives, implements and obstacles—generate perspectival deformations, project reflections of themselves and mirages and shadows on other things, emanate glows, halos, echoes, and reverberations that captivate our eyes and ears, and constitute the pleasure of seeing and hearing. As we make our way through the display of objects and obstacles, our eyes wander in this emanation of doubles, this pageantry of images. And when we see members of our species we discern from a distance a graceful carriage and stride, and from closer the attractiveness or unattractiveness of a face. In its form, contours, and complexion, a face looks opaque or vibrant, composed or askew, dull or buoyant, beautiful or plain or ugly. A face is an aesthetic form from the start. At six to eight weeks of age, sometimes earlier, infants respond with a smile to the adult who faces them with a smile. Throughout life we see in the faces of others loci of benevolence and pleasure. Their surfaces are not only expanses of susceptibility and suffering; on them radiate pleasures that lighten and delight our glance.

In the visible form of a face, in its beauty or ugliness, we divine, Immanuel Kant observed, character. In the attractiveness of its form and the vibrant hue of its complexion, a face looks noble, serene, gracious, compassionate. In the ugliness of its features and pitted complexion a face looks brutal, intrusive, insensitive, cruel.

7. For Levinas when someone faces me, he situates him- or herself at a distance, as other; there is confrontation and opposition between the same and the other. Within the encounter with someone who faces me, I am backed up to myself, he says, unable to turn away or to flee (*OB*, 104). It is before the other that I find myself here, and find myself endowed with powers and resources; it is before the other who appeals and demands that I am the rich one. I find myself existing before the other, for the other, responsible for his or her needs, unendingly—and responsible for those for whom the other is responsible. The other exists unendingly dependent on me. This conception distorts my position in a world where there are companion human beings.

There is a vertigo and loss of sense of self when we gaze into someone's look. The more we gaze at someone's face the more it becomes our face too. We spontaneously look where her eyes turn; as soon as she speaks we pick up the tone of her voice, and the sound level, pacing, and rhythms of our voice join hers. As she speaks her words are immediately inside us, directing our thoughts and our words, so that we so often find ourselves finishing her sentences for her. We have to force ourselves to not smile with the one who smiles at us; in laughter our individual identity dissolves. We see the tears of another with our distress.

When we are working together at a task, or simply strolling in the woods, we intermittently glance at each other's faces, glances that convey neither summons nor orders. We glance at one another while watching a television drama together, while looking at paintings and sculpture in a museum, while watching a sunset over the ocean. Our glances meet, life makes contact with life, pleasure stirs.

When there is no longer anything the doctors and nurses can do, we remain with the dying one, gazing into her eyes and she gazing into ours, accompanying someone who is going nowhere.

8. How or why is the other, for whose needs I am responsible, someone of my kind—a human being? Must there not be an underlying recognition of kinship? Is this not a recognition that I exist in a human community, where other humans are companions in a world? We have argued that the recognition of need occurs within a recognition of the positive plenitude of a living being that exists of itself, a recognition of the goodness and importance of that being. The recognition of the goodness and importance of human beings includes a recognition of the goodness and importance of life, of my life.

The Locus of the Ethical Imperative

1. For Immanuel Kant, thought—as soon as it begins to think—finds itself required to think the universal and the necessary. Thought, if it is to be coherent and consistent, must be rational. The imperative for the universal and the necessary is not a law or a program the mind puts on itself; thought finds itself already subject to, and affected by, the rational imperative.

Levinas sees that someone who faces me orders me to orient the resources of my perceptual field to him or her. What appears to me, exists for me, and is now cast as appearing and existing for another. The objectivity of the perceived environment is founded on intersubjectivity (*TI*, 209). The rational imperative is imposed by the empirical encounter with someone who faces me, and the encounter with a third party who integrates his perception of my environment and that of someone who faces me.

Levinas does not address the objection that an objective structure is not simply the collation of multiple perspectives relative to multiple subjects, or that the validity of logical laws transcends the psychological laws that govern specifically human mental processes.

2. Levinas's ethics of absolute responsibility for the individual who faces me conflicts with the assessment of responsibility in social, economic, political, and professional ethics.

Levinas designates as the third party someone who faces this couple: me and the other who faces me. This third party includes all those who face us and face him. The third party is an outside witness to my encounter with someone who faces me.

There is an ambiguity in Levinas's account of the third party. As a concrete locus of an imperative, he is an individual who exposes his needs to the couple consisting of me and the one who faces me. He orders the resources available to us to his needs.

But the third party is also someone who has to answer for the needs of all those who face him. Levinas then says that the third party introduces an ordered distribution of resources. He is an outside witness who assesses, reasons, and calculates. He is the agency of distributive justice. He is the voice of the institution, the economy, the profession, the political order, the state (*OB*, 161). For Levinas the obligatory force of the regulations that govern economic, social, juridical, and political institutions do not devolve from social contract. Instead they are based on the encounter of each individual with another who requires and orders his assistance, and on still others who face the one who faces that individual.

There is conflict between my responsibility to those I encounter, to my family, and to the third party. A father in the suburbs purchases expensive sports equipment for his children with funds that would supply food for slum dwellers in his city. A doctor in a refugee camp allots herself a ration of food and lodging superior to that which an equitable distribution among all would determine, under the alleged justification that she must marshal her strength to aid the others. Then she also allots a superior ration to her children.

In fact there is a gaping abyss between the demands put on me by an individual who faces me and the measured obligations I incur in participating in economic, social, juridical, and political institutions and exchanges. Levinas affirms that in the face-to-face encounter with another human I find myself responsible for the unending succession of his needs and wants, and for all those who face him and all those who face those who face him. But as a citizen of the State, I am, or am represented by, a third party; I find myself in the position of judge who subjects others to my orders and subjugates them. To responsibly, that is effectively, ensure the equitable distribution of resources requires the use of force. The essential means of the State are constraint and violence: taxes, expropriations, fines, exclusion, imprisonment, execution, and war.

If I do commit myself to the unlimited and unending responsibility toward someone who faces me, do I not therewith withdraw from economic, social, juridical, and political responsibility? Levinas does not explain how the ethics of the economic, social, juridical, and political community derives from the unlimited and unending responsibility I have toward someone who faces me and does not simply negate that responsibility.

3. Levinas's philosophical method excludes the ethics that would be imposed by the world order or by the ecological order in which human animals share the terrestrial environment with other species of life. The world order, the environment, are shown to be constituted for subjectivity by subjectivity and do not command subjectivity.

Levinas's phenomenological description of the environment gives way to a constitutive analysis. The environment is described as it appears to me, exists for me. Then Levinas proceeds to explain how the home base is constituted by my subjective acts of taking position somewhere, establishing it as a zone of tranquillity and rest by returning to it and recollecting myself there. He explains how things are constituted by acts of circumscribing their contours and detaching them from the ground and stabilizing them in and about the home base. Things are *meubles*—movable goods, furnishings. They exist for my use and my enjoyment, and lay no claims on me. Levinas takes no note of the other mammals, birds, reptiles, and fish in the environment.

Levinas's conception of the environment about me, appearing for me as existing for me, makes dramatic and radical his conception of another human who faces me as radically other, other than me and other than the whole of the perceived environment.

But, we object, things that appear to me appear to exist in and of themselves, prior to and independent of my consciousness of them. I perceive things as exterior to me, already there when I came upon the scene. They appear as substances clothed and enclosed by their contours, indifferent to me. Their character as *meubles*, my possessions, appears as a transitory accidental trait. My existence as a conscious organism appears to me to depend on the prior and independent existence of the earth and its geological composition, climate, and ecosystems. And things order me. We attend to each implement to see how we have to handle it. A river, a path direct my advance; a rock, a washout obstruct it. There are imperatives in things.

Phenomenology of Need and Obligation

Exclusion of Other Species

1. Levinas does not elaborate a phenomenological description of other forms of life with which we human animals share the planet. As phenomena they

would be constituted as entities existing for me and as such would have no ontological otherness.

2. Levinas also separates the human species from all other species of life with the introduction of God. When someone faces me, need opens upon further need unendingly. This dimension of unendingness—infinition of the appeal made to me, the demand put on me—Levinas identifies as God.

We argue that the life in an organism is not the negativity of want and need in a material system that opens it on the environment to satisfy its needs. Life is the production of energies in excess of needs. The needs of an organism are superficial and intermittent, and satisfiable. If we then deny the unendingness, infinition of need, we no longer find an absolute otherness in another human who faces me and no longer find the absolute separation of the human from the other species of life.

In fact, God enters Levinas's discourse from outside philosophy. He specifies God—the monotheist God. He explicitly excludes the sacred and the gods of pagan religions. It is not the phenomenology of the life-world or the phenomenology of religion that will produce this exclusion.

We find ourselves with two questions: Is the appeal and demand put on me in the face of another God? Does God, the monotheist God, appear only in the human face?

The Phenomenology of Need

The physiology that took perception to result from the impact of an external stimulus led to conceiving the perceptum as a plenum—collation, or structure, of sense data. Levinas's phenomenological account of the perception of need is original and important.

But I do not see need only in the human who faces me. To perceive anything—a water jug, a building, a tree, a fish—is to perceive its inner cohesion and coherence, its inner plenitude, and also to perceive the ground it needs to support its position, the light and air it needs, the space it needs to move, the water in which it swims, the substance it needs to sustain itself.

We perceive what a being is lacking to maintain itself. We perceive the fissure opened in the wall that threatens to destabilize the wall in a violent storm such that the House of Usher would collapse and sink into the tarn. We see the ancient temple being dismantled by the descending roots of banyan trees. We perceive the desiccated roots of the young fruit tree upended by a storm. We perceive the wilted leaves of the roadside vegetation in a drought.

We see the broken leg of our horse, the hunger of an orphaned lamb. Their needs are exposed and afflict us. We see the pain of a wounded deer, the agony of a beached whale, the vulnerability of a down-covered baby jay fallen from its nest in the rain.

This perception is not simply the recording of a negativity, an absence. The perception reverberates in our sensory-motor body; it awakens a diagram of position and movement that would supply for the need, that would provide support, nourishment, protection, repair. We do not see the mountain spring without seeing how plastic bags that the wind has blown into it are choking it. We do not see a deer caught in the branches of a tree in the flooding river without envisioning how it could be freed and how we could free it. We discover our powers in the measure that we explore our environment and discover, every step of the way, what the things require.

At the same time the perception of their vulnerability and mortality awakens in us a sense of our powers to capture them, subjugate them, kill them.

The Alterity of Other Species

When a being exterior to me orders me, he appears, in Levinas's conception, as not another one like me but other than me. Levinas locates the otherness of someone who faces us in the appeal he makes to us and the demand he puts on us in the need he exposes to us. We have argued that the negativity of need appears in the antecedent positivity of the fullness of an organism that is there. The positive fullness of someone in whom life has achieved strength, health, and sensibility, someone who has contracted skills, honesty, and care call for my attention and command my respect.

When we perceive the need and affliction of someone of another species, we see the fullness of an organism existing exterior to us and that maintains itself by itself. We see that other life perceive what we perceive, perceive the things of its environment as exterior, independent of it and as real as it is. In an antelope, a heron, a dolphin we perceive organisms whose complexity and functioning our specialized biologists, neurologists, and geneticists only partly understand and whose beauty and behavior attract our attention and order our response.

Our spontaneous responses to the natural world are awe and wonder: awe before those whose grandeur exceeds our power to apprehend and measure; wonder before those whose intricate constitution and complex behaviors induce our contemplation and curiosity. "There is something wonderful and wonder-inspiring in all the complex forms of animal life,"[2] Martha Nussbaum notes.

We perceive the mountains and rivers, the forests and the clouds, the flowering prairies and the moss-covered tundra as good and important for us. We perceive birds and butterflies, antelopes and seagulls as good and important for us. We perceive them and interact with them intermittently and we know that they go on existing beyond our view, that they have existed before we came on the scene. We see that they are good and important in themselves, for themselves. In our wonder before them we see that it is good that they flourish. Beyond perceiving the need that puts demands on us, we contemplate the flourishing that we should allow or promote.

There are things that are important in a practical layout, an environment, a cultural history, an intellectual construction. But importance is also an irreducible category; there are things that are important in themselves. Life is important in itself, although we could not argue that it is important for the cosmic order. In the sequoia forests we see that they are important, although they may not be important to the lumber industry or indeed to the environment. The Grand Canyon is grand, grandiose of itself. Over and beyond their possible utility for human understanding and enterprises, we recognize the importance of protecting Iguazu Falls and Mammoth Cave from commercial development, of protecting the ancient temples and artworks, and the sacred sites of long-forgotten religions. That there are zebras and hedgehogs, fireflies and orchids is important.

What I Have to Do

Individuals of other species encounter us and interact with us. Our companion dog or horse addresses us in his or her hunger. With cries and struggle they seek to order us off when we inflict pain on them, as do cattle and sheep being driven to the slaughter. The neighborhood birds come to the feeders we set up for them. They defend their nests against our encroachment. We call all animals and birds that we have not domesticated "wild"; in fact, they are wary of us because we continually terrorize them with our weapons, tools, games, and noise. In places where humans are enjoined from troubling them, the Galapagos Islands, Kruger Park in South Africa, they interact with us without fear.

We come upon needs, hungers and wounds, exposed to us in living beings who exist on their own, exterior to us. These needs show what has to be done. Seeing them awakens in us diagrams of movement that would respond to these needs, that would support, nourish, protect, heal. They make us aware of what we can do.

Our powers and resources are limited; we cannot be held to respond to the needs of everyone we encounter. Needs that are urgent command priority. The importance of a being in urgent need may well prevail over the importance of projects in which we find ourselves engaged at the time.

What has to be done becomes what I have to do when I am the one who is there and has the resources. This child in the Amazon needs urgent medical attention, and I am the one who has the money at my disposal to fly her to a hospital. I provide food for my companion dog who lives with me, and I put out seed for the birds in my yard when the landscape is sealed by the ice storm. Coming upon an ivory-billed woodpecker, thought to be extinct for sixty years, I alert the press and launch the movement to protect its habitat from loggers and developers. I come upon a still-smoldering cigarette butt in the sequoia forest.

Ethical and Juridical Theories

The Experience of Obligation and the Theory

1. The phenomenological analysis locates an experience of obligation when we encounter individuals of other species. Our thought is motivated to formulate maxims that can guide our behavior with other species. We elaborate ethics and bodies of legislation.

2. Philosophies of animal welfare or rights, as well as jurists, seek to elaborate a coherent and consistent system of maxims and rules regulating our behavior with other species. They locate ethical obligation in general principles. One is the principle that consciousness in an organism gives moral standing and rights to be treated properly. Personhood endows a being with rights, and other species may be persons. Another principle is that living beings should be allowed to flourish to the extent of their capabilities. It is wrong to needlessly cause suffering in humans as in other species. Other animals are not to be treated as property for humans to use and dispose of as they like.

   Such principles entail condemnation of sport hunting, use of other animals for entertainment, fur coats, animal testing for duplicative household products and cosmetics. They may also condemn use of other animals for food or for medical experimentation.

3. But the reasoning that derives from these principles engenders perplexities. If we base rights on personhood, self-consciousness, or capabilities, human infants and people with severe cognitive disabilities would fall below chimpanzees, bonobos, and dolphins. Biologists have established that the capabilities of humans—language, self-consciousness, rationality, autonomy—differ from those of other species only in degree.

   To which species are we to recognize rights? Which are excluded from being treated as property or commodity? Mollusks? Insects? The minuscule organisms and ecosystems that cannot be seen with the naked eye?

Biologists recognize that mammals, birds, reptiles, and fish can feel pain, but they do not affirm that other species do not.

There is conflict between the needs of predator species and those of prey. Pet cats that are allowed outdoors kill from 1.4 billion to 3.7 billion birds in the continental United States each year. But cats that are kept indoors are fed a meat diet, supplied from slaughterhouses. What reasoning would induce us to protect prey from predators in nature?

Invasive species—such as insects, rabbits, and feral dogs—destroy native species and ecosystems. To preserve native species in the Galapagos, extermination campaigns targeted feral goats, pigs, and dogs.

Conflict occurs between the needs of humans and those of other species. In practice, we justify the killing of animals of other species that endanger our lives or our means of livelihood, such as our agricultural holdings. The struggle to preserve declining populations of chimpanzees, hippopotamuses, elephants, and tigers conflicts with the needs of growing human populations in the areas where such species live. When we allow the use of other animals for food in desert or arctic climates, we grant priority to the needs of humans. We likewise do so when we accept the use of other animals in medical research, even accepting the infliction of pain and mutilation.

The still increasing human population has led to the factory farming of cattle, pigs, sheep, and poultry for human food. The industrial production of meat constitutes a huge segment of economies. These animals and birds are genetically modified, castrated, force-fed, and restricted in their movements in order to produce the maximum quantity of meat in the shortest time.

These problems are like those that the ethics and jurisprudence concerning human rights and welfare confront. How are the rights affirmed for humans who are capable of language, self-consciousness, rationality, and autonomy extended to infants, the mentally deficient, or patients with advanced Alzheimer's disease? At what point of gestation does a fetus become a person with rights? How do we determine whether a mother and fetus are not viable together? How do we decide who receives what treatment when the resources for extremely expensive medical treatment are limited, or when organs available for transplant are limited?

The Uneasy Juncture of Theoretical Norms and Practical Concerns

The application of ethical principles is limited by practical concerns. Among ethical and juridical thinkers and in the public there is broad consensus that needless cruelty to other species is to be prohibited. There are laws regulating the welfare of companion animals and species kept in zoos and used in the entertainment industry. There is growing attention to the welfare of animals used in medical and cosmetic research. There is growing attention to needless cruelty in the confinement and slaughter of cattle, pigs, sheep, and poultry in the factory farming industry. Protected from predators and diseases, they could live prosperously and be killed painlessly. It would require an enormous cultural and psychological change, and involve a vast transformation of our economies, to convert populations from carnivorous to vegetarian diets.

There is also general agreement among thinkers that the natural environment must be protected. Unpolluted water and air are essential for the well-being of species, as well as for our own. The more biological ecosystems are studied, the more evident it becomes that it is important to maintain biodiversity. Humans will have to take on the role of intelligent management of the environment, for humans are present everywhere on the planet and their activities everywhere impact the environment. Extraction and use will have to be conjoined to resource management and renewal, as well as protection for species whose possible pharmaceutical use is hitherto unknown, and for species whose use for human enterprises is hitherto inconceivable. But the interests of industry encroach on environmental principles.

Conflict between the Encounter and the Theory

There is also conflict between the responses that are motivated by encounters with individuals of other species and the ethical and legal systems that are constructed for the rights and welfare of species. The ethical and legal systems of regulations, which aim to establish distributive justice between species, humans and others, in limited resources, are elaborated as from outside the encounter, as by Levinas's third party.

But we find again the force of obligation in our encounter with individuals. We expend considerable resources to care for our ailing or aging companion dog, iguana, or parrot. We also expend disproportionate resources on an orphaned owl or fawn we find in our backyard. We endorse the devotion of considerable resources to preserve certain endangered species with which, through the media, we develop personal interest and fascination.

The size, elegance, and spectacular courtship rituals of the fifteen species of cranes have long fascinated people in Japan, China, Siberia, and Africa. In 1938 the total population of whooping cranes, native to North America, was down to sixteen. The effort to preserve this species involved aerial tracking to locate their breeding grounds, the establishment of a captive population whose keepers have to be costumed as cranes, much trial and error in learning how to incubate and successfully rear offspring, and a spectacular project to induce juvenile cranes to follow an ultralight plane to a new migration route. While the species is still critically endangered, the population in 2015 has now risen to 620. One can argue that the funds and resources devoted to the whooping crane project could have been more rationally used on habitat preservation and recovery and, indeed, general conservation education.

Phenomenology of Interspecies Community

The distinctive contribution we found in Levinas is the phenomenological analysis of an empirical encounter in which an appeal is made, an order addressed to me. We have been guided to extend the phenomenological analysis to the empirical encounter with individuals of other species.

When we consider the general principles that determine obligation in ethical and legal systems, we find that they do refer back to the experience of obligation in an empirical encounter. Since Bentham, thinkers have invoked our visceral reaction to seeing other animals suffer. Factory farms and slaughterhouses have taken legal measures to ensure that their operations are outside of public view, and animal rights campaigners have believed in the power of showing the actual suffering inflicted to sway public opinion. Richard Posner invokes the force of instinct, our instinctual revulsion against cruelty to animals. He believes that this instinct is strong enough to continue to motivate more and more public concern about the cruelty of sports hunting, animal testing for luxury products and nonessential animal testing for pharmaceuticals, and the cruel conditions of factory farming.[3]

Martha Nussbaum invokes wonder before individual animals of other species that we encounter—a wonder that motivates a longing to know more of them, and a will to see them flourish. Many urban dwellers encounter the variety of species of life in modern zoos, which awaken in them a concern that other species be protected and their forms of life enabled to flourish.

However, to be horrified at the sight of another's pain and suffering, or to be filled with wonder are irreducible experiences, which seems to locate them in the register of feeling. Feeling has been conceptualized as subjective, private, passive, recording pleasure and pain, rather than as true or false, permissible or prohibited. We argue that the phenomenological analysis of an encounter with an empirical individual elucidates the structure and dimensions of the experience and the obligation embedded in it. Perception is not just the recording of positive sense data or of stretches of extension filled with sensory quality. The perception of need, exposed in a human who faces us or in the presence of an individual of another species, awakens in our sensory-motor body the diagram of an initiative to protect, support, nourish, repair, or heal. Every perception distinguishes what is important in the perceptual field from what is accessory or incidental, and may indicate an urgency that is more important than whatever projects I may be pursuing for my own interests or benefit.

Ethical experience does not start with the perception of need. The phenomenological analysis should begin with the observation that we share the world with human and nonhuman companions—5,000 species of mammals; 10,500 species of birds; 17,000 species of reptiles and amphibians; 33,000 species of fish. Our sense of wonder before the natural world affirms the importance and goodness of our life and of the multiple species of life. The existence of multiple species of life is good for us; they serve as our food, and we have become more aware of the importance of biodiversity in an environment in which we can thrive. We also recognize in wonder the importance and goodness of multiple species of life inherent in them, and that which benefits them. Though we do not seize them for our utility, to perceive icebergs and sunsets, sequoias and water lilies, whales and butterflies, flying squirrels and flying fish is to affirm their existence and importance. The wonder that contemplates them issues in a quest for knowledge about them; it is nowise an irrational feeling. Wonder issues in active respect.

Notes

1. See Eric Weil, *Logique de la philosophie* (Paris: Vrin, 1950).
2. Martha C. Nussbaum, "Beyond 'Compassion and Humanity,'" in *Animal Rights: Current Debates and New Directions*, eds. Cass R. Sunstein and Martha C. Nussbaum (Oxford, UK: Oxford University Press, 2005), 299–20 (306).
3. Richard A. Posner, "Animal Rights: Legal, Philosophical, and Pragmatic Perspectives," in *Animal Rights: Current Debates and New Directions*, 51–77 (69–70).

CHAPTER 3

Vulnerable Lives

Levinas, Wittgenstein, and "Animals"

BOB PLANT

It is not in the dog that the phenomenon of the face is in its purity.

—Emmanuel Levinas, "The Animal Interview"

[T]he way in which animals are similar to and different from one another and in relation to man . . .

—Ludwig Wittgenstein, "Remarks on Frazer's *Golden Bough*"

Levinas's remarks on "the animal" are deeply anthropocentric, and arguably speciesist. Nevertheless, they raise some important questions regarding the relational possibilities between human beings and particular forms of animal life. Drawing on the later Wittgenstein, in this essay I suggest that our ordinary dealings with members of (many) other species are much richer than talk of "animals" *in general* implies.[1] The discussion is divided into the following six sections: (1) First I argue that while Levinas overstates the "radical otherness" of the other, he is right to emphasize the ethical claim made on me by the other's vulnerability as a fleshy, finite creature. (2) I then critically discuss Levinas's allusions to "animals" and the priority he places on human suffering. For although Levinas insists that animals do not have a "face" in the full ethical sense, he confesses that he does not know if and when *specific* types of animal (notably the snake) can be said to have a face and thereby demand a "welcome." (3–4)

31

Drawing on the later Wittgenstein, in the following two sections I explain the
significance of Levinas's aforementioned hesitancy regarding particular forms
of animal life. I do this by reconstructing what Wittgenstein calls having an
"attitude towards the soul" of another. Developing Wittgenstein's remarks, I
argue that the relational possibilities between human and nonhuman others are
shaped by our respective forms of embodiment—as Wittgenstein observes, we
are most hesitant when encountering animals who least "resemble" ourselves.
In this sense at least, Wittgenstein's work (like Levinas's) is anthropocentric.
I suggest, however, that it is a significantly more hospitable anthropocentrism
than Levinas's. (5) In this section I return to suffering—which is central both
to Levinasian ethics and to Wittgenstein's notion of having an attitude toward
a soul. Notwithstanding the central role suffering has in our ethical life, I argue
that we can make sense of another's *vulnerability* without that committing us to
the belief that they possess the neurological structure necessary for feeling *pain*.
(6) Finally, I address two worries one might have about the approach taken
in this essay: first, concerning whether Wittgenstein's piecemeal, descriptive
approach—namely, his attempt to ascertain what we can/cannot meaningfully
say in particular circumstances—is inherently parochial (for who are "we" who
can/cannot say this or that?); and second, whether trying to determine who/
what qualifies as an "other" is itself unethical. In conclusion, I suggest that a
degree of anthropocentrism in our ethical lives is unavoidable, but that more
or less welcoming forms of anthropocentrism are possible.[2]

1. Pain and Suffering

According to Schopenhauer, pain, misfortune, want, and boredom are not the
exception in human life but the rule. Indeed, the view that evil is a privation
of good gets things precisely backward.[3] But one does not have to accept this
notoriously gloomy portrait of life to acknowledge the distinctive hold suffering has on us. Leaving aside the various forms of emotional and psychological distress we routinely undergo, physical pain remains a constant threat in
everyday life, and occurs at the limits of most bodily sensations. (It is a striking
fact that whereas relatively few regions of our bodies produce pleasure, most
are susceptible to pain.) Not only do my own pains insist on being attended
to, they are commonly accompanied by onerous questions: Why am I feeling
pain? When will it stop? How might I ease it? Will it return? Is this merely
a symptom of something more serious? Such questions call for, though rarely
receive, immediate, unequivocal answers.

There are, of course, many other notable features of suffering.[4] But the
general point I want to emphasize here is that in suffering one's very exis-

tence can become a burden. Thus, of his experience of torture, Améry recalls how "flesh" soon became his "total reality" (*ATL*, 33). For not only are our rational and perceptual capacities disrupted by extreme physical suffering, here we invariably find ourselves reduced to making "sounds anterior to learned language" (*BP*, 54)—namely, "animal" noises. In pain one finds oneself rooted to the here-and-now as "the world ceases to be the locus of purposeful action" (*AB*, 75). Indeed, all those things that ordinarily give our lives meaning and value are, more or less temporarily, "destroyed when there is that cracking and splintering in the shoulder joints" (*ATL*, 40). In this way pain renders me both wordless and worldless[5]:

> At the exquisitely exact point of optimal torture . . . nothing is significant except the pain and its cessation. At that point the victim of torture has no morals, no religion, no politics, no family, no world, no subjectivity. . . . The victim is only pain, that is, only flesh. . . . In suffering, the body contracts upon itself, curls up within itself in agony and blind pain, and turns itself into flesh. In suffering, the body contracts into the immanence of flesh. (*AE*, 206)

We should not, however, conclude that these features of suffering apply only to the horrors of torture. For the everyday pains of toothache, migraine, trapped nerves, and so on similarly reduce us to "flesh"—albeit to differing degrees of intensity and transience.

Clearly, then, one's own suffering makes a powerful claim on one's attention. But what about others' suffering? Does that also make a claim on us? To this question Levinas offers an unequivocally positive response. In broadly phenomenological terms, he attempts to explain how the plight of others makes a distinctively ethical claim on us—or more precisely, on *me*. (This latter emphasis is crucially important for Levinas, for it is *I* who is singled out as responsible—*as if* God spoke to me.[6]) And yet, for all his talk of responsibility for the vulnerable other who "faces" me, Levinas's quasi-theological terminology often obscures the issues. Whatever the rhetorical force of his characterizing the other as "absolutely other" (*CPP*, 55), "infinitely transcendent, infinitely foreign" (*TI*, 194), an "astonishing alterity" (*EN*, 101), and the one with whom "I have nothing in common" (*BPW*, 27), caution is needed here for at least three reasons: (1) It is markedly unclear how my responsibility for the other could arise from their "absolute otherness." For assuming that such a *radically* "other" other would even register on my perceptual, cognitive, and/or affective radar, why would such an encounter have anything distinctively *ethical* about it? Why would the other not instead provoke mere epistemic befuddlement, aesthetic wonder, and/or comic incongruity? (Caputo is surely right that it is "the face of *suffering* which puts teeth into . . . [the other's] mystery and prevents us from confusing the mystery with an object of poetic reverie" [*RH*, 277, my emphasis].) (2) As we will see shortly, Levinas's "other" is not an inherently enigmatic creature; on the contrary, for him, only *human beings* qualify as "others."[7] But if that is right, and we thereby possess some basic capacity to distinguish between human beings and "animals," it is misleading to claim that the other is "absolutely different" (*BPW*, 27). (3) In his various remarks on the face, Levinas's highly metaphorical—and often overtly spiritualized[8]—vocabulary diverts attention from the other's mundane vulnerabilities as a singular, finite being. Consider, for example, the following cautionary remarks:

> You turn yourself toward the Other as toward an object when you see a nose, eyes, a forehead, a chin, and you describe them. The best way of encountering the Other is not even to notice the color of his eyes! When one observes the color of the eyes one is not in social relationship with the Other. The relation with the face surely can be dominated by perception, but what is specifically the face is what cannot be reduced to that. (*EI*, 85–86)

Levinas is doubtless right to oppose the *reduction* of the other's "face" to an assemblage of distinguishing features. (Wittgenstein will say much the same.) But it is not clear why noticing the color of the other's eyes thwarts or derails the ethical relation. After all, as a singular embodied creature facing me, the other is never without such surface qualities—just as she is never without age, gender, size, a particular behavioral repertoire, or configuration of limbs and sense organs. Acknowledging this much does not commit us to the view that she is somehow *reducible* to such features. Likewise, when Levinas suggests that the face encompasses "the whole body—a hand or a curve of the shoulder" (*TI*, 262), that "all the naked and disarmed mortality of the other" (*EN*, 232) lies in the nape of her neck,[9] and that "the whole human body is . . . more or less face" (*EI*, 97), we can make sense of this without evoking anything mysterious. (In a drunken stupor, a man passes out on the train seat opposite me. Slumped over, his belly protrudes from beneath his shirt. In this immodest exposure, all his "naked and disarmed mortality" is revealed.) It therefore seems to me that there is a tension between Levinas's quasi-theological hyperbole and his avowed interest in the concrete details of prephilosophical experience.[10] In this essay I will not try to resolve this tension. Rather, drawing on Levinas and the later Wittgenstein, I want to focus on the mundane corporeality of intersubjective life—in our relations both with other human beings and with "animals." But before turning to Wittgenstein, let me briefly outline what I find most insightful in Levinas's ethics.

In everyday social intercourse I do not encounter the other as a speci-men of a species, an instance of humanity, or an individual of a genus.[11] Nor is he adequately characterized as a rational, autonomous, and/or moral "agent," or an anonymous, generalized "other" to whom I attribute personhood, rights, interests or dignity. Rather, the other who faces me makes an ethical claim on my attention simply by *being there* in her concrete singularity.[12] Specifically, Levinas maintains, the other silently commands: "Thou shalt not kill."[13] This is not, however, merely a general injunction against murder,[14] for the face of the other also appeals: "Do not kill me, do not abandon me, do not let me suffer."[15] From where does the ethical authority of this command/appeal originate? Not in the other's power or strength, but rather in her inherent fragility as a fleshy creature who ages, falls ill, suffers, and dies.[16] Accordingly, Levinas insists that the other concerns me in the most banal facts of material life—not least in her need for shelter and nourishment.[17] (Indeed, I might even be called on to give food from my own mouth![18]) In this crucial sense, then, ethics "has meaning only among beings of flesh and blood" (*OB*, 74). For what sort of ethical life could immortal, invulnerable beings have? What could they possibly "give one another," and how could they "help one another" (*EI*, 97)?[19]

This emphasis on the "flesh and blood" reality of others provides a valu-able counterweight to the fanciful abstractions and intuition-pumps routinely employed by moral philosophers. For here Levinas draws our attention back to the banalities of human life that underlie our ethical theorizing.[20] After all, it is easy to forget that the "elevation of human identity to the rank of transcendental subjectivity does not annul the effect which the penetration of metal can have, as a knife point or a revolver's bullet, into the heart of the I, which is but viscera" (*OGM*, 43).[21] As Caputo suggests, the force and urgency of ethical responsibility lie in the manifold "'accidents' that strike at us in daily life" (*TEE*, 111). As such, we should remember how little it takes for a life to come undone: "A stray bullet, a stray chromosome, a stray virus, a wanton cellular division—and the flesh is hopelessly ruined" (*AE*, 234). That we are fleshy, finite, vulnerable creatures is not *merely* a contingent, empirical fact about us. Nor is it of secondary importance to (purportedly) deeper metaphysical considerations. On the contrary, our being preciously pathetic[22] constitutes the mundane conditions of possibility for ethical life. What then is the appropriate response to all this? Not more theorizing, but simply "offering relief, lending a hand. Without why. Because. Because flesh is flesh, because flesh calls to flesh" (*AE*, 237).[23] What Levinas variously describes as the "goodness of everyday life" (*AT*, 107), "individual goodness, from man to man" (*IR*, 81), and acts of "stupid, senseless goodness" (*IR*, 89)[24] occur in even the most oppressive circumstances.[25] But nothing guarantees their occurrence. Ethical life is an inherently fragile affair, no matter how much theoretical reassurance we may crave.

In the view I have briefly sketched here, ethical responsibility is elicited by others' vulnerability—not least by bodies in pain.[26] If that is right, then perhaps, as Caputo suggests, our primary focus ought to be on the "disasters," "broken bodies and damaged lives" (*AE*, 32–33) that punctuate ordinary life, not on what might constitute the Good Life. After all, while conceptions of the Good are notoriously diverse, if not incommensurable, the aforementioned disasters have an "ominous sameness" insofar as they involve "spilled blood, limp bodies, broken minds, damaged lives" (*AE*, 41). If the effects of suffering are pretty much always the same—namely, "all the pressing matters of our everyday concerns are suspended" (*RH*, 277)—then might our inextricable helplessness not bind us together?[27] Might compassion not arise "precisely from the sense of a common fate," from our suffering a common "comfortlessness" (*RH*, 259)? To what extent Levinas would endorse Caputo's suggestions is debatable. What is undeniable, however, is that here he would want to remind us of a crucial asymmetry between my own suffering and the suffering of others. For I can often find some redeeming sense in my own trials and tribulations; for example, by accommodating them into a larger narrative of divine punishment and spiritual refinement.[28] Such "grand designs"[29] need not, of course, be theological. I might instead see my own suffering as a necessary part of some greater humanitarian cause, and thereby "preserve an attitude of dignity" (*TO*, 69) in the pain I undergo. I might even declare from an available mountaintop that what does not kill me only makes me stronger. But while these hermeneutic strategies are live possibilities for *me*, Levinas insists that there is a "radical difference between *the suffering in the other* . . . and suffering *in me*" (*EN*, 94). Of course, the other is free to accommodate her own suffering into such grand explanatory-justificatory narratives. But this is *her* business; it is not something *I* can legitimately demand *of* her. Indeed, Levinas maintains that the "source of all immorality" lies in the "justification of the neighbor's pain" (*EN*, 99)—hence the inherent dangers of theodicy.[30]

Having discussed the respective claims my own and others' suffering make on me, let us now turn to animal suffering.[31]

2. The Plight of Animals

As already noted, on Levinas's estimation, only human beings qualify as "others." He does not, however, deny that animals matter. Not only does Levinas acknowledge that we often feel "pity" for members of other species, he considers it patently wrong to make animals "suffer needlessly." But a lot hinges on the qualification "needlessly" here. For while he sees the suffering of other human beings as fundamentally useless, in Levinas's view, animal suffering is sometimes necessary—not least when it benefits *us*.[32] In his account then, we have no positive duty of care toward animals, only a negative duty to avoid causing them unnecessary (needless) harm.[33] Accordingly, Levinas insists that whatever ethical concern we might feel for animals derives from our responsibility for other human beings. In particular, our responsiveness to animal suffering arises from the "transference of the idea of suffering to an animal," for it is only "because we as men know what suffering is that we can also have this obligation" (*AI*, 4) to animal life. So, for example, while we "cannot entirely refuse a dog the face," "[i]t is not in the dog that the phenomenon of the face is in its purity." Indeed, no animal has a "face" in the full "ethical sense" (*AI*, 3).

Why does Levinas say this? Because animals are essentially concerned with their own "persistence in being." In their primitive egoism, the life of animals is therefore a "struggle . . . without ethics" (5).[34] Only for us (human beings) can *another's* welfare take precedence over our own. Indeed, we are assured, the human being is an entirely "new phenomenon" (4), and this, Levinas maintains, is his "entire philosophy" (5). Levinas's view of "animals" is thus part of a much broader, and markedly bleak, conception of nature.[35] In fact, he claims that were I motivated by my natural "animal perseverance in being" (*OGM*, 152), then my primary inclination would be nothing short of *murderous*.[36] It is only through the ethical claim made on me by the other (human being) that this primitive drive for violence is challenged, and my "right to be"[37] called into question. Ethics, we are therefore told, is essentially "*against nature*" (*DCC*, 60). Given all of this, I think that Wood is right to suggest, not only that Levinas's ethics is offered as "an antidote to what he believes to be man's fundamentally murderous natural disposition," but that "the animal" represents "the condition that man must overcome" (*TC*, 132). Before proceeding, I want to say something more specific about nonhuman suffering.

It is often thought that the suffering of "animals" is less deep, and therefore less morally troublesome, than the suffering of (most) human beings. This view seems plausible insofar as only we are vulnerable to debilitating guilt, profound boredom, fear of ageing and illness, just as only we agonize over the causes and consequences of the brute physical pains we share with (some) other species.[38] By contrast, the suffering of animals is "uncomplicated" (*AL*, 256), not least because they only ever suffer *in the moment*. (As Schopenhauer puts it, the animal is "the present incarnate" [*EA*, 45].) Still, even assuming this is true of *all* forms of animal life, should we conclude that animals are inherently better off than (most) human beings in matters of suffering? Not obviously so. For as noted earlier, we can often find some redeeming sense in our own suffering by accommodating it into a larger explanatory-justificatory narrative. But such "grand designs" are presumably not available to other animals. Thus, when my Cairn terrier (Alfie) is in pain, he *simply suffers*; his pain is always, for him, without any transcendent value, meaning, or purpose. In that very specific sense, Alfie's suffering might be described as "uncomplicated." However, it is precisely *this* fact that makes his suffering so awful—both for him and those who care about him. For not only is Alfie unable to accommodate his own trials and tribulations into an explanatory-justificatory narrative, I cannot offer him the sort of comfort and reassurance I can offer (most) other human beings. Without doubt, a great deal of our (human) suffering is compounded by the beliefs, fears, and anxieties we have about it. But it does not follow—at least, not in any straightforward way—that animals are inherently better off in this regard. Mindful of this point, let us now return to Levinas.

Although Levinas's assessment of "the animal" *in general* is pretty gloomy, his remarks on animal life are not wholly negative. Thus, recalling his wartime incarceration by the Nazis, Levinas tells us of Bobby—a stray dog who briefly entered the lives of the prisoners.[39] Not only did Bobby's arrival provide momentary relief from the daily misery of camp life, Levinas notes that while the prison guards and villagers who passed by the camp saw only "prisoners," "Jews," or "the contaminated carriers of germs" (*IR*, 41), "[f]or him [Bobby] there was no doubt that we were men" (*DF*, 153); *he* "evidently took us for human beings" (*IR*, 41).[40] Elsewhere, Levinas acknowledges that the complexity of our "attraction" (*AI*, 4) toward different animals suggests a parallel between the lovable "animality" of children and dogs,[41] and explicitly states that "the ethical extends to living beings" (4). But of equal interest here, I think, is the tentativeness with which he responds to specific questions asked by his interlocutors. For Levinas openly admits that he does not know when "the human appears [in nature]" (5), and likewise concedes: "I cannot tell you at what moment you have a right to be called 'face'" (4). He is similarly hesitant about what can meaningfully be said of particular forms of animal life. Thus, while Levinas insists that animals *as such* do not have a "face" in the full "ethical sense" (4), when asked if an animal can be considered as another who must be welcomed, he confesses: "I do not know whether one comes across [the face] in the snake! I do not know how to answer that question, since more specific [phenomenological] analyses are needed" (4). (As we will see later, Levinas is less equivocal regarding insects.)

Although Levinas's work is deeply anthropocentric, if not speciesist,[42] his remarks on animal life are not without broader philosophical interest. Thus, as previously noted, Levinas maintains that our concern for animal suffering arises from the "transference of the idea of suffering to an animal," for it is only "because we as men know what suffering is that we can also have this obligation [to animals]." But what, we may ask, does it mean to *transfer* the idea of suffering to other animals from our prior knowledge of human misery? Is the "human" paradigmatic in the way Levinas here suggests? Indeed, if human beings are an *entirely* "new phenomenon" (4) in nature, then how is it even possible to transfer the "idea" of suffering *from* the human *to* the animal? Could we also transfer this "idea" to microbes, viruses, trees, stones, or rivers? Or rather, is our understanding of pain and suffering (among other things) "formed in responses to animals and to human beings together" (*TPD*, 60)?[43] Drawing on the later Wittgenstein, this is what I want to explore in the next two sections.

3. An Attitude toward a (Human) Soul

Like Levinas, Wittgenstein does not offer a detailed, systematic account of human-animal relations. There is one passage, however, that is frequently cited by commentators: "If a lion could talk, we could not understand him" (*PI*, p. 223). Not unreasonably, this remark is often taken to imply a *radical* difference between human beings (specifically as language-users) and animals. But this reading sits uncomfortably alongside many other things Wittgenstein says, both about animal life and what is "primitive" in human life.[44] Indeed, the idea of a radical separation between the human and animal realms jars against some of his broader philosophical ambitions. For throughout his later writings, Wittgenstein sketches more or less extraordinary scenarios[45] in order to foreground those mundane features of life we habitually neglect.[46] More specifically, these piecemeal "reminders"[47] are intended to help "our gaze to rest on certain phenomena" we routinely dismiss as "corresponding to a low state of intelligence" (*PO*, 389).[48] Against philosophers' predilection for explanatory-justificatory theorizing, and essentialist "craving for generality" (*BB*, 17), Wittgenstein thus focuses our attention on particular, concrete cases. (Indeed, most often he talks, not of "animals" *in general*, but of cats, dogs, squirrels, crocodiles, spiders, fish, orangutans, or flies.[49]) Although Wittgenstein's reminders are offered in a variety of contexts, what interests me here are those pertaining to the concrete details of intersubjective life. As will become clear later, there are important correlations between what he says of interhuman and human-animal relations.

In *Philosophical Investigations*, Wittgenstein distinguishes between having an "attitude towards a soul" and believing that the other has a "soul." This is what he says.

> "I believe that he is suffering."—Do I also *believe* that he isn't an automaton?

It would go against the grain to use the word in both connexions . . .

Suppose I say of a friend: "He isn't an automaton"—What information is conveyed by this, and to whom would it be information?
To a *human being* who meets him in ordinary circumstances? . . .

"I believe that he is not an automaton," just like that, so far makes
no sense.

My attitude towards him is an attitude towards a soul. I am not of
the *opinion* that he has a soul . . .

The human body is the best picture of the human soul. (*PI*, p. 178)

In a similar vein elsewhere, Wittgenstein writes: "The face is the soul
of the body" (*CV*, 23). I take Wittgenstein's point to be something like this:
Whatever the vagaries of history and culture (which, of course, should not be
trivialized), our everyday understanding of, and responsiveness to, other human
beings occur against an unquestioned backdrop of "common behaviours" that
constitute part of "the natural history of human beings" (*PI*, §415).[50] For example,
barring extraordinary circumstances, we do not see an anxious, angry, or tender
facial expression as a mere assemblage of nose, eyes, ears, and mouth, or as the
"distribution of matter in space" (*CV*, 82). Indeed, it would be markedly odd to
see another's "facial contortions" and then make *inferences* to "joy, grief, boredom"
(*Z*, §225). (It would be similarly bizarre to describe another's writhing in pain,
cowering in fear, or jumping for joy in purely geometric terms.[51]) Normally, we
do not have to decipher others' bodily gestures and facial expressions; rather, we
see consciousness in another's face—and even "a particular *shade* of consciousness" (§220). Seeing another's face "as sad, radiant, bored" is not therefore a
hypothetical-speculative matter, the result of reasoning by analogy,[52] or even
something we choose to do, but rather it happens "immediately" (§225).[53] That
we commonly respond to others without conjecture, hypothesizing, argument
or justification is, broadly speaking, what Wittgenstein means by having an
"attitude towards a soul."

But this is only part of the story. For notwithstanding Wittgenstein's aver-
sion to moral theorizing, his reminders often have an ethical dimension. This
is perhaps unsurprising given that the human face and body constitute what
might be called a "moral space" (*WEA*, 115) in providing the locus of those
expressions that lie at the heart of ethical life.[54] Wittgenstein thus invites us
to imagine someone whose facial expressions jolted between just five positions,

and asks whether a fixed smile would "really be a smile." He then responds: "'Smiling' is our name for an expression in a normal play of expressions.—I might not be able to react as I do to a smile. It would e.g. not make me smile myself" (Z, §527). Of course, this does not only apply to smiling.

> "Grief" describes a pattern which recurs, with different variations, in the weave of our life. If a man's bodily expression of sorrow and of joy alternated, say with the ticking of a clock, here we should not have the characteristic formation and pattern of sorrow or of the pattern of joy. (PI, p. 174)[55]

Likewise, this time of pain, Wittgenstein writes,

> The concept of pain is characterized by its particular function in our life.

> Pain has *this* position in our life; has *these* connexions; (That is to say: we only call "pain" what has *this* position, *these* connexions).

> Only surrounded by certain normal manifestations of life, is there such a thing as an expression of pain. Only surrounded by an even more far-reaching particular manifestation of life, such a thing as the expression of sorrow or affection. And so on. (Z, §§532–34)

While there is doubtless a story to be told about the cultural history of pain, the "position" suffering has in human life also includes features of our shared natural history.[56] That I respond in *these* ways to *these* events—that pain has *this* "position" in my life—is shaped by general facts of human embodiment, including what happens outside our control beneath the surface of our skin.[57] I am, after all, a finite creature whose flesh is easily torn, limbs easily broken, and organs easily ruptured, whose behavior is not wildly idiosyncratic, and so on. These are not isolable, *merely* empirical facts. For we can no more decide to abolish the concepts of "pain" and "suffering" from our lives[58] than we can radically revise the normal manifestations of life within which expressions and attributions of "pain" (among other things) make sense. There is a point at which, when trying to imagine a radically different form of human life, we are no longer imagining a recognizably *human* life at all.[59]

Clearly, the "position" and "connexions" pain has in our lives do not only pertain to one's *own* suffering. For not only am I ordinarily affected by the mere presence of another human being,[60] their suffering in particular makes a claim on me. (As Levinas puts it, wherever "a moan, a cry, a groan or a sigh" of pain occurs, there we find "the original call for aid, for curative help" [*EN*, 93].) To illustrate, Wittgenstein imagines a distraught infant holding his cheek and crying: "*One* kind of reaction to this is for the mother to try and comfort her child and to nurse him" (*PO*, 383). Here there is "nothing corresponding to a doubt whether the child is really in pain"—after all, infants have to learn how to dissimulate.[61] We are then invited to imagine another scenario: "The usual reaction to the child's complaints is as just described, but under some circumstances the mother behaves sceptically"; on occasion, she "shakes her head suspiciously, stops comforting and nursing her child—even expresses annoyance and lack of sympathy" (*PO*, 383). Although we might judge her to be insufficiently attentive, this woman's responses are not unintelligible. (She might simply be fatigued after a run of sleepless nights.) Finally, Wittgenstein sketches a more troubling case, describing a mother who is "sceptical right from the very beginning." Whenever her child cries, "she shrugs her shoulders and shakes her head; sometimes she looks at him inquiringly, examines him; on exceptional occasions she also makes vague attempts to comfort and nurse him" (*PO*, 383). What would we make of such responses? Well, we would presumably not think that she is simply being epistemically rigorous, nor would we describe her behavior as "skepticism." At the very least, we would not conclude that she had made a mistake one could correct with evidence or argument.[62] Rather, Wittgenstein suggests, we would think her "crazy" (*PO*, 383). This is not a crude folk-psychiatric diagnosis; Wittgenstein is simply registering the difficulty we would have finding our feet with someone who responded in these ways[63]—a difficulty that manifests itself in our having to *interpret* their behavior. It is significant that in such extraordinary cases we resort to reasoning, for what is lacking here are the appropriate *responses*.[64] Accordingly, Wittgenstein maintains that it is a "primitive reaction to tend, to treat, the part that hurts when someone else is in pain; and not merely when oneself is" (*Z*, §540). That is to say,

> The game doesn't begin with doubting whether someone has a toothache, because that doesn't—as it were—fit the game's biological function in our life. In its most primitive form it is a reaction to somebody's cries and gestures, a reaction of sympathy or something of that sort. (*PO*, 381)[65]

In short, our responsiveness to others' suffering is "not the result of thought," but what our thinking is "based *on*" (*Z*, §541).

Extraordinary circumstances aside, we do not deliberate about the reality of others' suffering. (Indeed, the ways we are cruel to others, or turn away from their suffering, tend to manifest a more or less tacit acknowledgment of their humanity.[66]) We might therefore say that responding to others' suffering is neither justified nor unjustified, neither reasonable nor unreasonable, but rather "something animal" (*OC*, §359). Of course, this is not to deny that in particular situations we might treat another's suffering with varying degrees of circumspection. But here, as elsewhere, we would need "grounds for doubt" (§122), or "reasons for leaving a familiar track" (*PO*, 379). In this sense, hesitancy in the face of others' suffering is parasitic on our "natural, instinctive . . . behaviour towards other human beings" (*Z*, §545).[67] What Wittgenstein describes as having "an attitude towards a soul" thus comprises those unthinking responses we have toward others.[68] And although this "attitude" can be strengthened or weakened by circumstance, it is not something one can choose to adopt or abandon at will.[69] Indeed, someone who routinely treated others' distress with suspicion (or who could muster such suspicion at will) would thereby lack the normal reactions that make ethical life possible.

Wittgenstein claims that it is a "primitive reaction" to attend to others' suffering, and I have suggested that this is central to having "an attitude towards a soul." But then what of our relations with nonhuman animals? This is what I want to discuss next.

4. Human and Animal Bodies

According to Wittgenstein, "instead of 'attitude toward the soul' one could also say 'attitude toward a human'" (*LWP2*, 38). Should we therefore conclude that such an "attitude" can only be had toward other human beings? Or can we speak of having an attitude towards the soul of an animal? I think we can—after all, Wittgenstein himself suggests that when "one sees the behaviour of a living thing, one sees its soul" (*PI*, §357). However, given the immense diversity of animal life, and the manifold differences between "us" and "them," we need to consider the possibilities of having such an attitude toward particular forms of animal life.[70]

As noted earlier, Levinas hesitates when asked if the face of an animal truly demands our "welcome." While his circumspection may not be entirely sincere,[71] I want to take it seriously. For as Wittgenstein reminds us, we often *do* experience "uncertainty" regarding "whether animals, particularly lower animals, such as flies, feel pain." He proceeds: "Indeed, aren't we really uncertain in our behaviour towards animals? One doesn't know: Is he being cruel or not?" (*RPP2*, §659). In a similar vein, he notes our hesitancy when encountering "animals that least resemble humans. (Jellyfish, for instance.)" (*LWP2*, §238). This allusion to "resemblance" is important. For elsewhere Wittgenstein remarks that "only of a living human being and what resembles (behaves like) a living human being can one say: it has sensations; it sees; is blind; is deaf; is conscious or unconscious" (*PI*, §281), and likewise: "Only of what behaves like a human being can one say that it *has* pains" (§283). In other words, what we can/cannot meaningfully say of other animals (whether they are "in pain," "sad," "frightened," "happy," and so on), and the relational possibilities between us and them, are shaped by "very general facts of nature" (p. 230). I take these general facts to include our respective forms of embodiment,[72] though the importance of the human form is routinely underestimated by philosophers. As Cockburn rightly suggests, we should not assume that ethical life must hinge on something more fundamental or metaphysical.

> The human body is subject to disease and is readily damaged by external forces in many ways. Further, no matter how much care an individual takes, death, and, with that, the disintegration of the body, is, in the end, inevitable. These facts play a crucial role in virtually all of our more important relationships with each other. (*OHB*, 76)

If such general facts of nature shape interhuman relations, then it is reasonable to suppose that they also play a significant role in our dealings with, and attitudes toward, other animals.[73]

I think Wittgenstein is right to draw attention to our uncertainty regarding whether some forms of animal life (perhaps especially "lower animals") suffer. However, this should not be exaggerated. For as he writes,

> What has a soul, or pain, to do with a stone? . . . Look at a stone and imagine it having sensations.—One says to oneself: How could one so much as get the idea of ascribing a *sensation* to a *thing*? One might as well ascribe it to a number!—And now look at a wriggling fly and at once these difficulties vanish and pain seems able to get a foothold here. . . . And so, too, a corpse seems to us quite inaccessible to pain.—Our attitude to what is alive and to what is dead, is not the same. All our reactions are different. (*PI*, §§283–84)[74]

Unlike the stone, in appropriate circumstances attributing "pain" to a fly can get a conceptual and practical foothold. Of course, this is not to suggest that we respond to the plight of insects (or other forms of animal life) and human beings in identical ways. It would, after all, be pretty odd for someone to be haunted by nightmares or so wracked with guilt that they attempt suicide after swatting a wasp, swallowing a fly, or stepping on a snail.[75] And yet we can make *some* sense even of these extreme responses.[76] (Contrast these cases with someone similarly traumatized by kicking a stone into a ditch or breaking a twig underfoot.) Here we should remind ourselves of the concern we often *do* show for "lower animals"; for example, we rescue flies from spiders' webs, feel ashamed (albeit momentarily) for soaking them in fly spray, and chastise our children for cruelly pulling off their wings. That we use the vocabulary of "rescuing," "shame," and "cruelty" in these contexts is important, for there is no equivalent terminology available to describe our ordinary dealings with stones or numbers.[77] (What would follow from ascribing "pain" to a stone? How would the plight of a number manifest itself?) Consider a parallel case: We do not feel pity for coal burning on a fire. But is this because we believe that coal is not conscious or sentient, does not have interests or rights? Or rather, is it because we cannot see how pity toward coal could be given and received? Is it of marginal importance that "You cannot rub the affected part because coal has no parts. You cannot hold its hand because it has no hands. You cannot be sickened by its writhing because it does not writhe" (*LCT*, 56)? Analogously, consider our attitudes toward vegetal life: While I evidently can exhibit varying degrees of care and concern for plants, is it a *merely* empirical fact that a tree "does not have an ear to whisper into, eyes to look into, or a shoulder to put one's arm around" (*MBF*, 489)?[78]

Although we can make sense of rescuing a fly, treating it cruelly, and even of feeling ashamed of our behavior toward it, what we can meaningfully say of our relations with specific forms of animal life is not unbounded. Can I, for example, console a fly in distress? And what would it mean to comfort an animal whose injuries I cannot tend to, who is too small and delicate to be touched without being damaged—or, indeed, too large and coarsely covered to feel my intervention?[79] Can I have a companion wasp or whale, or seriously declare my fondness for this particular ant or worm? While I can meaningfully talk of "loving" Alfie (my dog) as an individual with whom I share a unique personal history, what sense would there be in saying such things of animals whose natural life-span extends for just a few hours or days? For all our respective peculiarities, Alfie and I play and rest together, show mutual concern, tolerate and sometimes ignore one another.[80] Indeed, in his sheer bloody-mindedness, Alfie sometimes refuses to respond to my petitions. It is not a trivial fact that I cannot share these aspects of life with flies, beetles, spiders, snails, and many other creatures.[81] Of his own dog (Lupa), Pitcher thus talks of feeling "suffocating remorse" (*DCS*, 54) when once having handled her too roughly. Later he describes Lupa as "dignified" and having "great integrity," as not being inclined to "exaggerate her feelings or needs" (65), and as "magnificent" (123) in the way she handled her later illness and approaching death.[82] Pitcher subsequently recalls the reactions of himself and friend Ed to Lupa's euthanasia.

> Outside in the car, we two sat weeping, plunged into a world of grief. For days after that, tears would strike again, with no warning. Even now, I have to avert my eyes from certain sights—the scratches on the front door made by Lupa as she prepared herself to meet the onslaught of the incoming mail, the smudges she left on the wall next to her bed. And yet I can't think of removing these signs, these visible remnants of her life. I regularly dream of Lupa; so does Ed, and I suppose we always shall. But though she enriches our dream world, her death has left a great empty place in the center of our waking life. (127)

In a similar vein, Pitcher describes his relationship with Lupa as paradoxical in the sense that, on the one hand, he cared for her "as parents love and care for their child," but on the other, she was also (for him) "a mother figure." For as long as she was around, he felt "in some inexplicable way, if not exactly safe from harm, then at least watched over and generally speaking okay" (66).[83] While one might say analogous things about a variety of different creatures, one could not talk in this way of just any form of animal life. These examples could, of course, be multiplied. My point is that the general facts of nature (including forms of embodiment, behavioral repertoire, longevity, and size) that determine these relational possibilities are not merely empirical facts about "us" and "animals." Rather, they provide the bounds within which ethical life, in all its variety, is lived and made sense of.

There are undoubtedly many borderline cases in having an attitude toward the soul of an animal. Sometimes we simply do not know whether our concept of "suffering" (among many other concepts) can be applied in particular circumstances. Much will depend on whether the ascription of "suffering" parallels other cases of what we call "suffering" in the ordinary weave of life. This is not, however, to suggest that we *decide* to utilize or withhold such concepts. Whatever concepts might be, they are presumably not the sort of thing we can use as we wish—at least, not if we want to remain intelligible to others. It is perhaps more accurate to say that our unthinking responses to particular forms of animal life can be more or less circumspect and hesitant. Because the bounds of sense are not sharply delineated, there is no clear-cut, a priori way of demarcating between sentimentality, anthropocentrism, and anthropomorphism in our dealings with other creatures. Still, notwithstanding these cautionary points, it seems to me that Wittgenstein's piecemeal approach provides a valuable counterweight to what he diagnoses as our "craving for generality" (*BB*, 17). I do not want to deny that his emphasis on what resembles a human being is anthropocentric. It is, however, a significantly more hospitable anthropocentrism than Levinas's. I will return to this in section 6. Before that, let me say something about suffering and vulnerability.

5. Vulnerable Lives

As we saw earlier, corporeal suffering lies at the heart of Levinas's ethics. Thus, according to Atterton, the capacity to experience pain is a central criterion for who/what counts as an "other." Indeed, as he rightly notes, there is a "general agreement that an animal that cannot suffer or enjoy has no interests to harm or promote, and thus nothing I can do to it that can possibly take away from its welfare or do it any good . . . Thus I can be responsible only *for* a being that suffers." As such, Atterton concludes, "only beings capable of suffering can be said to be capable of provoking a response (and responsibility) that is Levinasian" (*LOM*, 641). Clearly, the capacity to experience and exhibit pain, to whom/what we can meaningfully attribute "pain," and how we are able to respond to others' pain, all contribute to shaping ethical life. But while Levinas seems unable to comprehend how an animal could make a fully ethical claim on us, Wittgenstein suggests that our talk of "pain" gets a conceptual and practical foothold with even a common house-fly. While I think he is right to remind us of our ordinary interactions with such "lower animals," Wittgenstein's emphasis on *pain* is potentially misleading. For one might conclude that meaningful attributions of "pain" depend on the neurological workings of particular species. And if that is right, then the "foothold" Wittgenstein alludes to may turn out to be illusory; we might simply be *mistaken* in attributing "pain" to flies (among many other forms of animal life). What I want to explore in the remainder of this section is the extent to which we can have an attitude toward the soul of an animal that does not hinge on their capacity to experience pain.

Without doubt, increased scientific understanding of different species can make us more or less ethically responsive toward them.[84] This does not, however, seem to be what interests Wittgenstein. After all, on his view, having an "attitude" toward another human being is a more primitive affair than any particular beliefs one might have about him. It therefore seems reasonable to suppose that our responsiveness toward nonhuman animals need not depend on the beliefs we have about them. While Wittgenstein talks explicitly of "pain" getting a foothold when we see a wriggling fly, we can, I think, make sense of another's *vulnerability* independently of their capacity to feel pain. To illustrate what I have in mind, consider the following scenarios: One day, walking in the woods, you see someone willfully destroying spiders' webs, stamping on snails, or pulling the wings off butterflies. Alternatively, imagine witnessing the frenzied activity of wasps around a nest that someone has just set alight, or discovering that your neighbor keeps goldfish in individual glasses of water rather than a fish tank. In these (and similar) scenarios, whatever concern we might feel for such creatures does not seem to hinge on the belief that spiders, snails, butterflies, wasps, or goldfish actually experience *pain*. Here, then, we might say that pulling the wings off butterflies is "cruel," not because of any pain caused, but because this is "the wanton mutilation of a living thing" (*GE*, 179).

This idea is attractive but difficult to unpack. Thus, while Hacking claims to be immensely fond of insects, he confesses that he "cannot see the souls of ants or spiders." More specifically, Hacking "cannot much resonate with their bodies"; at most, he "can reason by analogy and draw tepid inferences, attributing pain to ants, or fear and loathing to spiders." In a similar vein, of wasps, he remarks: "from their behaviours I can get a glimpse of a life, but it does not carry me far, for although their bodies are beautiful, they do not have bodies through which I can sympathize, to which I can respond as a fellow creature" (*SOC*, 712). I think Hacking's difficulties are real and important. Indeed, Levinas seems to encounter the same sort of difficulties with insects. For after admitting that he does not know precisely when one has the right to be called "face," Levinas similarly concedes,

> I do not know whether one comes across it in the snake! [Laughter]. I do not know how to answer that question, since more specific analyses are needed. Not in the flea, for example. The flea! It's an insect which jumps, eh? [laughter]. (*AI*, 4)

Levinas's laughter is neither incidental nor, I think, merely an expression of flippant anthropocentrism. Rather, for him, it would be as comically incongruous to talk of the "face" of an insect as it would be to talk of "the joy and sorrow, etc., of fish" (*RPP2*, §29), or of one's dog as "looking forward to Christmas" or "fearful of Judgment Day." As previously discussed, I can meaningfully talk of "sharing a life" with Alfie in his irreplaceable singularity—a life of companionship, mutual concern and affection, and so on. But I cannot, except perhaps as a joke, say such things of his fleas, ticks, or worms.[85] We often experience varying degrees of curiosity, fascination and/or aesthetic pleasure regarding "lower animals"—as Levinas rightly notes, our "attraction" toward different forms of animal life is "complex" (*AI*, 4). And in many circumstances we struggle to resonate with their bodies in the way Hacking describes. Perhaps, however, we can begin to make sense of responding as a "fellow creature" in at least some of these cases. Let me explain what I have in mind.

In a short essay documenting the last moments of a moth's life, Virginia Woolf reports feeling pity for his "frail and diminutive body." Of this "marvellous" and "pathetic" creature, she proceeds.

> It was as if someone had taken a tiny bead of pure life and decked it as lightly as possible with down and feathers, had set it dancing and zigzagging to show us the true nature of life. Thus displayed one could not get over the strangeness of it. . . . Again, the thought of all that life might have been had he been born in any other shape caused one to view his simple activities with a kind of joy. (*DOM*, 166)

Having momentarily settled down in the sunlight, the moth then struggled to resume his "dance."

> After perhaps a seventh attempt he slipped from the wooden ledge and fell, fluttering his wings, on to his back on the window sill. The helplessness of his attitude roused me. It flashed upon me that he was in difficulties; he could no longer raise himself; his legs struggled vainly. But, as I stretched out a pencil, meaning to help him to right himself, it came over me that the failure and awkwardness were the approach of death. I laid the pencil down again. (*DOM*, 166)

Woolf soon realized that there was nothing she could do besides watch the "extraordinary efforts made by those tiny legs against an oncoming doom." After a brief pause, the moth's legs fluttered again: "It was superb, this last protest, and so frantic that he succeeded at last in righting himself." Moved by such a "gigantic effort on the part of an insignificant little moth," Woolf then saw the unmistakable signs of death approaching.

> The body relaxed, and instantly grew stiff. The struggle was over. The insignificant little creature now knew death. As I looked at the dead moth, this minute wayside triumph of so great a force over so mean an antagonist filled me with wonder. . . . O yes, he seemed to say, death is stronger than I am. (167)

Whatever anthropomorphism these passages contain, Woolf's account is not wildly fanciful or sentimental. Two things in particular are worth highlighting here: (1) When she describes being roused by the moth's "helplessness," Woolf makes no mention of his *pain*. Nothing she says here seems to hinge on the assumption that this animal possesses the inner neurological structure necessary for feeling pain. In this way we can begin to see, not only what having an attitude toward the soul of an insect might mean, but more specifically, what it is for another creature to be *vulnerable* regardless of their capacity to experience pain. (2) When Woolf describes the moth as "pathetic" and "marvellous" (166), we need not take this to mean that he was pathetic *and in addition* marvelous. Rather, the moth's being pathetic and marvelous are internally related, and much the same can be said of human beings. For as fleshy, finite creatures we are exposed to an inevitable (and always possible) death, just as we are vulnerable to physical damage and illness, hunger, thirst, excessive heat and cold, the natural degeneration of old age, not to mention an array of disappointments, regrets, fears, and frustrations. None of us are immune to these frailties. But again, as I have been suggesting throughout this essay, these are not *merely* empirical facts about our natural history. Rather, our being "precious and pathetic" constitutes the mundane conditions of possibility for ethical life. Unlike invulnerable, incorporeal, immortal beings, for us everything is "preciously precarious" (*LAB*, 146).[86] But like Woolf's moth, we are not precious *and in addition* pathetic; these are no more discrete traits than our vulnerability is an unfortunate appendage to our humanity. (As Levinas quips: "The body does not happen as an accident to the soul" [*TI*, 168].) That we are creatures of flesh and blood who are born, require nurturing and protection, grow old, suffer illness and die are very general facts of nature that provide the bounds within which human life, in all its variety, is lived. And particular forms of animal life share much of this with us.[87]

6. Who Are We? Who Is the Other?

Before concluding, I want to briefly consider two related worries one might have about the approach taken in this essay:

First, in attempting to describe our everyday practices, and thereby ascertain what we can/cannot meaningfully say in specific circumstances, Wittgenstein's "reminders" may seem unduly parochial. For who, we might ask, are the "we" who can/cannot meaningfully say this or that?[88] Undoubtedly, the Wittgensteinian approach can lead to more or less questionable stipulations. (For example, when Wittgenstein claims that "the word 'hope' refers to a phenomenon of human life"

(*PI*, §583),[89] he neglects the fact that the words *hope* and *hopeful* are regularly used with regard to (some) animals—not only by sentimental, anthropomorphizing fools.[90] On a more explicitly ethical point, Gaita maintains that we "cannot respond to what happens in the abattoir as we respond to murder" (*TPD*, 211),[91] while Margalit insists that "animals do not have accusing eyes" [*TDS*, 112].) Should we therefore conclude that, in the broadly Wittgensteinian view I have tried to develop, what we can/cannot meaningfully say of our relations with other animals are merely conventional? Not if that means that one could decide to henceforth start talking of "sharing a life" with a worm or "loving" a flea in its unique, irreplaceable singularity. We can make perfectly good sense of having special attachments and responsibilities to particular animals. But what would we make of someone who described their "relationship" with a frog, snail, or goldfish in the way we commonly talk of our relationships with beloved dogs? And even if it turns out that what "we" can/cannot meaningfully say in particular circumstances is more or less local, this is not a trifling fact. For it says something crucially important about our cultural form of life, and what *we* can/cannot make sense of in the sayings and doings of others.

Second, another objection may be that trying to determine who/what qualifies as a morally considerable "other" is itself ethically problematic. After all, might not "anything . . . take on a face" (*FBA*, 127)?[92] But then what would it mean to see " 'life itself,' in each of its forms, as addressing us" (*TC*, 140–41)? Could we seriously describe "a stray chromosome, a stray virus, a wanton cellular division" (*AE*, 234) as singular "others" who "address" us? And if so, what would follow from that? As previously suggested, the bounds of sense are not rigidly demarcated. But this is not to say that there are no boundaries in operation here. For it is not a trivial—or merely *conventional*—fact that we cannot meaningfully talk of "pity," "compassion" or "cruelty" with regard to anything we choose.[93]

There is something attractive in the thought that we could, with suitable effort and ingenuity, radically change our dealings with other animals—beyond, I mean, altering our dietary habits, and such like. But there is a danger of hubris here. Clearly, we can become more attuned to other forms of animal life, especially if we spend time in their company. But how far does the empathic imagination extend? Is it infinitely malleable? We should not pretend that abstract, a priori theorizing can answer these sorts of questions. Here, at least as a start, we can only look at particular concrete cases and try to ascertain what is meaningful for us to do and say of our relations with other creatures. Perhaps, without a measure of anthropocentrism, talk of "ethical responsibility for the other" becomes empty—or "like an engine idling" (*PI*, §132). Perhaps the challenge that faces us is not one of eradicating anthropocentrism from ethical life, but of fostering more hospitable forms of anthropocentrism.

7. Afterword

At the time of writing this essay, Alfie and I have shared a life for just over six years. Living in close proximity with one another, I have spent a significant part of that time watching him, looking into his eyes—as he looks back and watches me.[94] I find myself wanting to say that I now see a trace of him, not only in the eyes of other dogs, but in many different forms of animal life. (To what, if any, extent this is merely an anthropomorphic projection on my part I do not know.) What is it I see, or at least think I can see, here? It is tempting to say, their shared "animality." But that is potentially misleading. For what I see here does not differ fundamentally from what I see in the face and body of another human being. In Alfie's eyes (though not only his eyes) I want to say that I see "all the weakness, all the mortality, all the naked and disarmed mortality of the other" (*EN*, 232). It is not patently absurd to say something similar about a wriggling fly or a dying moth.[95]

Abbreviations

AB   Drew Leder. *The Absent Body*. Chicago, IL and London: University of Chicago Press, 1990.

AE   John D. Caputo. *Against Ethics: Contributions to a Poetics of Obligation with Constant Reference to Deconstruction*. Bloomington and Indianapolis: Indiana University Press, 1993.

AL   Michael Leahy. *Against Liberation: Putting Animals in Perspective*. London and New York: Routledge, 1994.

ATL   Jean Améry. *At the Mind's Limits: Contemplations by a Survivor on Auschwitz and Its Realities*. Trans. Sidney Rosenfeld and Stella P. Rosenfeld. London: Granta Books, 1999.

ATT   Jacques Derrida. *The Animal That Therefore I Am*. Trans. David Wills. New York: Fordham University Press, 2008.

AV   Doug Halls. "Agency, Vulnerability, and Societas: Toward a Levinasian Politics of the Animal." In *Facing Nature: Levinas and Environmental Thought*. Eds. William Edelglass, James Hatley, and Christian Diehm. Pittsburgh, PA: Duquesne University Press, 2012, 41–65.

AWM   Mary Midgley. *Animals and Why They Matter: A Journey around the Species Barrier*. Middlesex, UK: Penguin Books, 1983.

BB   Ludwig Wittgenstein. *The Blue and Brown Books*. Oxford, UK: Basil Blackwell, 1969.

BP   Elaine Scarry. *The Body in Pain: The Making and Unmaking of the World.* New York and Oxford, UK: Oxford University Press, 1985.

CHA   Martha Nussbaum. "Compassion: Human and Animal." In *Species Matters: Humane Advocacy and Cultural* Theory. Eds. Marianne DeKoven and Michael Lundblad. New York: Columbia University Press, 2012.

CV   Ludwig Wittgenstein. *Culture and Value.* Trans. Peter Winch. Oxford, UK: Blackwell Publishers, 1994.

DC   Tony Milligan. "Dependent Companions." *Journal of Applied Philosophy* 26, no. 4 (2009): 402–13.

DCS   George Pitcher. *The Dogs Who Came to Stay.* New York: Dutton, 1995.

DM   John D. Caputo. *Demythologizing Heidegger.* Bloomington and Indianapolis: Indiana University Press, 1993.

DH   David Wood. "*Comment ne pas manger*—Deconstruction and Humanism." In *Animal Others: On Ethics, Ontology, and Animal* Life. Ed. H. Peter Steeves. Albany: State University of New York Press, 1999, 15–35.

DOM   Virginia Woolf. "The Death of the Moth." In *Mortalism: Readings on the Meaning of* Life. Ed. Peter Heinegg. Amherst, NY: Prometheus Books, 2003, 165–67.

DW   Rush Rhees. *Discussions of Wittgenstein.* Bristol, UK: Thoemmes Press, 1996.

DWW   Nancy Scheper-Hughes. "Death without Weeping." In *Death, Mourning, and Burial: A Cross-Cultural* Reader. Ed. Antonius C. G. M. Robben. Oxford, UK: Blackwell, 2008, 179–93.

EA   Arthur Schopenhauer. *Essays and Aphorisms.* Trans. R. J. Hollingdale. London: Penguin Books, 2004.

FA   Peter Atterton. "Facing Animals." In *Facing Nature: Levinas and Environmental Thought.* Eds. William Edelglass, James Hatley, and Christian Diehm. Pittsburgh: Duquesne University Press, 2012, 25–39.

FBA   Matthew Calarco. "Faced by Animals." In *Radicalizing Levinas.* Eds. Peter Atterton and Matthew Calarco. Albany: State University of New York Press, 2010, 113–33.

FF   Peter Atterton. "Face-to-Face with the Other Animal?" In *Levinas and Buber: Dialogue and Difference.* Eds. Peter Atterton, Mathew Calarco, and Maurice Friedman. Pittsburgh, PA: Duquesne University Press, 2004, 262–81.

GE   Raimond Gaita. *Good and Evil: An Absolute Conception* (2nd ed.). London and New York: Routledge, 2004.

GDT   Emmanuel Levinas. *God, Death, and Time.* Trans. Bettina Bergo. Stanford, CA: Stanford University Press, 2000.

IEP   Michael Marder. "Is It Ethical to Eat Plants?" *Parallax* 19, no. 1 (2013): 29–37.

IM   Mikel Burley. "Immortality and Meaning: Reflections on the Makropulos Debate." *Philosophy* 84, no. 4 (2009): 529–47.

LAB   Jorge Luis Borges. *Labyrinths: Selected Stories and Other Writings*. London: Penguin Books, 1970.

LC   Ludwig Wittgenstein. *Lectures and Conversations on Aesthetics, Psychology and Religious Belief*. Oxford, UK: Blackwell Publishers, 1994.

LCT   Richard W. Beardsmore. "If a Lion Could Talk . . ." In *Wittgenstein and the Philosophy of Culture*. Eds. K. S. Johannessen and T. Nordenstam. Vienna: Verlag Hölder-Pichler-Tempsky, 1996, 41–59.

LHR   Bob Plant. "Levinas and the Holocaust: A Reconstruction." *Journal of Jewish Thought and Philosophy* 22, no. 1 (2014), 44–79.

LOM   Peter Atterton. "Levinas and Our Moral Responsibility toward Other Animals." *Inquiry: An Interdisciplinary Journal of Philosophy* 54, no. 6 (2011): 633–49.

LOP   Michael Marder. "The Life of Plants and the Limits of Empathy." *Dialogue* 51, no. 2 (2012): 259–73.

LWM   Norman Malcolm. *Ludwig Wittgenstein: A Memoir*. Oxford, UK: Clarendon Press, 2001.

LWP1   Ludwig Wittgenstein. *Last Writings on the Philosophy of Psychology*, vol. 1. Trans. C. G. Luckhardt and Maximilian A. E. Aue. Oxford, UK: Basil Blackwell, 1990.

LWP2   Ludwig Wittgenstein. *Last Writings on the Philosophy of Psychology*, vol. 2. Trans. C. G. Luckhardt and Maximilian A. E. Aue. Oxford, UK: Basil Blackwell, 1993.

MBF   David Cockburn. "The Mind, the Brain and the Face." *Philosophy* 60, no. 234 (1985): 477–93.

MN   D. Z. Phillips. "My Neighbour and My Neighbours." *Philosophical Investigations* 12, no. 2 (April 1989): 112–33.

MQ   Rush Rhees. *Moral Questions*. Basingstoke, UK: Macmillan Press, 1999.

OB   Emmanuel Levinas. *Otherwise than Being or Beyond Essence*. Trans. Alphonso Lingis. Dordrecht, the Netherlands: Kluwer Academic Publishers, 1994.

OC   Ludwig Wittgenstein. *On Certainty*. Trans. Denis Paul and G. E. M. Anscombe. Oxford, UK: Blackwell Publishers, 1999.

OHB   David Cockburn. *Other Human Beings*. London: Macmillan, 1990.

PI   Ludwig Wittgenstein. *Philosophical Investigations*. Trans. G. E. M. Anscombe. Oxford, UK: Basil Blackwell, 1958.

PO   Ludwig Wittgenstein. *Philosophical Occasions: 1912–1951*. Indianapolis, IN and
        Cambridge, UK: Hackett, 1993.

RFGB   Ludwig Wittgenstein. "Remarks on Frazer's *Golden Bough*." Trans. John Bev-
        ersluis. In *Wittgenstein: Sources and Perspectives*. Ed. C. G. Luckhardt. Bristol,
        UK: Thoemmes Press, 1996, 61–81.

RFM   Ludwig Wittgenstein. *Remarks on the Foundations of Mathematics*. Trans. G. E.
        M. Anscombe. Oxford, UK: Basil Blackwell, 1994.

RH   John D. Caputo. *Radical Hermeneutics: Repetition, Desconstruction, and the Her-
        meneutic Project*. Bloomington and Indianapolis: Indiana University Press, 1987.

RPP1   Ludwig Wittgenstein. *Remarks on the Philosophy of Psychology*, vol. I. Trans.
        G. E. M. Anscombe. Oxford, UK: Basil Blackwell, 1980.

RPP2   Ludwig Wittgenstein. *Remarks on the Philosophy of Psychology*, vol. II. Trans.
        C. G. Luckhardt and M. A. E. Aue. Oxford, UK: Basil Blackwell, 1980.

SOC   Ian Hacking. "On Sympathy: With Other Creatures." *Tijdschrift voor Filosofie*
        63 (2001): 685–717.

SW   Simone Weil. *Simone Weil: An Anthology*. London: Penguin Classics, 2005.

TAC   William Earle. *The Autobiographical Consciousness: A Philosophical Inquiry into
        Existence*. Chicago, IL: Quadrangle Books, 1972.

TC   David Wood. "Thinking with Cats." In *Animal Philosophy: Ethics and Identity*.
        Eds. Peter Atterton and Matthew Calarco. London and New York: Continuum,
        2004, 129–44.

TCR   Stanley Cavell. *The Cavell Reader*. Ed. Stephen Mulhall. Cambridge, MA:
        Blackwell, 1996.

TDL   Nancy E. Baker. "The Difficulty of Language: Wittgenstein on Animals and
        Humans." In *Language, Ethics and Animal Life: Wittgenstein and Beyond*. Eds.
        Niklas Forsberg, Mikel Burley, and Nora Hämäläinen. New York: Bloomsbury,
        2012, 45–64.

TDS   Avishai Margalit. *The Decent Society*. Cambridge, MA and London: Harvard
        University Press, 1998.

TEE   John D. Caputo. "The End of Ethics." In *The Blackwell Guide to Ethical Theory*.
        Ed. Hugh LaFollette. Oxford, UK: Blackwell Publishing, 2000, 111–28.

TMS   Peter Winch. *Trying to Make Sense*. Oxford, UK and New York: Basil Blackwell,
        1987.

TPD   Raimond Gaita. *The Philosopher's Dog*. London and New York: Routledge, 2003.

UAA   Roger Wertheimer. "Understanding the Abortion Argument." *Philosophy &
        Public Affairs* 1, no. 1 (1971): 67–95.

UD	Kenneth J. Shapiro. "Understanding Dogs through Kinesthetic Empathy, Social Construction, and History." In *Social Creatures: A Human and Animal Studies Reader*. Ed. Clifton P. Flynn. New York: Lantern Books, 2008, 31–48.

UDC	Clinton R. Sanders. "Understanding Dogs: Caretaker's Attributions of Mindedness in Canine-Human Relationships." In *Social Creatures: A Human and Animal Studies Reader*. Ed. Clifton P. Flynn. New York: Lantern Books, 2008, 59–74.

WD	Bob Plant. "Welcoming Dogs: Levinas and 'the Animal' Question." *Philosophy & Social Criticism* 37, no. 1 (2011): 49–71.

WEA	B. R. Tilghman. *Wittgenstein, Ethics and Aesthetics: The View from Eternity*. Albany: State University of New York Press, 1991.

WFR	Edward F. Mooney and Lyman F. Mower. "Witness to the Face of a River: Thinking with Levinas and Thoreau." In *Facing Nature: Levinas and Environmental Thought*. Eds. William Edelglass, James Hatley, and Christian Diehm. Pittsburgh, PA: Duquesne University Press, 2012, 279–99.

WL	Bob Plant. *Wittgenstein and Levinas: Ethical and Religious Thought*. London and New York: Routledge, 2005.

Z	Ludwig Wittgenstein. *Zettel*. Trans. G. E. M. Anscombe. Oxford, UK: Basil Blackwell, 1990.

Notes

1. On the problematic locution "animals"/"the animal" *in general*, see *DH*, 29; *ATT*, 23–24, 31–32, 34, 40–41, 47–48, 59, 89–90, 126, 135.

2. As I hope will become clear later, what this welcoming involves will depend on specific, concrete cases.

3. See *EA*, 41–42, 45.

4. For example: (1) While we often suffer from the loss of pleasure, we feel little (and only momentary) relief when our pain ceases. (2) Although I might regret the opportunities for pleasure I never had or missed, I do not usually have a corresponding positive feeling about the suffering I never had or avoided. (3) When in extreme and/or chronic pain, not only can I barely remember *not* being in pain, imagining being free from pain in the future becomes near impossible—and when imaginable, often irrelevant to my current suffering. (4) Whereas feeling well is generally difficult to characterize, feeling unwell tends to have distinctive, identifiable qualities.

5. See *AE*, 205.

6. See *AT*, 27.

7. See *ATT*, 12, 106–7, 112.

8. See *PN*, 95.

9. See also *OS*, 102.

10. See *IR*, 159–60.

11. See *TMS*, 174; *OGM*, 10; *EN*, 9; *TEE*, 118.

12. On the added complication of the "third party" see *WL*, chap. 7.

13. See *EI*, 86, 89, 92; *CPP*, 55.

14. See *IR*, 53.

15. See *OS*, 44.

16. See *EI*, 86; *OS*, 102, 158; *EN*, 145.

17. See *IR*, 52.

18. See *GDT*, 188.

19. On mortality and a meaningful life see *TAC*, 220.

20. In this sense at least, moral theorists resemble "the crowd that gathers around the scene of an accident" (*TEE*, 111).

21. As Caputo notes, even when philosophers do discuss embodiment, they tend to presuppose an "athletic, healthy, erect, white male body, sexually able and unambiguously gendered, well-born, well-bred" (*AE*, 194).

22. See *LAB*, 146; *TAC*, 216–17.

23. Here, we might say, justification *comes to an end* (see *OC*, §192, 563).

24. See also *OB*, 54; *AT*, 108; *IR*, 81.

25. See *LHR*.

26. See *DM*, 167–68.

27. See *RH*, 288; *AE*, 54.

28. See *EN*, 95.

29. See *EN*, 96.

30. See *EN*, 97.

31. Although I will not discuss this, Derrida is right to note that human and animal suffering is not due to a common ability or power, but rather to a shared passivity; a "not-being-able" (*ATT*, 27).

32. See *FF*, 279; *LOM*, 646; *FA*, 38.

33. See *FF*, 272.

34. Interestingly, Levinas here sees something Darwinian in Heidegger's *Dasein* (see *IR*, 136, 145; *AI*, 5).

35. For example, Levinas talks of the "brutish dumbness" (*CPP*, 55) of animals, and describes the "sounds and noises of nature" as "words that disappoint us" (*OS*, 148).

36. This is a curious notion, not least because nonhuman animals (unlike their human counterparts) do not normally murder members of their own species.

37. See *OS*, 92; *OGM*, 171, 175; *EN*, 143, 145, 148; *IR*, 225.

38. Likewise, as Nussbaum notes, only human beings suffer from "anthropodenial," for "no animal hates being an animal, wishes not to be an animal, tries to convince itself that it is not an animal" (*CHA*, 156; see also 166–67).

39. For more on this see *WD*. Although Levinas admits "myself, I don't have much to do with animals" (*AI*, 1), it is perhaps not incidental that his most positive remarks on nonhuman life (namely, Bobby) are autobiographical.

40. When Levinas describes Bobby as "the last Kantian in Nazi Germany," he presumably wants to stress the unconditionality of Bobby's response to the prisoners. But,

of course, Bobby's response is fundamentally un-Kantian insofar as he lacks the "brain needed to universalize maxims and drives" (*DF*, 153; see also *ATT*, 114). Leaving that aside, Levinas maintains that the individual who manifests "saintliness" is someone who is "attached more to the being of the other than to his own." (Indeed, in this sense, ethical responsibility is "unreasonable.") But if that is right, then why don't Bobby's actions qualify as "saintly"? In him is there not also "something other than pure Being that persists in being" (*AI*, 3)?

41. Levinas maintains that "[t]he child is a pure exposure of expression insofar as it is pure vulnerability; it has not yet learned to dissemble, to deceive, to be insincere. What distinguishes human language from animal or child expression, for example, is that the human speaker can remain silent, can refuse to be exposed in sincerity . . . The animal is incapable of this duplicity; the dog, for instance, cannot suppress its bark, the bird its song. But man can repress his saying" (*DCC*, 64–65). But Levinas is simply wrong when he asserts that the dog "cannot suppress its bark," as anyone who has lived with dogs will attest.

42. See *FF*, 263; *LOM*, 634. Precisely what "speciesism" amounts to, and why it is troublesome remains contestable. I will not discuss that here.

43. See also *LCT*, 55–58; *TPD*, 69–70; *HB*, 147.

44. For example, Wittgenstein suggests that linguistic expressions of pain are not reports on one's inner experience, but rather new forms of "pain-behaviour" which *replace* more primitive forms—such as "crying" (*PI*, §244). If that is right, then there is nothing *fundamentally* different between my linguistic pain-behavior and my dog's squeals of pain. See also *PI*, §343; *RPP2*, §644, 689; *Z*, §§391, 540–41, 545; *PO*, 373, 377, 381, 387; *LC*, 13; *CV*, 26, 31, 73; *RFGB*, 67, 72; *OC*, §§287, 359, 475, 477–78.

45. Wittgenstein thus adopts a quasi-"anthropological" method (see *RFM*, 220; *DW*, 101).

46. See *PI*, §415; p. 56 footnote; *RPP1*, §46; *OC*, §617.

47. See *PI*, §89, 127, 253. Insofar as he attempts to remind us of "the *kind of statement* that we make about phenomena," Wittgenstein describes his approach as "grammatical" (§90). But we should not construe "grammatical" too narrowly. For our sayings and doings are inextricably intertwined—hence Wittgenstein's introduction of the term *language-game* (§23).

48. See also *CV*, 26; *OC*, §287.

49. See *TDL*, 47.

50. See also *PI*, §206, p. 230; *Z*, §§387–88; *RFM*, 94.

51. See *PI*, §285; *Z*, §218. Likewise, I do not describe my *dog's* writhing in pain, cowering in fear or jumping for joy in such geometric terms either. On a related point see *AWM*, 31.

52. See *Z*, §218, 220, 537, 542.

53. See *TDS*, 94–95; *SOC*, 689.

54. See also *PI*, §583, p. 174; *Z*, §527, 594; *LWP1*, §966; *MBF*, 491; *OHB*, 77; *TDS*, 99.

55. See also *Z*, §594.

56. Even the dedicated masochist does not find the pain of kidney stones or migraines sexually arousing.

57. See Gaita's remarks on the "physical details of sexuality" (*TPD*, 192).

58. See *LWP2*, 43–44.

59. For an excellent discussion of this in relation to debates about the un/desirability of immortality, see *IM*.

60. See *SW*, 187; *TMS*, 146–47, 150; *OHB*, 5–6.

61. See *OC*, §160, 283.

62. Imagine that, after we had presented this woman with reasoned arguments or scientific evidence, she suddenly declared, "Ah! *Now* I see what was awry with my behavior!" Would we then trust her?

63. Clearly, cultural context can play a significant role here (see, for example, *DWW*). Cavell asks whether others *must* be judged "crazy" when their "reactions are at variance with ours?" After all: "It seems safe to suppose that if you can describe any behaviour which I can recognise as that of human beings, I can give an explanation which will make that behaviour coherent, i.e., show it to be imaginable in terms of natural responses and practicalities." Perhaps, "if I say 'They are crazy' or 'incomprehensible' then that is not a fact but my fate for them." In other words, here "I have gone as far as my imagination, magnanimity, or anxiety will allow; or as my honor, or my standing cares and commitments, can accommodate" (*TCR*, 38). My point, however, is that our need to "give an explanation"—and the effort involved in doing so—in such extraordinary cases is *itself* significant insofar as it highlights the fact that, ordinarily, no such explanation is needed.

64. On a related point see *TDS*, 96. Note also Wertheimer's remarks on Catholic and Liberal attitudes toward abortion (see *UAA*, 73–76, 83–85).

65. On the "response" and "reaction" see *ATT*, 8, 10, 32–33, 52, 84, 89.

66. See *TDS*, 109–11.

67. See also *PO*, 449; *OC*, §10. Phillips maintains that "unsympathetic responses" to others' pain and distress are "equally primitive" (*MN*, 117; see also 118–20, 125), and we should not therefore assume that these must be "parasitic" (121; see also 132) on sympathetic responses. Indeed, he insists, our "unsympathetic reactions to others . . . are part of what Wittgenstein meant by an attitude towards a soul" (123). I agree that we must not focus solely on those cases where sympathy is elicited; certainly I might feel "relief" (120) that another's suffering is not mine. Likewise, "recoiling" and "moving away" (121) from others' distress, or even "ignoring" (125) them might be described as "primitive reactions." But even here, I suspect that the ways in which we respond *unsympathetically* to others' suffering most often exhibit a more or less tacit acknowledgment that their suffering makes a moral claim on us and that we should help.

68. See *TMS*, 144, 146–47; *TDS*, 109; *TPD*, 59–60.

69. See *TMS*, 149.

70. Of course, we should not trivialize the differences between human and non-human forms of life, or our responsiveness to each (see *TPD*, 35–36; *GE*, 114, 186; *ATT*, 30, 126, 135; *CHA*). But in acknowledging these differences, we must also resist

the temptation to characterize "animals" as inherently impoverished—namely, as *lacking* something (see *DH*, 20; *TDL*, 64).

71. See *FF*, 271; *LOM*, 642, 644–45; *FA*, 33, 36.

72. See *UAA*, 92; *MBF*, 491.

73. As Gaita suggests: "[W]e do not think of behaving towards goldfish or insects in the way we behave towards our cats and dogs, but I suspect it is *not their objective differences in themselves* that matter to us so much as *the relations those features make possible for us*" (*TPD*, 37, my emphases). Here then we must take seriously "the body's part in the constitution of our concepts" (184).

74. Interestingly, Wittgenstein considers even the concept of a "living being" as more or less indeterminate (see *Z*, §326).

75. See *GE*, 180.

76. I therefore think it is misleading to say that "it is not even intelligible that a person should wish to kill himself because he had killed . . . insects, and it would show moral failings rather than virtue if they should want to do it having killed an animal" (*TPD*, 164).

77. See *PI*, §§282–83.

78. There is more to say about our relations with vegetal life (see *WFR*, 292; *IEP*, 30–31; *LOP*, 264)—assuming, of course, we can legitimately talk of "vegetal life" *in general* (see *IEP*, 36). Still, one might reasonably wonder what being "receptive" to the "otherness" of plants, or extending them a "welcome" (34), would actually involve.

79. I think Milligan is wrong that the "opacity and elusiveness" of specific types of animal life (for example, whales) have nothing to do with their size (*DC*, 405).

80. See Shapiro's remarks on the noninferential, "direct and immediate" (*UD*, 35) nature of play with his dog Sabaka, and Sabaka's need for reassurance after misbehaving (40–42).

81. Rhees recalls how one of his dogs (Tim) would "show his distress and come to me with his distress." He proceeds: "Doing something or making sounds to which I responded, and vice versa: that I could call him, and that I could be sure of getting a response from him in certain ways. This has a lot to do with the ways in which I was affected by his cries before his death. It is one of the ways in which the death of such an animal is different from the death of an insect, in which I cannot even imagine any such relation" (*MQ*, 170).

82. See also *DCS*, 129–30.

83. On the various ways we talk about companion dogs, see *UDC*.

84. Although I will not discuss this here, it is worth remembering that, unlike domesticated dogs, many animals do not tend to display their suffering in outward behavior—though increased respiration is a good indication that they are in pain.

85. There is, I think, something deep and comic in Wittgenstein's remark: "If fleas developed a rite, it would be based on the dog" (*RFGB*, 73). Indeed, it is notable that he took jokes very seriously (see *PI*, §111; *LWM*, 27–28).

86. See also *TAC*, 216–17.

87. And, of course, we share much else. As Shapiro notes, "like us, nonhuman animals are intentional beings who move in purposeful ways, who run into barriers,

reach for things and find other things unreachable; who also posture, gesture, effect, and manipulate" (*UD*, 44–45).

88. See *LCT*, 58; *DH*, 16. For example, *we* would find it bizarre to think that any animal could be held legally and/or morally culpable for its actions (see *MQ*, 199). (When a dog is destroyed after mauling a child, his destruction is not a form of *punishment*; we do not hold him accountable in that way.) But we should not forget that in various places at various times animals have been sent to trial for their perceived "crimes" (see *AV*, 41–42). On a related point see *CHA*, 149, 155–56.

89. See also *RPP1*, §314; *LWP2*, §357.

90. See *AWM*, 57.

91. See also *TPD*, 164, 197–98; *GE*, 117.

92. See also *LOM*, 643; *FA*, 27, 33; *WFR*, 280.

93. See *PI*, §583, 650, p. 174; *RPP2*, §29; *TPD*, 71.

94. On the animal "look" see *ATT*, 3–5, 11, 13–14, 29, 57, 59, 90, 107.

95. Thanks to Peter Atterton and Mikel Burley for extremely helpful comments on an earlier draft of this essay.

CHAPTER 4

Dog and Philosophy

Does Bobby Have What It Takes to be Moral?

PETER ATTERTON

. . . [W]ithout ethics and without *logos*, the dog will attest to the dignity of the person.

—Emmanuel Levinas, "Name of a Dog or Natural Right"

There has by now been a considerable amount written on *the question of the animal* in the work of Levinas. Most authors seem to feel that Levinas was wrong not to consider animals in his ethics—which he termed "humanism of the other man"—and that at least some animals are in fact Others for whom we are responsible.[1] In this essay I intend to go one step further: I shall argue that animals are also capable of being responsible for the Other. My argument will not depend on the now extensive literature on animal prosocial behavior and cognitive ethology (see Bekoff and Pierce's admirable book *Wild Justice* and references therein[2]), but will start with an exposition of Levinas's essay "Name of a Dog or Natural Right."[3] The essay is not only the locus of Levinas's major discussion of animality in his corpus, it is also the only occasion of which I am aware when Levinas explicitly attributes to an animal—a dog—a moral capability that he elsewhere reserves exclusively for human beings. This makes the essay illuminating not just for the light that it sheds on the question of whether animals can be moral, but also for the way it manifests a certain tension in Levinas's work between what appears to be a novel way to think about the possibility of animals being moral subjects (I do not say "moral *agents*"[4]) and the profound human exceptionalism that Levinas's analysis throws radically into question. This will be followed by a philosophical development of the theme of animal morality within a broadly Levinasian framework. The problem I have set myself here is to show that there are no gross philosophical or conceptual impediments that stand in the way of ascribing a moral intention or meaning to certain animal behaviors. On the contrary, from a phenomenological standpoint such an ascription even appears compelling.

"Une transcendance dans l'animal!"

This "Name of a Dog" calls for infinite commentary, and with all the requisite patience.[5]

—Derrida, *The Animal That Therefore I Am*

"Name of a Dog or Natural Right" is widely known for the story of Bobby, the stray dog who befriended Levinas and the other Jewish prisoners during their internment in a POW camp in Germany during World War II. Among the many interesting features of the essay is Levinas's oft-quoted claim that Bobby was "the last Kantian in Nazi Germany," which seems paradoxical on the face of it, but, as we shall shortly see, has not always been properly understood. The essay as a whole, however, is ostensibly concerned with an exegesis of the biblical verse (Exodus 22:31):

> You shall be men consecrated to me; therefore you shall not eat any flesh that is torn by beasts in the field; you shall cast it to the dogs. (cited *DF*, 151)

Since this seems to have to do more with the laws of kashrut than with the putative rights of animals it is not surprising that that many commentators tend to gloss over Levinas's exegesis, either ignoring it completely or dismissing it as belonging to Levinas's confessional writings rather than to his proper philosophical corpus. Although this is understandable, the wholesale neglect of the Jewish dimension of Levinas's thinking in the essay under discussion is misguided. In the foreword to *Beyond the Verse*, Levinas writes: "the verses outlined in the Holy Scriptures have a plain meaning [*sens obvie*] which is also enigmatic."[6] The task that Levinas sets himself in the essay is to extricate from the "plain" meaning a meaning that is hidden within it, an implied (or "enigmatic") meaning. Thus, though the Bible has a largely negative attitude toward dogs in particular[7] and doesn't explicitly address animal rights and correlative

human duties in the modern sense of the terms, it does provide a framework
in terms of which Levinas analyzes this contemporary debate. It also serves as
a transition from the exegetical question that dominates the first half of the
discussion to the story of Bobby that will occupy the remainder of the essay.

The "plain" meaning of Exodus 22:31 is consistent with legislation elsewhere
in the Bible (for example, Leviticus 22:8; Deuteronomy 14:21) that forbids Jews
to eat animals killed by other animals. Noting that such dietary restrictions are
often dismissed by modern readers as being too concerned with what goes into
a person's mouth and not enough with what comes out of it,[8] Levinas suggests, however, that there may be purely psychological or *aesthetic* reasons for
refraining from eating the meat of animals whose death has been caused by
other predators: "This spectacle suggesting the horrors of war, this devouring
within species, will provide men with the artistic emotions of the *Kriegspiel*.
Such ideas make one lose one's appetite!" (*DF*, 151) The same revulsion is also
present at the meal table as one is about to plunge one's fork into the Sunday
roast: "There is enough, there, to make you a vegetarian again" (*DF*, 151). This
is perhaps the closest we get to Levinas's formulating an argument for why we
should not eat animals, though he can hardly be said to be calling for anything
more than a *restriction* on our meat-eating: "There is, at least, enough there to
make us want to *limit* [*limiter*], through various interdictions, the butchery that
every day claims our 'consecrated' mouths!" (*DF*, 151; emphasis added). All of
this is beside the point, however, for the question of the consumption of meat
belongs to the "plain" meaning of the text, whereas the true goal of the essay
is to seek a philosophical interpretation (i.e., "metaphysical meaning" [*BV*, xiii])
behind the plain reading. Levinas finds it in connection with the dog: "It is
the dog mentioned at the end of the verse that I am especially interested in. I
am thinking of Bobby" (*DF*, 151).

Who, then, is the dog mentioned at the end of the verse—the one that
reminds Levinas of Bobby? Levinas could not be more emphatic: "in Exodus
22:31, the dog is a dog. Literally a dog!" (*DF*, 152). The necessity for making this clear arises because, says Levinas, "we are always [*toujours*] taking the
name of a dog in the figurative sense" (*DF*, 152; modified translation). Levinas
gives several illustrations of the tendency to use the word *dog* in a figurative
sense, all of them humorous, though one not-so-funny illustration that he may
also have had in mind, though he doesn't mention it, was the tendency in the
Middle Ages to use the dog as a symbol of religious impurity in the religious
conflict between Jews and Christians.[9] Although Christians mainly used this
symbol to insult Jews, Jews themselves were not averse on occasion to reflect it
back on Christians.[10] For example, the famous rabbinical exegete, Rashi, com-
menting on Exodus 22:31, wondered whether it would be permissible to give
or sell meat that is "unclean" (*treif*) to a Gentile because "he [the Gentile] is

also similar to a dog, or perhaps a dog [in Exodus 22:31] is meant literally?"[11] Rashi concluded that the dog in Exodus 22:31 is indeed to be understood "literally" and that God told the Jews to give meat that is *treif* to the dogs as a "reward" (*sakar*). In keeping with this tradition, Levinas too argues that meat is something that the dog is *owed*: "Beyond all scruples, by virtue of its happy nature and straightforward canine thoughts [*droites pensées de chien*], the dog transforms all this flesh cast to it in the field into good flesh. This feast is its right" (*DF*, 152; modified translation). This removes the suspicion that the image of the dog is a metaphor in Levinas's text, but it does not resolve our perplexity at "the paradox of a pure nature leading to rights [*droits*]" (*DF*, 152). *What features do dogs have by their nature that makes respect for their right to food appropriate?* As a way of answering this question, Levinas again invokes "the hermeneutics of the talmudic Doctors," which he says uncovers "some forgotten dogs lying in a subordinate proposition in another verse from Exodus" (*DF*, 152). Here is Levinas's gloss of the passage in question.

> In Chapter 11, verse 7, strange dogs are struck by a stupor or by a light [*stupeur ou de lumière*] in the middle of the night. They will not bark! [*Ils n'aboieront pas!*] But around them a world is coming to an end [*un monde s'achève*]. For this is the fatal night of the "death of the first-born" of Egypt. Israel is about to be released from the house of bondage. Slaves who served the slaves of the State will henceforth follow the most high Voice, the most free path. It is a figure of humanity! Man's freedom is that of an emancipated man remembering his servitude and feeling solidarity for all enslaved people. A rabble of slaves will celebrate this high mystery of man, and "not a dog shall bark" [*"pas un chien n'aboiera"*]. At the supreme hour of humanity's inception—and without ethics and without *logos*—the dog will attest to the dignity of the person. [*A l heure suprême de son instauration et sans éthique et sans logos, le chien va attester la dignité de la personne.*] This is what the friend of man means. A transcendence in the animal! [*Une transcendance dans l'animal!*] And the clear verse with which we began is given a new meaning. It reminds us of the debt that is always open. (*DF*, 152; modified translation)

The interpretation of Exodus 22:31 as a reward for the behavior of dogs during the release of the Israelites from slavery seems to make for a nice story, but we know from experience that there is no *possibility* that actual (i.e., "literal") dogs would have remained silent during such an upheaval.[12] Levinas knows this because elsewhere he declares that "[t]he animal is incapable of . . . duplicity; the dog, for instance, cannot suppress its bark, the bird its song."[13] This, of course, is pure dogma on Levinas's part (think of the plover bird and its broken wing display[14]), but if we accept Levinas's claim that the dog cannot *naturally* suppress its bark (police dogs, for example, can indeed be trained not to bark), then evidently its bark must be suppressed, if not by training, then by preternatural means, *a miracle no less*. Not only is this untenable, according to the religious skeptic, but even if it were true, it would hardly be a suitable resolution of "the paradox of a *pure* nature leading to rights," which Levinas's invocation of Exodus 11:7 was supposed to solve.

Levinas is aware of the objection and appears to concede its legitimacy: "But perhaps the subtle exegesis we are quoting gets lost in rhetoric?" (*DF*, 152). What is needed is a discussion grounded in the kind of behavioral evidence that could support the attribution of moral transcendence to an animal—even though no objective certainty seems to be possible here since morality, as Levinas understands it, involves a motive that is inscrutable even to the subject whose motive it is. Levinas's response is to offer a story taken from real life that he clearly sees as isomorphic with the tale of Exodus 11:7, the story of his experience as a Jewish slave laborer in Germany, 1940–45:

There were seventy of us in a forestry commando unit for Jewish prisoners of war in Nazi Germany. An extraordinary coincidence was the fact that the camp bore the number 1492, the year of the expulsion of the Jews from Spain under the Catholic Ferdinand V. The French uniform still protected us from Hitlerian violence. But the other men, called free, who had dealings with us or gave us work or orders or even a smile—and the children and women who passed by and sometimes raised their eyes—stripped us of our human skin. We were a quasi-humanity [*une quasi-humanité*], a gang of apes. A small inner murmur, the strength and wretchedness of persecuted people, reminded us of our essence as thinking creatures, but we were no longer part of the world. Our comings and goings, our sorrow and laughter, illnesses and distractions, the work of our hands and the anguish of our eyes, the letters we received from France and those accepted for our families—all that passed in parenthesis. We were beings entrapped in their species; despite all their vocabulary, beings without language. Racism is not a biological concept; anti-Semitism is the archetype of all internment. Social oppression [*L'oppression sociale*] itself, merely imitates this model. It shuts people away in a class, deprives them of expression and condemns them to being "signifiers without a signified" and from there to violence and fighting. How can we deliver a message about our humanity which, from behind the bars of quotation marks, will come across as anything other than monkey talk? (*DF*, 152–53; modified translation)

Notice that in the very process of challenging humanist assumptions about the moral superiority of humans by ascribing transcendence to animals, Levinas's essay resorts to some of the very same assumptions. The passage makes it clear that Levinas views the comparison of humans to animals as a form of degradation and dehumanization. As David Clark has pointed out: "Levinas . . . is informed by conventional assumptions about animality that make it impossible for him straightforwardly to attribute dutifulness to a creature that is not human."[15] He goes on to say, "Even when Levinas disrupts the boundaries constituting the human . . . he reinscribes the boundaries defining the animal as if his critique of humanism remained more or less in a certain anthropological space."[16] Derrida too observes that Levinas's description "doesn't appear to break with the traditional reference to the ape" (*ATT*, 118).

I mentioned earlier that "Name of a Dog" marks a tension in Levinas's work between the view of animals as moral subjects and the perception of them as morally inferior beings in comparison with human persons. In Levinas's essay, animals are interstitial beings, neither persons nor things, occupying a twilight world (in French *entre chien et loup* [*DL*, 214]), simultaneously embodying a strange admixture of transcendence and immanence. I do not believe that this tension can ultimately be resolved; but this is perhaps not that important. Of much greater significance is the fact that, even if Levinas ultimately shows himself unwilling to abandon the human-animal distinction, what he actually says about "*Une transcendance dans l'animal!*" does much to undermine it. As Matthew Calarco has correctly pointed out, "If animals are also capable of being-for-the-Other, then the chief dividing line between the human and the animals threatens to vanish in Levinas's discourse."[17] The question is not whether Levinas himself seeks a radical subversion of the human-animal distinction; he clearly does not. It is whether his ethics conflicts with his ultimate *approval* of that distinction, which I shall argue it does. So, while I agree with Derrida when he writes in reference to the dog Bobby (see below) that "the traverse of this dog remains without precedent, without consciousness, and without future within the discourse in which it appears" (*ATT*, 99), I disagree with the claim that the attribution of transcendence to animals runs up against what he calls "internal limits" (*ATT*, 99) in Levinas's discourse. On the contrary, it seems to me that the logic of Levinas's ethics, far from providing grounds for those who argue that there are significant differences between humans and animals as far as ethics is concerned, presents us with what perhaps is the only serviceable basis for thinking that certain animals might also be capable of ethics of a Levinasian variety.

The story of Bobby is recounted immediately following the passage cited above:

> And then, about halfway through our long captivity, for a few short weeks, before the sentinels chased him away, a wandering dog entered our lives. One day he came to meet this rabble as we returned under guard from work. He survived in some wild patch in the region of the camp. But we called him Bobby, an exotic name, as one does with a cherished dog. He would appear at morning assembly and was waiting for us as we returned, jumping up and down and barking in delight. For him—it was incontestable—we were men. [*Pour lui—c'était incontestable—nous fûmes des hommes*]. (*DF*, 153; modified translation)

Levinas's main motivation for introducing Bobby into the account is presumably to draw a stark contrast between the way the guards and villagers treated Levinas and the other prisoners, and the way Bobby treated them. Whereas the guards and villagers saw them as animals ("a gang of apes"), Bobby, Levinas says in the strongest terms possible ("it was incontestable"), saw them *as* "men." I will come back to this dismally unphilosophical utterance concerning what Bobby thinks—and its profoundly un-Levinasian implications—in the second part of this essay.

Is Levinas then suggesting that Bobby is a full-blown moral agent? In fact, though he attributes to Bobby qua dog the Kantian capacity to attest to the "dignity of persons," he also shows up the naivety of attributing to Bobby the ability to act on principle. Consider the final paragraph of the essay under discussion.

> Perhaps the dog that recognized Ulysses beneath his disguise on his return from the Odyssey was a forebear of our own. But no, no! There, they were in Ithaca and the Fatherland. Here, we were nowhere. This dog was the last Kantian in Nazi Germany, without the brain needed to universalize the maxims of its drives [*universaliser les maximes de ses pulsions*]. He was a descendant of the dogs of Egypt. And his friendly barking [*son aboiement d'ami*], his animal faith, was born from the silence of his forefathers on the banks of the Nile. (*DF*, 153; modified translation)

Levinas's description of Bobby as a "Kantian," the last of its kind in Germany at that time, has been challenged by Derrida, who asks: "But how can one ignore that a Kantian who doesn't have 'the brain needed' to universalize maxims would not be a Kantian, especially if the maxims in question are maxims of 'drives' that would have made Kant bark. Bobby is thus anything but Kantian" (*ATT*, 114). Clark too sees here some kind of contradiction on Levinas's part: "Bobby remains inwardly deficient. . . . Because he lacks the knowhow and the liberty truly to stop himself from acting in a way that cannot be universalized, he is only a kind of simulation of goodness."[18] And Guenther similarly writes: "And yet, Levinas immediately limits the compliment to Bobby; for as an animal 'without the brains [etc. . . .]' the dog is just a dog, deprived of language and reason, incapable of truly responding to others."[19]

These criticisms are totally misguided. The ambivalent character of Levinas's appeal to Kant is to be conceded without substantially taking anything away from Bobby's capacity to be moral. For there is an alternative construction to be put on Levinas's claim that Bobby cannot universalize maxims: that it be understood as a claim not about Bobby's incapacity for ethics *but about the character of the ethics that Bobby does have a capacity for.* In other words, that Bobby's "Kantianism" should be treated not as the capacity to adopt universalizable maxims, for example, but as the capacity for "respect." In an interview with *Le Monde* in 1984, Levinas says: "I like the second formula of the categorical imperative, the one that speaks of 'respect [for] the man in me and in the Other.' In this formula we are not in pure universality, but already in the presence of the Other" (*IR*, 163; modified translation[20]). I have discussed the proximity between Levinas and Kant on an earlier occasion and must forego a discussion of it here.[21] What I wish to stress is that what unites Levinas's and Kant's views on ethics is not respect as action (*observantia*), that is, acting on the basis of an (impersonal) reason, but respect as feeling (*reverentia*) that the Other has the capacity to arouse and which, says Kant, "presupposes the sensuousness and hence the finitude of such beings on whom respect for the moral law is imposed."[22] In this view, Bobby's "friendly barking" stands to the presence of Levinas and the other prisoners somewhat as the Same to the Other in the face-to-face relation: an *immediate* response to the proximity of the Other "before understanding" ("*avant d'entendre*") (*OB*, 113; cf. also 12; 150). And that this is so would be demonstrated by the fact that Bobby does not have "the brain needed to universalize the maxims of his drives."

In what follows I shall be defending the view that Bobby has what it takes to be a Levinasian moral subject despite his lacking "ethics" and "*logos*." The basic argument here is very simple: it is that whatever cognitive abilities humans have that Bobby lacks are essentially irrelevant to the question of whether Bobby has the ability to enter into a relation with the Other face to face because the face to face as such does not involve the exercise of judgment-employing concepts.

Bobby as a Levinasian Moral Subject

What has just been said about Bobby not having "the brain needed to universalize the maxims of his drives" (though I have students who also can't apply Kant's formula of universal law) should not prejudice the case against Bobby having a variegated mental life. *The problem is to say what sorts of thoughts Bobby is capable of and whether they include the type of thinking that would count for or against an attribution of ethical subjectivity.* Because Bobby obviously cannot tell us directly in words what he is thinking, we have to infer it from his behavior. The especial danger involved in making such inferences, however, is anthropomorphizing. Indeed, in at least one place in "Name of a Dog" Levinas appears guilty of doing just that—and this, ironically, by radically *overestimating* Bobby's cognitive capabilities. Recall the passage we quoted earlier in which Levinas says the following about Bobby:

> He would appear at morning assembly and was waiting for us as we returned, jumping up and down and barking in delight. For him—it was incontestable—we were men.

In an interview in 1986, Levinas gives what is substantially the same account of Bobby recognizing Levinas and the others as "men," though he weakens the claim just a little bit.

> But when we used to come back from work, very relieved, he welcomed us, jumping up and down. . . . [T]his dog *evidently* took us [*nous prenait*] for men. (*IR*, 41)

It is difficult to see how Bobby's behavior could suffice for ascribing to Bobby the belief that Levinas and the other prisoners are *men*. To say that it does is to say far more than the evidence will actually support. Does Bobby have the canonical conceptual resources for identifying men? Does he even have concepts? You have a canonical concept of something if you are able to classify something as a particular *kind* of thing. This requires the ability to abstract from perceptual features that enable you to discriminate *F*'s from non-*F*'s (e.g., shape recognition) and know something *about* all *F*'s. In other words, it requires the capacity to discriminate *F*-ness. So, to have a concept *man*, for example, you must have the concept of a persisting physical object that is an animal, perhaps characterized by an erect posture, a highly developed brain, the capacity for abstract thought and reason, and the ability to use language. While there may be no definitive list of associated concepts needed have to have the concept *man* (*person*, member of the species *Homo sapiens*, etc.), there are a certain number of them that you need to have or you don't have the concept at all. Does Bobby have any of them? Obviously the theoretical and methodological problems in ascribing mental states to animals is too large a question to be dealt with here,[23] but I think we can say without provoking too much controversy that, whatever might be going on inside Bobby's head, we can assume that it is not content or belief that coincides with *our de dicto* way of representing the world, at least in the sense that animals do not possess concepts as we do.

But even if we were, contrary to fact, justified in ascribing to Bobby the concept *man*, it would be an entirely pyrrhic victory in the context of Levinas's ethics. We would indeed learn something extraordinary about dogs, namely, that there exists a *de dicto* content-ascription that correctly describes that way they represent the world, but we would learn nothing substantive about their capacity for *ethics*, at least as Levinas defines it. Why not?

Throughout his career, Levinas remained "obsessed" (*OB*, 55, 77, 84, 85, 89, 112, 123, 144, 192) by the otherness of the Other. This otherness was cashed out in terms of the claim that the Other cannot be known or identified by being subsumed under a universal concept. To subsume the Other under a concept is precisely to miss the uniqueness or "singularity" (*OB*, 18, 83, 86, 100, 106, 108, 129, 153, 176, 190, 194) of the Other, his or her irreducibility to any concept that *I as a thinker am able to think and account for*. This is why Levinas can say in *Totality and Infinity*: "The collectivity in which I say 'you' or 'we' is not a plural of the 'I.' I, you—these are not individuals of a common concept. Neither possession nor the unity of number nor the unity of concepts link me to the Stranger, the Stranger who disturbs the being at home with oneself" (*TI*, 39). Later in *Totality and Infinity* Levinas explicitly says that ethics is "an experience that is not commensurate with any a priori framework—a conceptless experience" (*TI*, 101). So, even if Bobby did have the right kind of canonical concept that enabled him to recognize Levinas and his fellows as "men"—which we have already seen is questionable—*it would not address any of the substantive ethical issues that are at stake*. Like the identity thinking of the racist and anti-Semite that "shuts people away in a class, deprives them of expression and condemns them to being 'signifiers without a signified'" (*DF*, 153), Bobby would have missed "the face," which expresses itself for its own self *in propria persona*.

The Levinasian subject does not need to recognize the Other as instantiating this or that concept but is only required to pick the Other out from among its thingly environment. You might say that ethics for Levinas is *discriminatory without being recognitory*. Since the ethical relation between us is pre- or supra-conceptual, our lack of understanding or inability to find ourselves in each other is not an impediment to ethics; quite the contrary, it would be truer to say that it is rather its precondition, if ethics, as Levinas says, is a relation between two alterities that remain "infinitely foreign" (*TI*, 194) with respect to each other.

Therefore, whether or not Bobby has concepts that are the same as ours is quite simply irrelevant to ethics. It is the dog's very incapacity for (human) conceptualization that allows for the specifically ethical dimension of the welcome to come through: the welcome as the ability to respond to something different as other. Although we might not (and probably will never) be able to attribute the *de dicto* belief ("Levinas is a man") to Bobby, we shouldn't see this in any way a priori grounds for Bobby's exclusion from the community of so-called moral agents. Rather we should see it as potential grounds for his inclusion. As long as Bobby believes of Levinas that he is there, that is, as long as he is able to discriminate certain O's (where O is the Other) from some non-O's (e.g., rocks and trees), and, on account of that discrimination (i.e., perception of O), is morally motivated to act in a manner that is characteristic of the kind of animal that Bobby is, which may include welcoming barking, tail-wagging, whimpering, and even altruistic behavior like defending O from attack by another animal or another O, then I think we can say without prejudice that Bobby has the capacity to "respond" to O in an ethical manner as Levinas defines it.

While this presupposes the ability on the part of the dog to do something that is at least discursive, namely, to discriminate, and perhaps progressively learn to better discriminate some O's,[24] it constitutes an exceptionally "low-grade" *ontological* component of recognition that, rather than vitiate the ethical relation, makes it possible in fact. What it does not require, to repeat what was said above, is the capacity to recognize Levinas and the other prisoners *as men*, avoiding the conceptualism and intellectualism inherent in the classifying awareness of being able to subsume particulars under a universal.

This obvious point has been overlooked by commentators who all too hastily attempt to reduce otherness to some kind of "alterity-content" (woman, Jew, Palestinian, etc.) despite Levinas's explicit disavowal.[25] Again this ability to discriminate in favor of the Other is nothing conceptual and does not require the use of language (*logos*) understood as apophantic discourse, "S is P." The nonconceptual perception does not have to be visual or haptic, which obviously bodes well for Bobby with his heightened capacity for hearing and, in particular, smell. The theme of invisibility is iterated many times by Levinas in *Totality and Infinity* (*TI*, 22, 35, 78, 243, 247, 248, 300). The following passage is exemplary:

> Invisibility does not denote an absence of relation; it implies relation with what is not given [in the manner of thinghood, property, or states of affairs], of which there is no idea. Vision is an adequation of the idea with the thing, a comprehension that encompasses. Non-adequation does not denote a simple negation or an obscurity of the idea, but—beyond the light and the night, beyond the knowledge measuring brings—the inordinateness of Desire. (*TI*, 34)

The singular, immediate representation of *what is there* without placing it within one or more classes is "blind" in the sense that it does not rest on any adequate idea, an idea that coincides with its object-ideatum (the Other). It does not lead to objective, that is, classificatory knowledge ("To think the infinite, the transcendent, the Stranger, is hence not to think an object" [*TI*, 49]), yet remains a relation with the Other. This special "thought" is not a concept but an affection toward other sensitive beings that Levinas calls "Desire" (*TI*, 31 passim), and which involves benevolence or concern antecedent to any sense of advantage or self-interest. It is not by chance that Levinas opens the argument in *Totality and Infinity* (after the lengthy introduction) with the chapter titled "Desire for the Invisible." Kant once famously said, "Thoughts without intuitions are empty, intuitions without concepts are blind" (*Critique of Pure Reason*, A51/B75). This "blind intuition" of the Other (Levinas's "conceptless experience") constitutes a type of transcendence, that is, a relation with what lies wholly outside the self, that goes "beyond thought," and which "is made in feeling [*le sentiment*], whose fundamental tonality is Desire . . . distinguished from tendency and need, [and which] does not belong to activity, but constitutes the intentionality of the affective order" (*CPP*, 623n4). It would take us too far afield to examine this affective order—including the whole range of social sentiments: empathy, sympathy, love, compassion—that Darwin, following Hume and Smith, placed at the foundation of morality, and which he saw as part of our (and the dog's) natural history.[26] Suffice to say that Bobby's "idea" of Levinas and the fellow prisoners does not amount to the recognition of them as "men," which would require the "brain" to subsume what he sees under the category *human*, which Bobby lacks, but constitutes an "intentionality of a wholly different type" (*TI*, 23) than the constitutive intentionality that we find at the basis of transcendental idealism in general. This intentionality is both world-directed (it is aimed at an object in the world and not a mere noema) and it is paradigmatically *de re*, since it aims directly at its object (*res*) rather than through a canonical understanding that the object (*human*) happens to fit.[27]

Is this not the paradigm of the ethical relationship between Same and Other? Not quite. For the relation to be ethics in Levinas's sense we need more than a *de re* thought about the Other. For it might turn out that Bobby is bereft of concepts altogether and thus it would be easy to be persuaded that every perceptual judgment that is genuinely world-directed and *de re* is a thought about the Other! Presumably if Bobby were to perceive the keyboard on which I am currently typing he would have no idea of what it is. Would that then constitute (for Bobby) acquaintance with the Other? But this leaves out an important component of Levinas's ethics, namely, the practical orientation that the ethical subject has through his or her acquaintance with the Other. Levinas calls this practical orientation many things: "being-for-the-Other," "responsibility," "saying," "obsession," and so on. Although the lexical meanings of these terms are hardly equivalent, what Levinas takes them each to denote is a response in and to the presence of the Other that can take myriad forms, but which all give rise to a type of ethical behavior, whether it be in the form of welcome, succor, or comfort.

For Bobby's behavior to constitute ethics, then, Bobby would have to be able to *respond* in the appropriate manner on seeing Levinas and the other prisoners. This is how Derrida puts it: "The said question of the said animal in its entirety comes down to knowing not whether an animal speaks but whether one can know what *respond* means. And how to distinguish a response from a reaction" (*ATT*, 8). What is the difference between a (mere) *reaction* and a (Levinasian) *response*? A reaction doesn't need to be backed up by thought (e.g., "phosphorus reacts with air"), whereas a response does (e.g., "the person responded to the news with alarm"). (Let's ignore for the purposes of discussion the inconsequential objection that the distinction is often blurred in ordinary English, as when we say that "the patient responded to treatment.") In other words, a reaction is conditioned by the relevant stimulus in a way that can be explained without any appeal to a psychological intermediary between the stimulus and the behavior. Reactions are fairly easy to detect: the resultant behavior is stereotypical (i.e., it always occurs in roughly the same form), it is the same for all members of the species, it is independent of the past experience or history of the individual, it cannot be varied once it is launched, it has only one function or purpose, and, finally, it is always caused or "triggered" by the same stimulus or set of stimuli.[28] In short, reactions do not require a psychological explanation that appeals to beliefs, desires, and perceptions.

Responses are just the opposite inasmuch as they allow the individual to respond flexibly and plastically to his or her environment. Imagine that Levinas and the other prisoners had always done as the guards had done when they saw Bobby and had chased him away. Can one then imagine that the dog would have been waiting for them, jumping up and down, each time they returned home from work in the forest? That would be absurd. A dog that has been mistreated by its "master" will respond differently from one that has been treated as "cherished" and will act accordingly. As Derrida writes: "For hunted, beaten, and slaughtered animals, we are also men, whom they identify only too quickly, regrettably as men" (*ATT*, 11). An individual with different desires and different beliefs, or whose brain is configured differently owing to a different personal history will respond to difference (the Other), well, *differently*!

Notice above I only said "flexibly and plastically"; I did not say "freely." In order to underline this distinction let us be perfectly clear about how, for Levinas, the response that provides all and any moral motivation for ethical behavior (responsivity, responsibility) is nothing that is freely chosen or willed. There is a widespread assumption, following Kant, that moral obligation presupposes freedom in the sense of the capacity to act independently of alien causes, that is, the ability to act in accordance with rational standards of one's own. Levinas totally rejects this assumption. He claims—and this is perhaps the most radical element of his ethics—that the Other obligates me prior to autonomous choice. As he once put it: "I can never escape the fact that the other has demanded a response from me before I affirm my freedom not to respond to his demand."[29] A Levinasian subject is someone who has a disposition to respond with an irrepressible and unchoosable responsibility to and in the presence of the Other as such. It matters little that the subject involved does not know what is going on. Levinas's ethics is supposed to tell us what is going on when we act ethically by ascribing to us a "content" ("the idea of infinity," "alterity," "saying," etc.) that neither we nor Bobby can entertain.[30] So, perhaps, to be told that Bobby is capable of acting morally—notwithstanding that like all animals (including humans?) he has no metaphysical free will—is not really objectionable in the slightest. Perhaps this is enough to credit him with a genuine ethical behavior as Levinas understands it. After all, Bobby's extreme passivity ("more passive than all passivity" [*OB*, 14 passim]), that is, his inability *not* to respond, is hardly an impediment to ethics if the motivation for the ethics precedes freedom. Rather, it would seem to be its genuine expression.

In what way does Bobby show himself irrepressibly responsive to Levinas and the other prisoners? In "Name of a Dog" Levinas twice mentions Bobby's vocalizations on seeing him and the other prisoners.

1. He would appear at morning assembly and was waiting for us upon our return, jumping up and down and barking in delight.

And:

2. [H]e was a descendant of the dogs of Egypt. And his friendly barking, his animal faith, was born from the silence of his forefathers on the banks of the Nile.

Looking at 2, I am not completely sure how the question of why Bobby barks when he sees Levinas is like the question of why dogs in Exodus 11:7 *do not bark* as the Israelites were about to leave Egypt. Taken literally, the only sense I can make of this is that Levinas regards dog barks as similar to what biologists call an "exaptation."[31] An exaptation is a behavioral trait that evolves because it served one particular function, but subsequently it may come to serve another. (A classic example is bird feathers, which initially evolved for thermoregulation but were later adapted for flight.) It has been hypothesized that barking originally evolved in wolves as a warning or threat to intruders, and has survived in dogs as a vestigial trait that has possibly hypertrophied due to the relaxation of the selection pressure for "silence" that is necessary in a wild predator.[32] The way I read 2 is that Levinas is suggesting that barking changed its function and became an important species of communication between dogs and humans. This seems highly plausible. Fifteen years ago a study was done that suggested that domestication and artificial selection effectively "changed dog barking to an effective communicative signal between dog and human."[33] The study showed that human listeners are highly adept at classifying the emotional content of barks in nonaggressive situations (walk, play, being alone) with a broad degree of consensus on the basis of auditory cues only. Indeed, humans are shown to have this "inborn"[34] ability, whether they have lived with dogs or not.

Seen in this light it is perhaps easy to understand why Levinas has no difficulty determining the suspected emotion of Bobby upon listening to Bobby's vocalizations when he, Levinas, and the other prisoners returned from work, and which he describes as "barking in delight." Indeed, even without auditory cues it appears no less possible to classify the emotional content of behavior of animals with a broad degree of agreement. Notably in the "Animal Interview," Levinas states,

[T]here is in our attraction, in a complex regard, in regard to an animal, an animal that is beautiful—*myself, I don't have much to do with animals*—but, there are those who love the dog, for example, and what they love in the dog is perhaps its childlike character. As though it were strong, cheerful, powerful, full of life, but because it doesn't know everything. And consequently, on the other hand, there is certainly there in regard to the animal, pity, is that not so? A wolf that does not bite—it is like that. One always loves in the

animal, the wolf, the memory of the wolf, the memory of the lion,
the dog, I don't know. In any case, there is there the possibility of
a specific phenomenological analysis, which cannot be used when
things are understood from the beginning. (*AI*, 4; emphasis added)

Since Levinas maintains that "phenomenological analysis" "cannot be
used when things are understood from the beginning," it is not surprising that
his discussion of Bobby's "descent" is extremely sketchy. Nevertheless, even
though it cannot tell us how Bobby's behavior emerged, that is, whether it is
a continuation or a relaxation of natural selection, phenomenology can be used
to throw light on the meaning of that behavior, at least in outline, in certain
instances. In his book *The Nature of Sympathy*, Scheler gives an account of how

> we can understand the experience of animals, though even in "ten-
> dency" we cannot imitate their manner of expression; for instance
> when *a dog expresses its joy by barking* and wagging its tail, or a bird
> by twittering. The relationships between expression and experience
> have a *fundamental* basis of connection. We have here, as it were,
> a universal grammar, valid for all languages of expression, and the
> ultimate basis of understanding for all form of mimes and pantomime
> among living creatures.[35]

If we doubt Scheler's conviction as to the existence of a "universal gram-
mar" that can provide the foundation of (all?) interspecific communication, we
can at least agree with the weaker claim that, even though we cannot hope to
speak the same "language" as animals, we can readily understand, at least in the
case of dogs, their suspected communicative signals. Scheler's heterophenomenol-
ogy thus has the merit of taking seriously a view to which Levinas also seems
committed and that contrasts clearly with, say, the phenomenology of Husserl.
This is the view that meaningful or expressive behavior can be predicated of
the other communicator prior to self-conscious thought or reflection. I do not
have to infer the experiences of others by noticing a resemblance between their
behavior and that of my own body (Husserl's "pairing" [*Paarung*][36]), which is
obviously inadequate when dealing with an animal that barks or has a tail, but
I can have awareness of those experiences *nonanalogically* simply by listening
to their vocalizations and watching their behavior. As Scheler said: "But that
'experiences' occur there [i.e., in others] is given for us *in* expressive phenomena—again, not by inference, but directly, as some sort of primary 'perception.'"[37] Thus, it was *in* the wagging of its tail, *in* its barks, *in* its jumping up

and down that Levinas was able to perceive directly that Bobby was happy to see *him and the others*.

In the same manner that humans are able to attribute to dogs very strong emotional content on the basis of auditory and visual cues, it is possible in many instances to recognize in animals the capacity to witness and respond to the suffering of others. Something that tends to be insufficiently stressed in discussions of the Exodus story—and Levinas's gloss is no exception—is that the slaying of the "first-born" of Egypt included *animals*: "And all the first-born in the land of Egypt shall die, from the first-born of Pharaoh that sitteth upon his throne, even unto the first-born of the maidservant that is behind the mill; and all the first-born of beasts" (Exodus 11:5).[38] Again, it seems wildly implausible to suppose that during such slaughter "not a dog will bark." As Calarco points out, "we need to pay specific attention to the *unique* ways in which animals themselves resist subjection and domination, even if their own efforts are not successful."[39] But it is likewise implausible to suggest that the loss of so many animals would not have been a source of considerable suffering not only for the Egyptians *but for the animals themselves*.[40] Here is a contemporary cognitive ethologist, Frans de Waal, speaking of the capability that certain animals have to bear witness to suffering and anguish in others, both conspecifics and members of nonrelated species: "There is increasing evidence, mostly in mammals but also in birds, that animals are sensitive to the emotions of others and react to distress in others by attempts to ameliorate their situation or rescue them."[41]

I shall ignore the galaxy of examples purporting to show that certain animals share with humans the capability to recognize strong emotions in others and respond to their distress by acting in ways that appear morally motivated by a concern to alleviate it, from ancient anecdotes of dolphins saving drowning fisherman, to a controlled experiment performed in 1964 that showed rhesus monkeys refusing to take food if doing so resulted in subjecting a painful electric shock to a companion,[42] to the story of Binti Jua the gorilla who saved the life of a three-year-old child who had fallen twenty feet into its gorilla enclosure.[43] I wish instead to focus on less dramatic or heroic acts in which an animal exhibits the capacity to alleviate suffering, *not by doing anything but just by just being there*.

Research on the now extensive use of "therapy dogs" is a clear testimony to the capacity of these companion animals to provide comfort to persons suffering from a wide range of physical and emotional problems. Carolyn Zahn-Waxler et al. write: "In observing parent-child interaction in the home we have seen emotionally distressed pets hovering over persons feigning distress in situations where we are measuring the *child's* capacity for empathy."[44] Deborah Custance and Jennifer Mayer also clearly expose the richness and depth of empathy in dogs.

> There are many different ways in which dogs could respond to an apparently distressed human. They could fail to respond at all and ignore the crying person; they could become fearful and avoidant, even approaching another calm human for reassurance; they could become alert and even act in a dominant manner towards an apparently weakened individual; they could become curious or playful; or they could approach and touch the distressed person in a gentle or submissive manner thereby providing reassurance or comfort. *The majority of dogs in the present study behaved in a manner that was consistent with empathic concern and comfort-offering. The dogs responded to their owner and the stranger when they were crying in a markedly differently manner compared to when they were humming or talking.* They oriented toward the person (i.e., looking at, approaching and touching them) significantly more during the crying condition than the humming or talking conditions.[45] (Emphasis added)

I imagine many readers may be less than surprised that an animal such as a dog or cat should be thought capable of providing therapeutic benefits. After all, a distressed human can help satisfy a need for love and affection when she or he touches, pets, or cuddles an animal. Therapy animals may also help to put the patient at ease since therapists appear less threatening when a friendly animal facilitator is present. But therapy dogs appear to be doing more than merely providing (what is perceived by the patient as) Rogerian "unconditional positive regard," that is, basic acceptance and support of the client regardless of what the client says or does. According to the Custance and Mayer study, the dogs were empathically concerned and prone to offer comfort to someone in distress. Why should an animal like a dog become "emotionally distressed" in the presence of someone who is also distressed? The proof that they are distressed is that they respond in a markedly different manner according to whether "their owner or stranger" was in distress or not. When the person showed their distress by crying, the dogs "oriented toward the person" significantly more than they did when the person was humming. This orientation included "looking at, approaching and touching them."

We are now in a position to recognize the significance of this "look," "approach," and "touch." In Levinas's ethics it is called *responsibility*, and consists in the predisposition to alleviate the Other's suffering simply because it is the Other. It would of course be ridiculous to dismiss the actions of the therapy dog as lacking the full weight and significance of Levinasian responsibility for the simple fact that none of the gestures involves giving a material thing *in a world*. Dogs, to be sure, are incapable of giving to the Other with "full hands" (*TI*, 205; *OB*, 42). But that has never been the question here.[46] Even Levinas seems to have realized that not all relations of responsibility involve material giving. From the eighties onward, Levinas was fond of repeatedly mandating the ethical imperative "not to let the other die alone" (*EN*, 131, 146, 169, 186). This duty is the duty we are left with when, in sickness and old age, the Other is literally dying.[47] Here it makes no sense to speak of "giving the bread out of one's own mouth" (*OB*, 142) to patients with advanced cancer undergoing a wasting syndrome characterized by poor appetite, anorexia, loss of weight, and asthenia. The best one can do for such patients at the end of life is enter them into a palliative care service focusing on providing patients with relief from the symptoms and stress of what is typically a terminal illness. The point remains firm: however much we (or I) can do to help someone to live, of itself this is not enough. There is also the duty, when the time comes, of helping someone die, which simply requires us (or me) to be there with them when they do. I shall spare the reader a discussion of the myriad case studies of therapy dogs assisting the dying and simply refer her to Michelle Rivera's moving book *Dogs and Dying: Inspirational Stories from Hospice Hounds*.[48]

It seems to me that the anthropocentric thesis that human beings are the sole preservers of the domain of morality would have to be made in the absence of empirical findings such as the above. Or else the dismissal of the above is the kind of sheer dogmatism of which Levinas himself appears guilty in the "The Animal Interview" when he says: "[T]here are people who will tell you . . . that it is in life that there is a certain sympathy regarding our life and that the ethical morality is a development of a purely biological phenomenon . . . I myself say, on the contrary, that in relation to the animal, humanity is a new phenomenon" (*AI*, 4). Since I have already criticized Levinas's anti-Darwinism elsewhere,[49] I will not rehearse it here. Let me just say that a severe problem with this is not only that it risks, by removing human morality completely from instinct, making ethics so much beyond our comprehension that Levinas can speak of it as a "miracle" ("The miracle of creation lies in creating a moral being" [*TI*, 89]), it utterly ignores or leaves unexplained the fact that human behavior appears continuous in many instances with prosocial behavior in other animals, including Bobby, whose welcoming behavior even Levinas could not fail to be impressed by.[50]

Conclusion

I conclude this essay with a review of some of the issues raised in it. The question is whether animals are capable of morality. Obviously, one wants to avoid anthropomorphizing and attributing to animals capacities that they don't have or share with us. This is why imputing to animals a traditional morality of universal obligations looks wrongheaded. Animals cannot universalize their maxims and are not free to act on them even if they could. But then it could be argued that human beings are not (metaphysically) free, and that even if they were this would not get to the heart of what ethics is about. The real question ought to be whether a theory like Levinas's that takes goodness as a matter of responding to the needs of the Other, outside of reason and freedom of the will, can be applied to certain types of animals. It is a question that, I have suggested, forces itself on us through a close and careful reading of the essay "Name of a Dog." The essay is remarkable for the very fact that it raises a question that is not treated anywhere else in his work, the scope and purport of which is profoundly anthropocentric. The question is whether Bobby, the welcoming dog that greeted Levinas and the other prisoners at the end of the day as they returned home from work, exemplifies the ethical gesture that Levinas elsewhere calls the face-to-face welcome of the other man. The argument here is not a simple-minded and unwarranted anthropomorphizing that falsely attributes to Bobby a concept of the human person as a holder of dignity and thus worthy of respect. More complicated is the story that we find in Levinas of the ethically motivated individual who is in a nonconceptual relation to the Other *as such*. A "nonconceptual" relation in Levinas is a relation with a particular not mediated by any universal concept. *To what avail then to be told that animals don't have ratiocination or general concepts as we do?* Levinas insists that the Other cannot be known or subsumed under a general concept. If we assume there is such a relation, that I can be in that relation to the Other in such a way that the presence of the Other provokes in me an idea or an affect that potentiates a response that is ethics, then from the standpoint of Levinas's ethics, Bobby's ethical relation with the human appears as an interesting interspecies configuration, nothing more.

Now I do not wish, by any means, to deny that there is a difference between how we respond ethically and Bobby's response. What I wish to deny are claims made by philosophers with regard to moral significance of that difference, for example, that because Bobby cannot talk or reason he is altogether incapable of morality. For Levinas morality begins in conscience, and perhaps it is only a matter of time before we can feel sure that nonhuman animals have one. For as Darwin was the first to point out, "Any animal whatever, endowed with well-marked social instincts, the parental and filial affections being here included, would inevitably acquire a moral sense of conscience, as soon as the intellectual powers had become as well-developed or nearly as well-developed as in man."[51] Morality, including such moral sentiments as empathy and sympathy, like all biological traits for Darwin, have evolved and are part of a biological continuum between humans and other animals whose differences are of degree, not of kind. An observation that I think is all too easily ignored is that those animals that are closest us, namely, dogs, perhaps more than any other animal, have a propensity to form more intense social bonds with and to elicit stronger expressions of affect from humans and to express them toward humans than to members of the same species (i.e., to other dogs). To be sure, this is not purely by chance. Dogs have evolved through selective breeding of precisely those behavioral traits that we so admire in them: loyalty, protection from predators (wolves?), defending humans, and so forth. But they also serve as an important reminder of the connection between human life and animal life, and the emotional needs—the need for empathy and friendship—that we share with a wide variety of other social mammals, perhaps even birds.

It is open for the skeptic to reply: But how do I know that Bobby feels what I feel when in touch with the Other? How do I know he has empathy or compassion when the "master" is sick, or feels joy and warmth when he is reunited after a period of absence? Against this, all that can be said is that we don't know for certain. But it would hardly be fair to draw the skeptical line at animals. In regard to humans, Levinas also speaks of the "mutual impenetrability of minds opaque as matter" (*EE*, 7). How do I know what the Other (human) is thinking? Levinas opens his magnum opus *Totality and Infinity* with the question of whether we are duped by morality. He then proceeds to spend the rest of the book using the phenomenological method to describe this experience that is irreducible to knowledge and that lies beyond ontology and the question "What is . . . ?," an experience that is true only in the sense that it is the *precondition* for truth and reason in general. Is it not, then, unreasonable to expect objective proof of the capacity for certain animals to be moral and to hold them to a higher justificatory standard for the attribution of morality than we do in the case of human beings? The claim that the dog is morally motivated is clearly corrigible, but this is so *not* because we are here talking about a dog rather than a human. It is because we are talking about morality.[52]

Notes

1. See, for example, John Llewelyn, "Am I Obsessed by Bobby? (Humanism of the Other Animal)," *The Middle Voice of Ecological Conscience: A Chiasmic Reading of Responsibility in the Neighborhood of Levinas, Heidegger and Others* (New York: St. Martin's Press, 1991), 49–67; David Clark, "On Being 'The Last Kantian in Nazi Germany': Dwelling with Animals after Levinas," in *Animal Acts: Configuring the Human in Western*

History, eds. Jennifer Ham and Matthew Senior (New York: Routledge, 1997), 165–98; Lisa Guenther, "Le flair animal: Levinas and the Possibility of Animal Friendship," *PhaenEx: Journal of Existential and Phenomenological Theory and Culture* 2, no. 2 (2007), 216–38; Matthew Calarco, *Zoographies* (New York: Columbia University Press, 2008), 55–77; Bob Plant, "Welcoming Dogs: Levinas and 'the Animal' Question," *Philosophy and Social Criticism* 3, no. 1 (2011): 49–71; Peter Atterton, "Levinas and Our Moral Responsibility Toward Animals," *Inquiry* 54, no. 6 (2011): 633–49.

2. Marc Bekoff and Jessica Pierce, *Wild Justice: The Moral Lives of Animals* (Chicago, IL: University of Chicago Press, 2009).

3. "Name of a Dog or Natural Right" was originally written for the collection published in honor the Dutch expressionist painter Bram van Velde titled *Celui qui ne peut se servir des mots*, ed. Pierre Alechinsky (Montpellier, France: Fata Morgana, 1975). It was reprinted the following year in the bimonthly Jewish journal *Les Nouveaux Cahiers* and in the second edition of *Difficile Liberté: Essais sur le judaïsm* (*DL*, 213–16). It was translated into English by Seán Hand (*DF*, 151–53). Hand chose to give his translation a nonliteral title: "The Name of a Dog, or Natural Rights," whereas I have used a literal one: "Name of a Dog or Natural Right." The title of the French original is: "Nom d'un chien or le droit naturel." In French, *nom d'un chien!* (without an article) is a mild expletive (like "doggone!") used as a euphemism for *nom de Dieu!* ("good God!"). Although the idiom does not carry over into English, I decided to translate it literally (i.e., without the definite article), in the hope that the reader coming to the text for the first time will understand that the essay is not about *the* name "dog," or the Adamic act of naming (i.e., giving a title to) animals (even though Levinas mentions that Bobby was given "an exotic name, as one does with a cherished dog"). What it is really about is not the name "dog," but dogs themselves. Moreover, the conjunction "or" (French *ou*) in the title suggests an equivalence or even a surprising identity between the dog and "the paradox of a pure nature leading to rights." Levinas is not trying to enumerate what are nowadays often referred to as "animal rights," but to justify a possible basis of those rights by grounding them in the propensity that the dog has for showing moral recognition. He is trying to make sense of the claim that a purely "natural" being, like a dog, could be owed anything (e.g., "flesh that is torn by beasts in the field") as a *moral right*. I make use below of Hand's translation, but have modified it when I considered that I could contribute a more appropriate translation of a word or phrase.

4. The distinction between moral agents and moral subjects is taken from a recent book by Mark Rowlands titled *Can Animals Be Moral?* (Oxford, UK: Oxford University Press, 2012). According to Rowlands, only moral agents are responsible for what they do and are thus deserving of moral praise or blame. This is because only moral agents are reflective scrutinizers of reasons for acting. Moral subjects, by contrast, do not engage in reflective scrutiny, which is why their actions cannot be praised or blamed, that is, morally evaluated. In the case of "nonrational" animals, Rowlands argues, they are motivated to act, at least sometimes, on reasons that have moral content, such as compassion, sympathy, grief, and so on, but are unaware of them as reasons for so acting. Specifically, my interest here is to use Levinas's work to identify the conditions under which it is legitimate to explain the moral behavior of an animal by way of a content

(subsumed under the general category of "alterity") that the animal "individual is incapable of entertaining" (48), that is, which are not available to conscious, rational scrutiny.

For an overview of the recent attempts to attribute moral agency to animals, see Grace Clement, "Animals and Moral Agency: The Recent Debate and Its Implications," *Journal of Animal Ethics* 3, no. 1 (2013): 1–4.

5. Jacques Derrida, *The Animal That Therefore I Am* (ed. Marie-Louise Mallet, trans. David Wills [New York: Fordham University Press, 2008], 115. Hereafter cited as *ATT*).

6. Emmanuel Levinas, *Beyond the Verse: Talmudic Readings and Lectures*, trans. Gary D. Mole (London: Continuum, 2007), xiii. Hereafter cited as *BV*.

7. See the collection *A Jew's Best Friend?: The Image of the Dog throughout Jewish History*, ed. Phillip Ackerman-Lieberman (Eastbourne, UK: Sussex Academic Press, 2014).

8. The allusion is to Matthew 15:11.

9. See Irven M. Resnick, "Good Dog/Bad Dog: Dogs in Medieval Religious Polemics," *Enarratio* 18 (2013): 70–97.

10. Ibid., 82.

11. Retrieved from: http://www.chabad.org/library/bible_cdo/aid/9883/jewish/Chapter-22.htm#showrashi=true.

12. As the English theologian John Gill (1667–1711) observed,

> If literally understood, it was a very extraordinary thing that a dog, which barks at the least noise that is made, especially in the night, yet not one should move his tongue or bark, or rather "sharpen" his tongue, snarl and grin, when 600,000 men, besides women and children, with their flocks and herds, set out on their journey, and must doubtless march through many places where dogs were, before they came to the Red sea. (*John Gill's Exposition of the Bible*, Exodus 11)

Retrieved from: https://archive.org/stream/JohnGillsExpositionOfTheBookOfExodusBroughtByPeter-johnParisis/JohnGillsExpositionOfTheBookOfExodus_djvu.txt.

13. Emmanuel Levinas and Richard Kearney, "Dialogue with Emmanuel Levinas," in Richard A. Cohen (ed.), *Face to Face with Levinas* (Albany: SUNY, 1986), 13–33 (29).

14. Not only are the totalizing implications of the use of the singular general term *the animal* in the context problematic, as Derrida has pointed out ("It follows that one will never have the right to take animals to be the species of a kind that would be named The Animal, or animal in general" [*ATT*, 31]), but there is a mountain of evidence produced by cognitive ethologists showing that many animals frequently use deception. See J. L. Gould and C. G. Gould, *The Animal Mind* (New York: Scientific American Library, 1999), 136–40, for a description of the plover bird's repertoire of tricks for distracting potential nest predators.

15. Clark, "On Being 'The Last Kantian in Nazi Germany,'" 42.

16. Ibid., 55.

17. Calarco, *Zoographies,* 56–57.

18. Clark, "On Being 'The Last Kantian in Nazi Germany,'" 64.

19. Lisa Guenther, "*Flair animal*: Levinas and the Possibility of Animal Friendship," *PhaenEx* 2, no. 2 (2007), 216–38 (217).

20. "J'aime la seconde formule de l'impératif catégorique, celle qui dit de 'respecter l'homme en moi et en autrui.' Dans cette formule, nous ne sommes pas dans la pure universalité, mais déjà dans la presence d'autrui." Emmanuel Levinas, *Entretiens avec Le Monde*, 1. Philosophies (Paris: Editions la Découverte et Journal *Le Monde*, 1984), 138–46 (146).

21. Peter Atterton, "The Proximity Between Levinas and Kant: The Primacy of Pure Practical Reason," *The Eighteenth Century: Theory and Interpretation* 40, no. 3 (1999): 61–77.

22. Immanuel Kant, *Critique of Practical Reason*, trans. Lewis White Beck (Indianapolis, IN: Bobbs-Merrill, 1956), 76, 79.

23. For an overview of these problems, see Collin Allen and Marc D. Hauser, "Concept Attribution in Nonhuman Animals: Theoretical and Methodological Problems in Ascribing Complex Mental Processes," *Philosophy of Science* 58 (1991): 221–40.

24. For an attempt to use the capacity to discriminate as a framework for understanding the conditions under which it is reasonable to attribute concepts to animals, see Collin Allen, "Animal Concepts Revisited: The Use of Self-Monitoring as an Empirical Approach," *Erkenntnis* 51 (1999): 33–40.

25. In 1979 Levinas added a new preface to *Time and the Other* (first published in 1948) in which he explained that he had *initially* sought the notion of transcendent alterity starting with an "alterity-content" that was femininity (see *TO*, 36). However, this is a route that is definitively abandoned by Levinas by the time he writes *Totality and Infinity*. As incontrovertible evidence that Levinas remained confirmed that the notion of an alterity-content was misguided, see also his remarks in a radio interview in 1982 in the aftermath of the massacres at Sabra and Shatila in response to the question of whether the Other (of the Israeli) was not "above all the Palestinian." Levinas prefaced his remarks by saying: "My definition of the other is completely different" (*LR*, 294). For an attempt nevertheless to apply Levinas's discourse of alterity to cultural and ethnic designations while restoring the notion of an alterity-content, see Robert Bernasconi, "Who Is My Neighbor? Who Is the Other? Questioning 'The Generosity of Western Thought,'" *in Ethics and Responsibility in the Phenomenological Tradition: The Ninth Annual Symposium of the Simon Silverman Phenomenology Center* (Pittsburgh, PA: Simon Silverman Phenomenology Center, Duquesne University, 1992), 1–31.

26. I have already made a preliminary attempt at doing this in my essay "Nourishing the Hunger of the Other: A Rapprochement between Levinas and Darwin," *Symplok* 19, no. 1 (2011): 17–33.

27. To use Russellian language (though Russell himself was talking about sense data), we could say that Bobby is *directly acquainted* with Levinas without any description or classifying awareness involving the employment of a conceptual scheme and logical relations.

28. See S. E. G. Lea, *Instinct, Environment, and Behavior* (London and New York: Methuen, 1984), 21–22.

29. Cohen (ed.), *Face to Face with Levinas*, 27.

30. That is to say, a thought that in a certain sense is thought in us because we are not responsible according to the standard operations of transcendental constitution. Levinas frequently refers to this thought as the "idea of infinity," a term he borrows from Descartes's Third Meditation to draw attention to a thought that the "I think . . . can nowise contain" (*TI*, 48) and that "thinks more than it thinks" (*TI*, 62).

31. The term was introduced in Steven J. Gould and Elizabeth S. Vrba, "Exaptation—A Missing Term in the Science of Form," *Paleobiology* 8, no. 1 (1982): 4–15.

32. J. A. Cohen and M. W. Fox, "Vocalizations in Wild Canids and Possible Effects of Domestication," *Behavioral Processes* 1 (1976), 77–92 (91).

33. See Péter Pongrácz et al., "Human Listeners Are Able to Classify Dog (*Canis familiaris*) Barks Recorded in Different Situations," *Journal of Comparative Psychology* 119, no. 2 (May 2005): 136–44 (142).

34. Ibid., 143. This might also be taken to suggest that not only has the domestication process selected for more human-oriented dogs that consistently bark in certain behavioral and emotional situations, but that dogs have exerted selective pressure on humans to be more receptive to their vocalizations.

35. Max Scheler, *The Nature of Sympathy*, trans. P. Heath (Hamden, CT: Archon, 1973), 11.

36. Edmund Husserl *Cartesian Meditations*, trans. Dorion Cairns (Dordrecht, the Netherlands: Kluwer 1991), § 51, 112.

37. Scheler, *The Nature of Sympathy*, 10.

38. The word *beasts* in the King James Version is a translation of the Hebrew word *bəhêmāh*, which according to Strong's *Concordance* means "beast; espec. any large quadraped or animal (often collective):—beast cattle." The *Pulpit Commentary* makes it clear that it also includes *dogs*:

> Not the first-born of cattle only, but of all beasts. The Egyptians had pet animals in most houses, dogs, apes, monkeys, perhaps cats and ichneumons. Most temples had sacred animals, and in most districts of Egypt, some beasts were regarded as sacred, and might not be killed, their death being viewed as a calamity. The loss of so many animals would consequently be felt by the Egyptians as a sensible aggravation of the infliction. It would wound them both in their domestic and in their religious sensibilities. (*Pulpit Commentary*, Exodus 11)

Retrieved from: http://biblehub.com/commentaries/pulpit/exodus/11.htm.

39. Calarco, *Zoographies*, 76.

40. "No one can deny," writes Derrida, "the suffering, fear, or panic, the terror or fright that can seize certain animals and that we humans can witness" (*AT*, 28). I would add: *and that animals themselves can witness.*

Does Bobby suffer? In the short essay "Name of a Dog" Levinas gives us no literal indication that he does. There are no descriptions of him exhibiting pain behavior (flinching and yelping) whatsoever. Instead, Levinas focuses on Bobby's jumping up and down and barking that he uncontroversially interprets as an expression of joy and happiness. But there is one brief comment that Levinas makes in "Name of a Dog," from which we can infer on the basis of Levinas's phenomenology of separation in *Totality and Infinity* that Bobby did indeed suffer. When introducing his account of Bobby he writes: "And then, about halfway through our long captivity, for a few short weeks, *before the sentinels chased him away*, a wandering dog entered our lives." That the guards had to "chase" Bobby away suggests that he was forcibly removed (presumably with gunshot). Along with the immediate fear that Bobby would have felt at the time, which could hardly be said to be a pleasant experience, there is also the suffering that the separation from Levinas and the others would have caused him. In *Totality and Infinity* Levinas writes: "Suffering is a failing of happiness; it is not correct to say that happiness is an absence of suffering" (*TI*, 115). We know or at least we believe that Bobby was happy in the company of the prisoners because Levinas tells us. "This little dog," he says in an interview, "welcomed us at the entrance of the camp, barking happily [*joyeusement*]" (*IR*, 40). Now, if happiness, which for Levinas is nothing spiritual but a sensible *joie de vivre*, is the default position ("I have to but open my eyes to enjoy the spectacle") that arises from our "animal condition" [*TI*, 116]) of having our material needs met, and, further, which makes possible the relationship with exteriority spoken of at length in section 2 of *Totality and Infinity*, then given Bobby's expulsion from the camp, akin to his world being turned upside down, where he now has to eat to live (remember we are talking about domesticated *Canis familiaris*), unless more is said, we are left to conclude that Bobby *suffered*. To equate happiness with the absence of suffering and say that as long as the guards didn't hurt Bobby as they chased him away (which is probably untrue at any rate) he did not suffer is precisely to get things back to front from a Levinasian perspective.

Argos also suffers. In Homer's poem he has "fallen on evil times." He used to be taken out by the young men when they went hunting wild goats, or deer, or hares, but now he is to be found "lying neglected on the heaps of mule and cow dung that lay in front of the stable doors till the men should come and draw it away to manure the great close; and he was full of fleas." Lying on a pile of cow manure, infested with lice, old and very tired, the image makes a stark contrast to the dog that once lived in Odysseus's "well-built mansion" (Homer, *Odyssey*, Book 17, lines 375–418). He dies soon after.

41. Kiran Moodley (December 23, 2014), "Do animals have morals and show empathy?" *The Independent*. Retrieved from: http://www.independent.co.uk/news/world/do-animals-have-morals-and-show-empathy-9940632.html.

42. Example taken from James Rachels, *Created from Animals: The Moral Implications of Darwinism* (Oxford, UK: Oxford University Press, 1990), 149–52.

43. Example taken from Bekoff and Pierce, *Wild Justice*, 1.

44. Carolyn Zahn-Waxler, Barbara Hollenbeck, and Marian Radke-Yarrow, "The Origins of Empathy and Altruism," in M. W. Fox and L. D. Mickley (eds.), *Advances in Animal Welfare Science 1984/85* (Washington, DC: The Humane Society of the United States, 1984), 21–41 (21).

45. Deborah Custance and Jennifer Mayer, "Empathic-like Responding by Domestic Dogs (*Canis familiaris*) to Distress in Humans: An Exploratory Study," *Animal Cognition* 15, no. (5 (2012): 851–59 (857).

46. The claim in *Totality and Infinity* (and the anthropocentrism is telling) that "No human or interhuman relationship can be enacted outside of economy; no face can be approached with empty hands and closed home" (*TI*, 172) simply does not apply to beings living "nowhere," as Levinas and the other prisoners were for five years ("But no! There, they were in Ithaca and the fatherland. Here, we were nowhere"). The most we can say is that fulfillment of the concrete duties of feeding, clothing, and sheltering the Other is usually sufficient for ethics, but by no means necessary. It is quite possible, especially if the Other has not physical but psychological needs, for ethics to involve no such material goods.

47. I say "literally dying" because there is a sense in which, if we are to believe Heidegger, as soon as I am born I am always already dying (*Sterben*) qua being-toward-death. Obviously, this is not the sense that is meant here. A healthy teenager is not "dying" in the sense that someone in hospice care with a terminal illness who is reckoned to have three months to live is dying. Heidegger does indeed distinguish Being-toward-death and what he calls "demise" (*Ableben*). It seems that when we reach the end of our lives, though as human we still never just "perish" (*Verenden*), we are literally dying in the sense that our biological functions are coming to an end. See Martin Heidegger, *Being and Time*, trans. John Macquarrie and Edward Robinson (Oxford: Blackwell, 1962), 247.

48. Michelle A. Rivera, *Dogs and Dying: Inspirational Stories from Hospice Hounds* (West Lafayette, Indiana: Purdue University, 2010).

49. "Nourishing the Hunger of the Other: A Rapprochement between Levinas and Darwin," *Symplok* 19, no. 1 (2011): 17–33.

50. The rejection of a biological basis for ethics is not perhaps objectionable in itself. After all, postmodernists, relativists, and many cultural anthropologists, while not denying that we share common decent with the African ape, are keen to point out that our primate origins do not determine the course taken by sociocultural evolution. As evidence of this they point to the tremendous variety of cultures on earth, the malleability of human existence, different mores, habits, customs, and laws, all of which have helped to transform our destiny and put us on a different track from that of our ape cousins. It is simply unreasonable, so they say, to assume that we can explain who *we* are today by reconstructing the process of evolution. The problem, however, is that Levinas does not believe that culture can explain our morality. He insists that "ethical truth is common" (*EI*, 115). In *Totality and Infinity* he states unequivocally: "When man truly approaches the Other he is uprooted from history" (*TI*, 52). It would appear therefore that in rejecting Darwinism, or at least the possibility of a Darwinian explanation for ethical behavior Levinas has given up his best ally against the dissolution of ethics into the very historico-cultural phenomenon or artifact that he wholeheartedly rejects.

51. Charles Darwin, *The Descent of Man, and Selection in Relation to Sex* (Princeton, NJ: Princeton, University Press, 1982), 71–72.

52. I wish to thank Wolfie, to whom so many of the ideas in this essay are indebted.

PART III

RESPONSIBILITY TOWARD ANIMALS

PART II

RESPONSIBILITY TOWARD ANIMALS

CHAPTER 5

Animals, Levinas, and Moral Imagination

Michael L. Morgan

Ethical and moral considerations play an important role in our everyday lives. I take it that this observation, for all its imprecision, is incontrovertible. One way of understanding Emmanuel Levinas's contribution to our understanding of human existence is that he sought to bring some clarity to this observation and indeed to provide it with a justification that makes sense of the priority of the ethical in a way that does not succumb to objections that can be raised against other purported justifications. Furthermore, it is well known that Levinas's account identifies one dimension of our interpersonal or social relations to perform these tasks; it is a dimension or aspect of all of our social relations and is associated with the second-person way in which these relations can be understood as "face-to-face," to use his terminology. One corollary of focusing on a dimension of our intersubjectivity that is second-personal is that this dimension involves both the self and the other in all their particularity and distinctiveness, their uniqueness. This is part of the reason that Levinas calls it "alterity" and "transcendence." But if this privileging of our particularity is a formal feature of all our interpersonal relations, the substantive or material content of this dimension is the other's claim against the self for acknowledgment, acceptance, assistance, and more—for what Levinas later calls its "infinite responsibility." Levinas calls this feature of the face to face "vulnerability" or "nudity" or "nakedness," and the crucial point about it is that it marks a kind of unqualified dependence that targets the self in all its particularity and "rivets" the self to the other as wholly responsible. It is this dimension of all our social relations, this normative and "transcendental"-like condition, which is ramified and orchestrated in our everyday lives in complex and highly contextual ways.[1]

Let us call the face to face the "ground" of our moral world, on the one hand, and the complexity of decisions, actions, norms, and other considerations that make up our everyday lives in the light of this dimension "our moral world," on the other. What I want to explore here is the scope or extent of this moral world and hence the sense in which its ground applies beyond human beings. Who or what is part of it? Who or what is excluded? And how are such questions answered? The questions are obvious and significant ones, and they have been asked often, not only about Levinas and his conception of the ethical. They are, moreover, not only unavoidable and important; in certain ways, they are fundamental. They touch on a host of problems about privilege, domination, partiality, and more, and for these reasons, the question of scope cannot be ignored. It ought to be addressed and appreciated for what it can tell us about Levinas's view and how it is itself located in our thinking and our lives.

It is obvious that Levinas's account of the character and priority of the ethical and moral normativity arises from and is grounded in a paradigm case. This case is constituted by person-to-person relations and relationships. There is an analogous primacy of the interhuman paradigm in Martin Buber's *I and Thou*. In fact, Buber frequently refers to dialogue and the I-Thou relation as the interhuman. It is well known that, in part I of the book, Buber gives a very prominent place to an example of I-Thou encounter between a person and a tree, and points out explicitly that the other in an I-Thou encounter can be either a human person or a natural object or a cultural object or work of art.[2] He also, on other occasions, recalls an intimate relation that he had as a youngster with a horse when he lived with his grandparents in Bohemia. Indeed, he uses this example, which he reports in "Dialogue" in *Between Man and Man*, to clarify how fragile and transient the I-Thou is and how it occurs that a Thou becomes an It in the course of the self's withdrawal and detachment from the intimacy and immediacy of the encounter.[3] I cite this comparison with Buber to point out that Levinas is not alone, when it comes to an account of human existence that is first-personal, dialogical, and interpersonal, in using the human case as a paradigm and yet leaving open the possibility for extending the range of the relation involved. To be sure, when Buber later, in the "Epilogue" to *I and Thou* written in the 1950s, returns to clarify and explain what such nonstandard cases of dialogue mean, his explanation may not be totally satisfying, and this may show that there is a continuing problem rather than a difficulty and a solution. But the ease with which Buber moved beyond the interhuman case to other types of relations and relationships, between a self or subject and other types of others—animals, even other natural beings, and artistic and cultural creations—suggests that Levinas might well have felt a similar ease and that including such beings in our moral world was not the problem. The difficulty is to account for how this can be done and how it ought to be understood. The challenge is not one of lived experience, including moral experience; it is an intellectual or philosophical one.

But the two issues may not be unconnected. That is, how desirable and even unavoidable it is for us to include certain beings in our moral universe, within the orbit of our moral sensibility and moral imagination, is not wholly divorced from the defense we might give, if called on to give one, of how and why this is so. Years ago, for example, in writing about arguments for and against abortion, Wayne Sumner made this point in a striking way. Sumner was addressing the question of how we ought to treat unborn fetuses, and naturally he turned to ask about the status of these fetuses.[4] In the terms that were used then, in the 1970s, and may still be used, the question Sumner examined was whether unborn fetuses are persons or not. The abortion question, he explained, is about two questions: Is abortion murder or unjustified killing? And is the fetus a person? If the act is not an act of unjustified killing or murder, then it might not be morally wrong, even if the fetus is a person; or if the act would be an act of murder, it might still not be morally wrong, if the fetus is not a person. The argument about abortion, that is, turned on two classification issues, one regarding the act, the other regarding the object of the act. Sumner's insight, which seemed so salient to me then and remains so today, is that with regard to the personhood of the fetus, the relevant ways of determining that status or standing all concern moral or ethical questions. That is, including the fetus in our moral universe is not a matter of applying ethically independent features or characteristics, say, biological ones, as if the notion of a person is a biological concept, and then taking this classification and giving it a moral or ethical significance. If personhood can be given a biological meaning, it is morally neutral, until other considerations are used to give it a moral mean-ing. The only sense of personhood relevant to how the fetus should be treated morally must be a moral sense. Or, to put it otherwise, unless the fetus is already part of our moral universe, unless we have moral attitudes about how to treat fetuses and what it is right or wrong to do to them, the status of the fetus is irrelevant to whether abortion is morally right or wrong. Surely, for example, being capable of being present visually and perceptually in front of me might be morally relevant to being part of my moral universe, but only if this applied to future generations and to deceased ancestors as well as to my contemporaries. To say that fetuses are not morally relevant because they are unavailable to public interaction with us all but only to the private experience of the mother may be objectionable for many reasons, but one of them must be that such a criterion would rule out too much and moreover implies a very narrow understanding of moral experience and moral imagination.

Sumner's insight regarding the status of being a morally relevant person is
that this is not a matter of the application of some morally neutral classification
scheme; rather, what is morally relevant is a matter of being present and having
standing in our moral world, and that is a matter of how we interact with such
beings or how we imagine that we might or should interact with them. It is
a matter of our interactions, as we have them or might have them. And if we
approach Levinas's understanding of the primacy of the ethical and the face to
face in this spirit, we ought to realize that the questions of whether there is a
place for animals in Levinas's moral world and whether animals have ethical
standing are matters of how we live with animals, how we interact with them,
and what place they occupy in our moral imaginations. It is not a matter of
how we classify animals for scientific purposes.

In particular, Levinas's conception of the ethical is about dependency
and responsibility; it focuses on feelings of concern, claim, and sympathy, not
because these constitute the face to face but rather because they are indicative
of or expressions of it. And these attitudes do not, of course, exhaust how we
relate to others in this way. In fact, they only point in the direction of what
is lived as a complex and nuanced fabric of interactions, some based on actual
experience and others suggested by what can best be called our "moral imagination." To put it simply, whether animals have a "face," in the Levinasian sense,
or whether we relate to animals in a second-person way, is not an a priori or
morally neutral matter. Rather it concerns where and how animals fit into our
moral world, which is about how that world is shaped and filled out. To confront the question of what Levinasian ethics tells us about our relations with
animals, we must ask what roles animals—of different kinds—play in our lives,
how we interact with animals, and what attitudes we have toward them and why.

In a recent book, Alice Crary has discussed these matters in terms of
the role of imagination and literature in our moral lives and in moral philosophy.[5] I have proposed that in order to understand how to think about animals
within the framework of Levinas's account of ethics, one should not look for
some morally neutral account of animals, their capabilities, and needs, and so
on, but rather should consider what Levinas's thinking suggests about how we
should deal morally with all the members of our moral world, as it were, and
about whether animals or at least certain animals might have standing in that
world. Crary makes this point about animals but also about ethics in general
by pointing to an assumption that is often made about ethics and by making
a distinction between what should take place "inside ethics" and what "outside
ethics." Her point is, as she writes: "Thinkers who address questions about
animals and ethics generally assume that [how we arrive at the empirical or
world-guided images of the lives of animals that we operate within ethics] is not

a task for ethics proper and that any acceptable empirical accounts of animal life that we use in ethics must be the products of disciplines independent of ethics such as the natural sciences" (*IE*, ix). That is, she came to realize that moral philosophers, in order to arrive at a "suitable empirical grasp" of humans and animals for ethical purposes, have thought that this was "the business not of ethics but of disciplines external to it" (*IE*, x). Crary argues that this approach is mistaken. Work in the humanities, literature, and the arts can provide ethical resources for arriving at such empirical and world-guided images. In her book, she considers both the general point of not going outside ethics in order to determine how human beings and animals should be viewed within the moral world and the specific point that imagination and literature can helpfully provide such resources within ethics.

What roles animals play in our lives and how we interact with them are clearly empirical matters. Clarifying our relations with animals always focuses on particular situations and contexts and with respect to very specific types of animals. It is no wonder that while the starting point for identifying such relations is to look at our actual lives with animals—with dogs and cats, horses and gorillas and more—it is important to go beyond such actual experience to situations and relations that arise in literature and film, for example, and that are the outcome of imagination and creativity.

Crary's strategy in arguing for locating animals as moral beings within ethics is metaphysical, in a sense, insofar as she argues for a "conception of reality capacious enough to include observable moral qualities" and then shows "that human beings and animals possess such qualities" (*IE*, 2). But showing this requires a "kind of empirical grasp of these lives." Furthermore, in order to do this responsibly, "we need to be open to exploring ethically loaded perspectives of sorts that we find expressed, for instance, in work across different fields in the humanities as well as in literature and other arts" (*IE*, 3).[6] Explicitly Crary claims that the "moral thought" she defends concerning this approach to "human-animal moral fellowship" occurs within ethics and not outside it; what it is to be a human being and what it is to be an animal, for the purpose of grasping their moral standing, are illuminated within our moral lives. After calling on works of fiction, Crary turns in her book to two accounts, one in a nonfiction book and the other in a documentary film, which deal with eating animals and the use of animals in experimentation, respectively, to show how "the kind of moral thought that interests [her] . . . [is] internal to powerful arguments against industrial farming and certain experimental practices with animals" (*IE*, 7). In short, like Sumner and his remarks on the moral status of unborn fetuses, Crary argues that the "moral standing" of animals is something to be grasped within ethics and internal to ethical argument and not outside them.

Crary's point can help us to articulate where to look for the ascription of moral status in Levinas. She argues that to grasp a being's moral standing we should not look to the sciences or to external knowledge, but rather to ethics itself and our ethical or moral engagements, for example, with animals and the disabled. Similarly with Levinas, the question of whether we have face-to-face relations with animals is not an a priori or theoretical matter concerning the kind of being an animal is or whether it has certain features or not. To simplify, what Levinas takes to be our infinite responsibility to and for others and the absolute or unqualified dependence of others on us are constitutive of a second-person relation each subject has with each and every "moral" other, as I shall call the other party. But theoretically or empirically identifying properties or qualities or features does not provide the route to determining whether the other is a "moral" other, that is, whether the animal other has a "face." How the self and the other engage with or act toward one another establishes whether there is such a relation or not. Calling the dimension of their interrelation the "face to face" or one of "infinite responsibility" identifies the normative and motivational character of that relation. It is, as it were, the transcendental condition that makes the relation a morally salient one. In the order of discovery, as it were, encountering the face does not come first; it is something we realize about a relation that already exists.

We can use Crary's expressions in the following way to clarify how to understand Levinas. Crary distinguishes between "thinkers who take human beings and/or animals to lack all observable moral characteristics as situating human beings and/or animals *outside ethics*" and "those who in contrast take human beings and/or animals to have moral characteristics that are open to observation as situating human beings and/or animals *inside ethics*" (*IE*, 11–12). Unlike for Crary, what we might call moral salience arises for Levinas only insofar as we relate to beings in a certain way. Hence, for him, we do not relate to another in a third-person way first of all, in terms of some mode of classification or other, qualified in one way or another, and then consider whether or not to relate to that being in a morally salient way for other reasons; rather we encounter the other or are related to the other always already in a morally salient way, and any subsequent descriptions, characterizations, and so forth occur within that morally salient relation. In one sense, then, no relation we have to others is wholly divorced from our responsibility to and for them, and no considerations of nature or context exclude a being from that ethical relation a priori.

There are three directions that Levinas might have gone in his thinking about the scope of our infinite responsibility to others. The first is to have held that only human persons are relevant others and that our relation to nonhuman objects, plants, and animals is of a different order. This kind of Platonic or

Kantian view has tradition behind it, but within Levinas's thinking there seems to be no reason for him to draw the line between others with moral standing, so to speak, and others without it. In *Totality and Infinity*, Levinas does take the self to constitute and cultivate its natural existence in a world of materials and resources, which it consumes, uses, and more. The claim of the other seems to arise only from other persons, and while language use, rationality, and so on do characterize the relation with other persons, these arise later and do not warrant exclusivity at the primordial level. A second direction would have been for Levinas to extend our responsibility to any and all other beings, no matter what kind of being they are. There is little evidence that he did intend our responsibility to others to extend this far, but this approach has the advantage of appreciating that in principle we have a second-person relation with any other thing, at least any other living being or any other being with needs and dependencies. A third direction would have been to take seriously his philosophical strategy as a quasi-phenomenologist with an ultimately transcendental purpose, to give an account of the primordial relation that grounds all our interactions, our experience, and our relationships as we actually engage in them in our ordinary, daily lives. In this third sense, then, to determine the moral standing of particular others, not only should one realize that everything about our relations to the other occurs *within ethics*, but also, to identify whether the particular being has moral standing at all requires that we turn to *ethics* in our ordinary lives, to grasp how we regularly relate to the other party in question. On this reading of Levinas, no beings are ruled out of moral consideration a priori; his account begins with the moral relations we do have as a matter of fact and proceeds to an understanding of what our moral relation means and the ground or condition without which we would have no normative character. Levinas's starting point, as it were, is not an unbounded ethical relation to everything; nor is it a privileged ethical relation to other persons; rather, it is a life of moral responsibility, however it actually is lived by us.

Moreover, there is an important impulse to which Levinas is responding, probably most seriously in his later work, *Otherwise Than Being*. This impulse addresses the thought that there is nothing and no one that could not in principle make a claim on any one of us, at any time, and in any circumstances. This certainly includes any person, no matter where or when tragedy strikes or a need arises, and might very well include animals in distress—say a dog, or even a deer or chipmunk hit by a passing car, or dogs mistreated and living in squalid surroundings, or circus animals confined and in distress. Levinas argues that moral responsibility is the most fundamental of our normative attitudes and that it is grounded in nothing beyond itself, no fact or feature or state of affairs. Responsibility as a claim or requirement arises in the second-person relation itself and is both "to and for" the person to whom the self relates. It is the other who needs the self, who depends on the self, and whom the self addresses—for any possible "other." And what "possible" includes here must surely extend as far as ordinary, everyday experience testifies and, as I will suggest shortly, it should extend into the territory explored in literature and film when it is the product of our moral imagination. In everyday terms, if we can imagine being drawn by the pain and suffering of a creature before us, we surely can take Levinas to have held that we encounter that creature face to face.

The core idea in Crary's attempt to show that animal and human life "falls 'inside ethics'" is "an argument for thinking that human beings and animals have moral qualities that lend themselves to empirical discovery" (*IE*, 31). For Levinas, a similar tactic would raise the question of what kinds of moral relations are present for human beings and animals in ordinary life, such that the presence of the face to face and infinite responsibility provides the condition for such normative relations. Crary's strategy is to articulate a conception of mindedness or a moral psychology that is derived from Wittgenstein and applies to both human beings and animals.[7] One might also, along these lines, show how various "thick moral concepts" apply to animals just as they do to human beings. Turning to Levinas, however, whose conception of ethics turns on our relationships with others, one might seek to show how our relations to animals include uneliminable moral considerations or features. In other words, we might consider how various relations with animals are "morally thick" in the sense that these relations are part of our common sense or ordinary relations with animals, and incorporate ineradicable moral dimensions.

For much of our married life, my wife Audrey and I had cats, and now, although we no longer have cats as participants in our immediate family life, one of our daughters and her family have cats that are very much members of her family. I do not believe it is simply a mistaken projection or confusion on our parts to think of our relations with these various cats as emotionally and morally rich. We still tell stories about how our last two cats, Blaze and Amanda, responded to events that were taking place in our home by showing displeasure or sympathy and made their preferences clear by reacting with affection and in other ways. For two years, when he was advanced in age, Blaze's kidney disease required that I give him pills and administer daily subcutaneous fluids. He was calmed and soothed by my singing only one song; his behavior made it clear that if I changed the melody, he was aware and disturbed by my experimentation with alternatives. He knew what he liked and found ways to communicate his preference to me. Not only were all of us able to tell when Blaze and Amanda were frightened, surprised, and enduring distress or pain; they also responded to our moods and conduct, avoiding us at times and tendering affection at others. To be sure, we might describe their behavior in terms of some kind of automatic mechanism or mere reactions, but by doing that we lose something of the "texture" or "nuance" of the behavior, something in the look of their eyes, in their posture, and in the delicacy or inflection of their bodily disposition. I have known many people who have had cats for years, and they regularly speak of such relations with their cats.

And what is true for cat people perhaps is even truer for dog-people. Dogs are often said to be aware of the moods and feelings of their owners, to recognize emotional changes, and to be educable, capable of learning in a way that can best be understood as conceptual and perhaps even rational. This means that we speak of a dog's behavior or conduct as conceptual in a sense, as involving a kind of generalization or categorization, and as the result of having come to treat an individual as a member of a kind and as deserving a certain kind of response. Crary calls on a scene from Thomas Mann's memoir about his life with his dog Bashan in order to illustrate the type of grasp or response that would count as being conceptual in this way. The scene involves Mann's attempt to describe Bashan's response to seeing a man shoot a duck for the first time. Mann's description tries to portray Bashan's sense of surprise, his starting at the sight of it, as if Bashan's uncharacteristic recoil and his being brought up starkly and abruptly were expressing questions like "What, what! *What* was that? In the name of a hundred thousand devils! *How* was that!" (cited *IE*, 113–14). Crary makes several points about Mann's description, most importantly that it attempts to describe Bashan as coming to grasp something that is new or unlike the common, everyday events and items that are utterly familiar to him, and that Mann's description and the event of Bashan's surprise are themselves common enough and not unusual. Such things happen all the time to dogs and those who care for them. That is, dogs (and cats, I would contend) regularly respond to experience by grasping and reacting to the novel and then by becoming familiarized to such events and things.

I have an ulterior motive, however, in calling attention to this moment in Crary's account. For this moment in her argument leads Crary to cite, in a footnote, the very famous and distinctive occasion in Levinas's writings, when he too calls attention to the behavior of a dog and the way that Levinas and others responded to that behavior. She takes Levinas's description to show what Mann's description of Bashan has shown: that dogs behave in ways we can describe as "dealing with kinds of things," that is, their behavior is conceptual in a sense. Here is Crary on Levinas.

> For a further illustration of dogs dealing with kinds of things, see Emmanuel Levinas's description of how, in a Nazi camp for Jewish

prisoners of war wearing the French uniform, in which he and others were treated as "subhuman, a gang of apes" by guards, a wandering dog clearly recognized them as men. (*IE*, 115)[8]

Crary's point here and in this chapter of her book is a very specific one. It is not about our relations with animals overall or even our relations with dogs. Rather, it is an attempt to show, via various examples, how common it is to take dogs and other animals as well to have some kind of conceptual ability. As she admits, there may be cases of canine behavior that could be explained in a way that does not involve concepts; it may be that she, Mann, and others in any given case are guilty of a kind of "sentimental projection" regarding the behavior of dogs. But even so, it is still possible to "say that a clear-sighted survey of the massive, millennia-old body of observation and testimony about the lives of dogs nevertheless speaks for attributing concepts to them" (*IE*, 118). And what applies to being conceptual also applies, I believe, to our relations with dogs and other animals and how we describe those relations. Some could be sentimental projections on our part, but there is a "massive" body of "observation and testimony" that suggests otherwise, that calls such relations by the names of "sympathetic care or concern" and "feeling affection" or "feeling pain" and "being trustworthy" and such, and that justify taking our relations to be value or moral based.

I have not drawn on Crary's argument on behalf of taking some nonhuman animals to have conceptual capacities in order to address this issue directly or to endorse her conclusion. Rather, my point concerns her approach. She uses testimony and literary examples in order to expose something about our everyday practices and in particular about animal behavior and our descriptions of it, the point of which is to defend "an image of animals as inside ethics." Similarly, I would argue, we might say that there is a mass of observation, testimony, and imaginative evidence that supports the thought that "dogs are capable of having moral relationships with others," as Crary puts it, and not only dogs but also other nonhuman animals.[9]

In this spirit, let us return to Levinas's well-known comments on his experience of the dog Bobby in the prisoner of war camp—a "forestry commando unit"—in Fallinpostel, near Magdeburg in Northern Germany. Here is a real dog and a real situation that tell us something about this dog's relationship with the prisoners in the camp and what it means to call the dog "the friend of man." There is, he says, "a transcendence in the animal" (*DF*, 152), and "transcendence" here refers of course to the otherness or alterity that lies in the other's face, that brings the claim of the other in the second-person relationship. In other words, what Levinas is about to describe is a situation with Bobby the dog that exposes the relationship with Bobby as morally involved or ethically inflected, in Levinas's broad sense of that term. On the one hand, Levinas calls attention to the fact that to those who gave the Jewish prisoners orders or who otherwise had dealings with them saw the Jews as "subhuman, a gang of apes" (*DF*, 153). As he puts it, in a sense "we were no longer part of the world"; rather, we were "beings without language" (*DF*, 153). On the other hand, for the dog that happened to enter their lives about halfway through their incarceration, "there was no doubt we were men" (*DF*, 153). Crary emphasizes the dog's treatment of the prisoners as human; Levinas, to my ear, emphasizes how the dog's greetings, his delight in seeing them, elicits a response from Levinas and his peers.[10] They name him; they call him "Bobby," and in so doing they accept him, acknowledge him in all his particularity, and in a spirit of appreciation for his welcome and his "friendship." In this way, Bobby's "transcendence" makes a claim on the prisoners; his encounter with them as human beings elicits their response to and for him. They never lose their right to recognition, and he gives them reason to respect it in him, which they do by naming him. Hence, the title of the little piece, "The Name of a Dog, or Natural Rights."

Enigmatically, Levinas ends his brief remarks about this availability of the ethical by saying two final things about Bobby. First, Bobby is "the last Kantian in Nazi Germany, without the brain needed to universalize maxims and drives" (*DF*, 153). How should we interpret Levinas here? Levinas and his fellow prisoners were in Germany, in Nazi Germany; they were in the Jewish section of a prisoner of war camp, and, as he describes their situation, they were treated by others as subhuman; others did not treat them with the respect shown to fellow human beings. But Bobby did. He welcomed them, delighted in their presence, in short showed them the respect due a being with shared moral standing. In this sense, as I read him, Levinas eulogizes Bobby as "the last remaining Kantian" in the German fascist state, even if he does not have the cognitive abilities to "universalize maxims." His response to the presence of the Jewish prisoners, his animated reception when they returned from work, was a response to them and not to a maxim or general principle; it nonetheless showed a respect for their moral status.

Levinas's second comment refers to Bobby as "a descendant of the dogs of Egypt" (*DF*, 153). Who are these "dogs of Egypt?" Earlier in the essay Levinas had commented on the dogs that appear in Exodus 11:7, on the night of the final plague, when the children of Israel are about to be released by Pharaoh in response to the "death of the first-born." Levinas refers to them as "strange dogs . . . struck by a light in the middle of the night. They will not growl!" (*DF*, 152). The text reports what God tells Pharaoh, that at midnight God will pass through Egypt and all the firstborn will die, from Pharaoh's child to those of slaves and even to those of the cattle. There will be wailing and grief everywhere, "but among the Israelites no dog will bark at any person or animal," which will be a sign that God has distinguished between Egyptians and Israelites. Levinas focuses on these dogs and their silence. What does it mean? How is the silence of the dogs a sign that God has distinguished between the Egyptians and the Israelites? And in what way is Bobby their descendant?

In order to answer these questions, we must begin with the dogs of the Israelites in Egypt and what their silence means, according to Levinas. Recall that the traumatic night of the Egyptians is, at the same time, the moment when Israel shall be liberated. The people will become a nation that remembers its past and yet is aware of its current freedom. As Levinas puts it, "Man's freedom is that of an emancipated man remembering his servitude and feeling solidarity for all enslaved people. . . . This is what the friend of man means" (*DF*, 152). That is, to be a "friend of man" or a person who takes responsibility for others who are in need or in pain or who are enslaved is to "feel solidarity" with people who are in bondage, which includes one's own past, in the case of the Israelites, where the solidarity is with one's own past, and all others who are similarly oppressed and who suffer. The silence of the dogs of Israel is in contrast to the wailing in Egypt at the death of their firstborns; it is a figure for the recognition of the liberation of people from slavery, oppression, and indifference, what Levinas calls "this high mystery of man" (*DF*, 152). The dogs do not growl at the pain and suffering of the Egyptians; they do not express despair and grief. They are silent in response to the impending liberation and the humanity of the Israelites. At this "supreme hour," the dogs of the Israelites "will attest to the dignity of the person" (*DF*, 152; modified translation).

Moreover, Bobby is the heir of these ancient dogs insofar as "his friendly growling, his animal faith, was born from the silence of his forefathers on the banks of the Nile" (DF, 153). That is, Bobby's "friendly barking," his joy and delight in welcoming the returning prisoners, is the legacy of the dogs whose silence was a response to the "mystery of freedom" and the humanity of the once-but-no-longer-enslaved people. Silence instead of wailing and despair; friendly frolic at the sight of newfound friends. All this bespeaks the relationship between people and a particular dog, a particular animal whose responses and needs are ethically salient; it is a kind of friendship of mutual acceptance, welcome, and respect.

How much can we build on the scaffolding of this slight essay, with its biblical exegesis and its concrete recollection? In *Inside Ethics*, Crary argues for a moral psychology and metaphysics that are broad enough to include nonhuman animals in our ethical world, and she supports these arguments with recollections of personal experiences with animals and interpretations of several literary episodes, most notably from Tolstoy, Coetzee, and Sebald. Neither concrete urgencies—for example, concerning using animals for scientific experimentation or the eating of animals—nor the abstract question of what is required to be an ethical other and have moral status become thematic for Levinas. What the single recollection at the heart of the little essay "The Name of a Dog, or Natural Rights" does do, however, is show that testimony on behalf of ethically inflected relations with nonhuman animals is available and that the upshot, for the seriousness of Levinas's ethical account of the human condition, is to underscore that it is not exclusive to human beings or to rational human agents. We ought not be indifferent or opposed to humane treatment and concern for others, and we ought especially to be attuned to the self-esteem and dignity of particular others. Such attitudes and responsibilities, moreover, can be directed at any other being, surely any other living being. Examples from life, literature, and film testify to whether in fact they do, and hence to whether nonmoral animals occupy places in our moral world as a matter of fact. Whether they do or not is a matter of what takes place *inside ethics* and how such beings present themselves to us.[11] In short, Levinas's account is compatible with a genuine moral concern for animals and with their concern for us, and it encourages taking responsibility for their well-being, nourishment, habitat, and more. But such responsibility occurs only when there are everyday normative relations between individuals and particular animals; when there are such relations, second-person ones, then underlying them is a dimension of moral responsibility that is present along with the everyday features and roles that otherwise characterize such relations. When we love our pets or come to the aid of a wounded animal, for example, this is the case.

This line of thinking is a very charitable one, however. Much of the time Levinas's treatment of the face to face is anthropocentric, at least in the way he presents it, and there are many moments when his presentation of the face to face, responsibility, and the ethical anticipates, at the transcendental level, what in ordinary affairs is manifest as a kind of fact-value distinction in a way that surely privileges the human.[12] Often by citing or alluding to a figure like Hobbes, Levinas suggests that the state of nature does itself lack a moral aspect, which only supplements it when we appreciate how second-person relations bring with them moral normativity. In this way, Levinas seems to be drawing a distinction between a dimension of moral value and normativity in our lives and a dimension that we associate with our natural, physiological, and physical character as beings often driven by needs and desires grounded in our natural existence. All of this suggests that nonhuman animals might well represent in his mind the dimension of human existence that we associate with some form of scientific naturalism. Commentators on Levinas have noticed this feature of his thinking, and in some cases, they treat it as decisive evidence that there is no room in his thinking for placing nonhuman animals within the domain of the ethical.[13]

My argument, however, is intended to show that this reading is too narrow; it treats the fact-value distinction or the distinction between the natural and the ethical as if it had a rigid, a priori scope, independent of how integrated our lives are and what our actual, lived interactions with animals are. The latter, to use Crary's expressions, occur *inside ethics* and not *outside*. In Levinas's terms, the moral standing of animals is not something one should doubt or credit independently of our ordinary ethical lives, even if our outside standards were some credentials for what kinds of others we can face and engage in a second-person way. In fact, there are no such credentials or requirements independent of our everyday lives and no a priori rules for what has moral standing in our lives and what does not. As Plant puts it, since the face to face can occur whenever there is embodied presence of one being to another, "it becomes even less clear why non-human animals—certainly Bobby, but perhaps even the snake—*cannot* be said to have a 'face' in the relevant ethical sense."[14]

Notes

1. For the general account of Levinas on which I am drawing, see Michael L. Morgan, *Discovering Levinas* (New York: Cambridge University Press, 2007) and *Levinas's Ethical Politics* (Bloomington: Indiana University Press, 2016).

2. See Martin Buber, *I and Thou*, trans. Walter Kaufmann (New York: Scribner's, 1970).

3. Martin Buber, *Between Man and Man*, trans. Ronald Gregor Smith (Boston: Beacon Press, 1961).

4. L. W. Sumner, *Abortion and Moral Theory* (Princeton, NJ: Princeton University Press, 1981), esp. chap. 6; see also "Toward a Credible View of Abortion," *Canadian Journal of Philosophy* 4, no. 1 (1974): 163–81; "A Matter of Life and Death," *Nous* 10, no. 2 (1976): 153–63.

5. Alice Crary, *Inside Ethics: On the Demands of Moral Thought* (Cambridge, MA: Harvard University Press, 2016). Hereafter cited as *IE*.

6. Showing how being human and being an animal give both moral standing is the burden of *Inside Ethics*, chapters 2–4. These are the philosophical heart of Crary's account, which employs an account of mind and behavior derived from Wittgenstein. Her use of literary accounts to illustrate how animals are seen to have such standing occurs primarily in chapter 6. Here she uses examples from Tolstoy, Coetzee, and Sebald to exhibit "important forms of human-animal moral fellowship" (*IE*, 6).

7. See *IE*, 39–40. As Crary puts it, she defends a view of mind "that represents aspects of mind as essentially tied to modes of behavior" and that uses "psychological

categories [that] resist any sort of meaningful reduction to physical terms because they have necessary references to ethically loaded conceptions of the lives of the—human or non-human—creatures to whom they apply" (*IE*, 61).

8. Crary is citing Emmanuel Levinas, "The Name of a Dog, or Natural Rights," in *Difficult Freedom: Essays on Judaism* (Baltimore, MD: Johns Hopkins University Press, 1990), 151–53.

9. In a footnote (*IE*, 120n58), Crary calls attention to the work of the poet and dog trainer Vicki Hearn as one valuable resource for such evidence. See Vicki Hearne, *Adam's Task: Calling Animals by Name* (New York: Harper Perennial, 1994). See also Raimond Gaita, *The Philosopher's Dog* (Melbourne, AU: Text Publishing, 2002), 40–42; and Alice Crary, "Freedom Is for the Dogs," in *Ethics, Society, Politics*, eds. Martin G. Weiss and Hajo Greif (Berlin, Germany: De Gruyter, 2013).

10. In an interview years later, in 1986, Levinas recounts the experience and explicitly says that this little dog, when he saw the prisoners returning from work, jumped up and down, excited, and welcomed them. "In this corner of Germany, where walking through the village we would be looked at by the villagers as *Juden*, this dog evidently took us for human beings. . . . [T]his little dog welcomed us at the entrance of the camp, barking happily and jumping up and down amicably around us" ("Interview with Francois Poirie," in *Is It Righteous to Be? Interviews with Emmanuel Levinas*, ed. Jill Robbins [Stanford, CA: Stanford University Press, 2001], 41).

11. This does not mean that relationships of concern or companionship are equally imaginable or possible with all kinds of living creatures and animals. In some cases, such relations seem very unlikely if not wholly out of the question. But different people have different aptitudes, sensibilities, and experiences. On these matters, see Bob Plant, "Welcoming Dogs: Levinas and 'the Animal' Question," *Philosophy and Social Criticism* 3, no. 1 (2011): 49–71 (esp. 58–60).

12. In one way for Levinas, the human does occupy a privileged place in the natural order, insofar as only with the human do we have moral experience or the experience of moral responsibility, as he understands it. When he says, for example, in "The Animal Interview," that "with the appearance of the human—here is my entire philosophy—that is, with man, there is something more important than my life, and that is the life of the other" (*AI*, 5), what he means is not that only human beings can matter to each of us but rather that only with human selves or subjects does the relation with the other involve the subject being aware that the other's life and well-being matters more than its own, that one's responsibility to and for the other is infinite or unlimited. In short, this does not rule out nonhuman animal others, but it does say that only human selves have the experience of moral normativity. Here, however, Levinas may be failing to appreciate what he and his fellow prisoners saw in Bobby's behavior.

13. For an exemplary paper that calls attention to this distinction and argues that Levinas's own views are limited in this way, see Bob Plant, "Welcoming Dogs" (cited earlier). Plant recalls a paper of Peter Atterton's in which Atterton distinguishes between what Levinas says and what his thinking involves, and Plant adds his own coda: "As Atterton rightly notes, whether Levinas himself does justice to the non-human realm is a separate question from 'whether a Levinasian ethics *ought* nevertheless to include the

other animal' ("Ethical Cynicism," p. 52). My feeling is that it *should*, but that in order to do this one would have to drop Levinas's antinaturalism (see Plant, *Wittgenstein and Levinas*, ch. 7)" (64n49). The distinction that Atterton draws and with which Plant agrees is certainly a right one to draw, but I disagree with Plant about Levinas's own commitment to naturalism; it is much more nuanced and attenuated than he seems to suggest.

14. Plant, "Welcoming Dogs," 60.

CHAPTER 6

Small Justice

The Rights of the Other Animal

JONATHAN CROWE

We owe things to animals. I mean: we have duties toward them. Animals, for their part, have rights with respect to us. This kind of language is a straightforward and compelling way of talking about our ethical relationship to animals. However, it invites two common objections. First, it is sometimes argued that since animals are incapable of engaging in moral discourse or holding duties with regard to other beings, they should not be regarded as bearers of rights.[1] The right-duty relationship, in this view, is necessarily reciprocal. Animals cannot show moral concern toward others, so they do not belong to the moral community.

A second objection concerns the relationship between ethics and justice. Ethics, it is sometimes thought, is concerned with interpersonal relationships, whereas justice considers institutions: duties, rights, and so on belong to the latter realm.[2] Furthermore, in this view, the topics must be distinguished. A theory of justice cannot simply restate the demands of ethics. It must make a place for nonideal theory, asking what institutions we should adopt on the assumption that people will not always behave well.[3] One question is what people owe to others, ethically speaking, but the issue of what rights and duties people hold is a separate issue.

I want to argue that these two worries rest on a common mistake. The mistake concerns the way they understand the moral community and its relationship to institutional justice. The mistake does not lie in thinking that people sometimes act unethically; this is indubitably true. Rather, the mistake lies in thinking that ethical and institutional questions can and should be separated. Interpersonal ethics, I will argue, supplies the basis for community and therefore for justice and law. Justice, then, is subsidiary to ethics; interpersonal relationships supply the foundations for just institutions. We must begin imagining justice on a small scale. The ethical theory of Emmanuel Levinas shows us how this might be done.

The Economy of Kindness

We often say that people who treat others cruelly are being *inhumane* or even *inhuman*. This wording suggests a deep link between human nature and kindness—a person who acts unkindly is not acting in a *human* fashion. What, then, is the link between being human and being kind? What are the limitations imposed on kindness by our humanity? Are we simply incapable of certain types of kindness—such as an unconditional kindness toward strangers, enemies, or nonhuman animals? Philosophers have long debated this issue. I want to begin with two contrasting viewpoints.

Friedrich Nietzsche had this to say about kindness in his book about human nature, *Human, All Too Human*.

> *Economy of kindness.* Kindness and love, the most curative herbs and agents in human intercourse, are such precious finds that one would hope these balsamlike remedies would be used as economically as possible; but this is impossible. Only the boldest Utopians would dream of the economy of kindness.[4]

What does Nietzsche mean when he questions the possibility of the economy of kindness? He seems to have in mind the partiality that humans often exhibit in their ethical thinking. We acknowledge those close to us as moral beings far more readily than we recognize strangers. Nietzsche's pessimism about the capacity of humans to overcome the natural limits of their empathy comes to the fore in a later passage.

> [T]he idea of one's "neighbour" . . . is very weak in us; and we feel toward him almost as free and irresponsible as toward plants and stones. That the other suffers *must be learned*; and it can never be learned completely.[5]

Nietzsche, then, sees the natural state of humans as characterized by indifference toward the suffering of others. Compassion, in his view, must be learned—and the difficulty of learning and retaining it makes kindness toward others very tenuous. There is, as such, a deep futility in our efforts to extend kindness beyond our immediate circle. We may profess to believe in universal kindness, but this reflects hypocrisy rather than a genuine commitment. The true economy of kindness is impossible to imagine.

We have, however, sometimes tried to imagine it. The most radical economist of kindness was Jesus, who commanded us to "love your neighbor as yourself."[6] The true radicalism of Jesus's teaching comes through not merely in the neighbor principle, but in his answer to the follow-up question: *Who is my neighbor?* Or, as Cain asks in Genesis, "Am I my brother's keeper?"[7] Jesus's answer is that your neighbors are not just your local community, but the whole of humanity: "I have other sheep that are not of this fold. I must bring them also, and they will listen to my voice. So there will be one flock, one shepherd."[8] The economy of kindness extends to strangers—and even your enemies: "[L]ove your enemies, do good to those who hate you."[9]

Jesus, then, was the radical Utopian whom Nietzsche no doubt had in mind. He taught that humans, despite their fallen nature, could be guided by a new commandment based on universal love.[10] Nietzsche, by contrast, thought such exhortations futile. He saw self-preservation as so ingrained in humanity that any claim to love another as oneself could only be self-deceiving. "We don't accuse nature of immorality when it sends us a thunderstorm," he says, so why do we call a callous person immoral?[11] Here, then, we have two contrasting views of human nature. Who is correct, Jesus or Nietzsche? Is it good or bad to dream of the economy of kindness?

It seems to me that Jesus has the better view. Nietzsche sees a form of pervasive self-deception in professions of altruism or universal compassion. However, I want to suggest the opposite is true: those who deny our capacity for kindness are deceiving themselves in order to avoid their ethical duties. There is no doubt that showing kindness toward strangers is highly demanding. As Nietzsche recognizes, it goes against our tendency to privilege ourselves and those like us. Deep down, however, we know it's wrong to be unkind. It is when we turn away from this knowledge, privileging comfort over conscience, that we fall into hypocrisy and bad faith.

Ethical Avoidance

It's hard to be kind to strangers, let alone our perceived enemies. We often struggle to love our fellow humans. What about the even more radical demand to be kind to nonhuman animals? A similar point applies in this context: we know it's wrong to mistreat animals, but sometimes it's convenient to pretend otherwise. The battle between comfort and conscience reappears at this level. We desire to deceive ourselves; we weave elaborate ruses; we conspire to evade our responsibilities. This sort of self-deception occurs on an individual basis, but it also has an important cultural dimension. There is often a form of *cultural rationalization* at work in such contexts. We find ways as a community to patrol the margins of our ethical world.

Our attempts to deny our ethical responsibilities to animals—not only our pets, but the animals who suffer from factory farming—are based on lies we tell to each other. We are like people casting about for reasons to reject an inconvenient suspicion. We sense the demand for ethical recognition that animals present to us, but we prefer to avoid the responsibility it entails. This kind of ethical avoidance is sometimes sustained by creating and maintaining *ethical blind spots*, areas of life whose ethical significance we avoid by hiding it from view. We may do this individually by refusing to direct our minds to a troubling ethical question. The same thing also occurs on a wider social and cultural level: the realities of factory farming are systematically hidden away so we need not confront them.

A second form of avoidance occurs where we justify our ethically problematic choices by creating *rationalizations* after the fact. The very act of asking the question, "Who is my neighbor?" signals the need to define the boundaries of the ethical community. This, in turn, gives us the capacity to deny certain beings any ethical status by rationalizing their exclusion. We grant to ourselves the power to decide *who counts and why*. Historical examples illustrating the seriousness of this issue are not hard to find. Communities have often decreed that women, slaves, and members of particular racial and cultural groups do not count for ethical purposes. Blacks did not count in antebellum America; Jews did not count in Nazi Germany. Pervasive discourses of cultural rationalization pushed them to the outer margins of ethics. It became all too easy not to count them.

These techniques of ethical avoidance have often been applied to humans, so it is no surprise we have also applied them to other species. Levinas links the two issues in "The Name of a Dog, or Natural Rights," when he reflects on his experience as a Jewish internee in a German prisoner-of-war camp. He describes how the gazes of "the other men, called free," who guarded the internees, "stripped us of our human skin" (*DF*, 153). "A small inner murmur, the strength and wretchedness of persecuted people, reminded us of our essence as thinking creatures, but we were no longer part of the world" (*DF*, 153). This kind of "social oppression" (modified translation) for Levinas, "shuts people away in a class, deprives them of expression and condemns them to being 'signifiers without a signified' . . . to violence and fighting" (*DF*, 153). Their ethical status is effaced by cultural rationalization.

Levinas contrasts the dehumanization of the internees by their captors with the affection and enthusiasm of the dog, nicknamed Bobby, who finds his way into the camp. It is Bobby, not the guards, who reminds the prisoners of their ethical status and human dignity. Levinas notes that Bobby has "neither ethics nor *logos*" (*DF*, 152); he lacks "the brain needed to universalize maxims and drives" (*DF*, 153). This might seem to call into question Bobby's own ethical standing.[12] However, Bobby's inability to rationalize renders him unable to push away the internees based on their Jewish identity. He simply recognizes them as fellow creatures and responds accordingly.

The cultural rationalization that excluded Levinas and his fellow inmates from moral belonging was, of course, perpetuated by Nazi dogma. Jews, it was said, were "subhuman"; for the greater good of the German people, they had to be eradicated. In this way, the Jewish neighbor is supplanted by the universal Jew; the individual is erased and replaced by a pure analytical category. Institutionally excluded from ethical consideration, members of such groups are pushed to the margins of social consciousness, perpetually situated at or beyond the borders of the moral community.

The Ethics of Suffering

Levinas's theory of ethics emphasizes what he calls the face-to-face encounter with the other. Our natural inclination from childhood is to place ourselves at the center of the world and view objects as existing for our enjoyment (*TI*, 134). The existence of other people troubles us, because we can no longer treat the world as ours alone: we must recognize other sentient beings, with their own desires, priorities, and outlooks (*TI*, 139). We may initially try to treat other people as mere objects, as means to our selfish ends. However, there is always something about them that eludes our grasp.

It is like the moment when, walking down a corridor, we see another person approaching us from the other end. At first, we may try to move around them as if they were a fixed object, but we are simultaneously aware that this is impossible: they might change course at any time. The other person demands recognition as a being with her own plans and purposes. She appears to us as an unpredictable, irreducible entity. The face to face, then, interrupts the coziness of the subject's inner world and compels her to acknowledge the demands of other people. Levinas calls it an "epiphany" in which "the sensible, still graspable, turns into total resistance to the grasp" (*TI*, 197). The face of the other reveals the subject's focus on self-enjoyment as capricious and arbitrary. Her freedom is rendered "inhibited," "guilty," and "timid" (*TI*, 203). The other commands respect; her gaze "paralyses power" (*TI*, 199).

The suffering of the other, Levinas observes, is not experienced as a mere "datum," but rather as something more primordial, akin to "revulsion" (*EN*, 91). He goes on to comment: "[T]he justification of the neighbors' pain is certainly the source of all immorality" (*EN*, 99). There are two important ideas in this statement. Levinas's remark emphasizes the fundamental place of suffering in ethics, but it equally takes aim at the role of cultural rationalization in covering over our ethical duties. The very idea of justifying my neighbor's suffering, according to Levinas, is an "outrage" (*EN*, 95).

It's hard for us to see another creature suffer. Suffering is hard to stomach—and this is exactly as it should be. We can't face it; we push it away; we try to hide it at the margins of our community. The point applies to both the suffering of the other human and the suffering of the other animal. We hide the reality of factory farming in order to avoid our responsibilities—if we were to openly acknowledge the ways animals suffer at our hands, we might feel compelled to do something about it. As Levinas notes, "We do not want to make an animal suffer needlessly . . . It is because we as [humans] know what suffering is that we can also have this obligation" (*AI*, 4). Ethical responsibility, then, involves guarding against the temptation to rationalize our actions, rather than engaging in good faith with the demands of other beings. This is the radical challenge posed by the economy of kindness.

We have become very good—terrifyingly good—at obscuring the suffering of animals. The factory farm is far removed from the typical consumer. People don't know—and choose not to discover—how their meat is produced. Many people continue to believe that meat is necessary for human nutrition, although millions thrive on vegetarian or vegan diets.[13] We exploit our distance from intensively farmed animals to keep them at the margins of our ethical lives. We are, in short, far too easy on ourselves. We live comfortably with things that should be hard to live with.

A person becomes our neighbor when we are familiar with their suffering. Thin walls make good neighbors. A neighbor who is close by is harder to live with, but an ethical life was not meant to be easy. Nietzsche, then, was partly right. That the other suffers must be learned—and it must be relearned, again and again. The neighbor principle lies deep within us, but it is far too easily forgotten. We must do our moral calisthenics, practice and nurture our natural sensitivity toward the suffering of other beings. We must invest in sympathy, mix it with our labor, trade in it, grow it, give it value, spread it around. We must circulate love like we circulate money. We must allow it to work from within to shape and direct our institutions.[14] And that would be the true economy of kindness.

Small Justice

What, then, is the relationship between kindness and justice? Is it unjust to be unkind? The relationship between ethics and justice raises deep questions within Levinas's theory. Some commentators have doubted whether Levinas really offers us a theory of justice.[15] They have puzzled over whether Levinas's ethics, which focuses on the interpersonal, can provide an adequate foundation for just institutions. There is an apparent problem here arising from the disjunction between the radical *particularity* of the face-to-face encounter and the *generality* we normally attribute to justice and law. The face-to-face encounter is particular in at least three senses.[16] First, the encounter with the other is primordial and therefore resists expression through terms and concepts. Ethics, for Levinas, appears prior to language and conceptual thought. We must seek to understand and express the significance of the face to face without reducing it to terms with which we are already familiar.

Second, the face to face signals a unique responsibility that rests on the subject alone. The ethical encounter forces the subject to acknowledge his personal capacity to respond to the other's demands. This yields a duty that nobody can share and from which no one can release him.

Third, each face-to-face encounter presents a radically new demand that reflects the other's singular nature. The subject must acknowledge the specific other who confronts her at that moment. This creates what Diane Perpich calls the problem of "singular justice: can there be an abstract principle or law that does justice to the absolute singularity of the other who faces me?"[17]

Levinas challenges us to reconsider our common assumption that justice begins at a general, rather than a particular level. I call the kind of justice suggested by Levinas's theory *small justice*. What, many commentators have asked, is the bridge between Levinas's account of ethics and his pronouncements on justice? How do we move from the concreteness of the face to face to the more general realm of institutions? The answer, I will argue, lies in the temporal aspect of the face to face. It is not so much that time provides a bridge between ethics and justice, as that time extends and deepens the ethical to the point where it transcends the face-to-face relation. The seeds of justice are, over time, already sowed at an interpersonal level. The challenge for justice is to recognize the radical potential of this ethical context.

Levinas's emphasis on the face-to-face encounter may give the impression that ethics is a succession of isolated moments. However, Levinas emphasizes that the face-to-face encounter does not occur in isolation. Rather, each encounter includes traces of prior ethical experiences. This "past that is on the hither side of every present" allows the subject to grasp, however tentatively and imperfectly, her responsibility for the other (*OB*, 10). Each encounter with the other involves a unique ethical demand, but these discrete "instants do not link up with one another indifferently." Rather, "the alterity of each face increases and deepens ever more profoundly" (*TI*, 283).

Each ethical moment contains, on its hither side, an indelible trace of the past. The subject's passive synthesis of these repeated encounters produces an overall attitude toward social life. Our memory of repeated encounters with the other therefore contains the beginnings of an ethical attitude that can, in turn, prepare the ground for legal and political discourse. Levinas reminds us that "nothing is lost" to the past; rather, "everything is consigned," "synthesized," or "assembled" into a "transcending diachrony" that resists the tendency to separate time into a series of events (*OB*, 9).

The temporally extended character of the ethical moment provides the foundation for a Levinasian account of ethical discourse. Diachronic time, Levinas argues, involves an iterative process of uncovering ethical meaning by means of a "memorable temporality." It does not "coagulate the flow of time" into a static set of themes and concepts, but rather provides an evolving hermeneutic backdrop against which ethical discourse can gradually take form (*OB*, 37). The synthesis of ethical moments experienced by the subject is "absolutely passive"; it gives rise to an "unrepresentable, immemorial, pre-historical" sense of our shared ethical responsibilities (*OB*, 38).

This temporally extended experience of ethics is repeated continually across a range of different social contexts. Community discourse therefore takes place against a shared hermeneutic backdrop. This produces an implicit orienting of the community toward a shared understanding of social life. It is this shared social sense of responsibility that leads Levinas to speak of an "astonishing human fraternity" (*OB*, 10). The diachronic orientation of ethics, for Levinas, "contains the secret of sociality" (*EN*, 169). It therefore paves the way for a shared discourse on justice and law.

Justice or the Other?

The story is well known. Albert Camus was asked in 1957 why he had not spoken out in support of the National Liberation Front's fight for independence in Algeria. He replied, "People are now planting bombs on the trams in Algiers. My mother could be on one of those trams. If that is justice, I prefer my mother."[18] Camus's statement was originally misreported by *Le Monde* as "I will defend my mother before justice." However, Camus's actual words are more ambiguous. The final sentence of Camus's remark states a conditional proposition: *if* that is justice, *then* I prefer my mother.

Like all conditionals, the meaning of Camus's statement depends crucially on the truth value of the antecedent. "If that is justice": well, is it or isn't it? Camus's comment is open to two different interpretations. If it is true that planting bombs on the trams in Algiers represents justice, then Camus prefers his mother to justice. However, if planting bombs on the trams is not justice, then Camus is not necessarily rejecting justice in favor of his mother. Rather, he can be interpreted as favoring an alternative conception of justice: one that does not justify bombing his mother.

It is possible, of course, that Camus himself was undecided between these stances. He may have been trying to say, "I don't know what justice requires here. However, regardless of the demands of justice, I know that I cannot support bombing my mother." This final interpretation places the onus on the interpreter to evaluate their own idea of justice in light of Camus's challenge. Does justice support placing bombs on the tramways? If so, a choice presents itself. What do I prefer: justice or my mother?

Can Levinasian ethics support a theory of justice? The academic debate on this issue can be partly understood in terms of the choice posed by Camus's statement. Levinas's account of ethics poses a challenge to traditional ideas of justice. We might imagine Levinas responding to mainstream views of justice with the comment, "If that is justice, I prefer the other." This response poses a twofold challenge to readers. Must justice be understood in that way? If so, which do I prefer: justice or the other?

Levinas's theory of ethics, with its interpersonal focus, is deeply at odds with a conception of justice focused on the institutional rights of the individual. This has led to a perception of Levinas's theory as challenging the very possibility of justice. The alternative view, however, is that Levinas offers us the tools to rethink justice. We do not have to choose between justice and the other, because true justice places the other at its center. A similar interpretation, of course, can be made of Camus. Only a perversion of justice requires a person to condone the bombing of his mother.

The Rights of the Other

Animals present a primordial claim for recognition; their suffering, in particular, requires a response. I said at the start of this chapter that we owe things to animals: that is, we have duties toward them. A duty, here, is a way of expressing the force of the other's ethical demand. I have a duty to recognize and respond to the suffering of the other animal; the other animal has a correlative right over me. It is important to be clear what is meant here by *correlativity*. The very idea of correlativity between duties and rights may seem problematic from a Levinasian perspective, since Levinas strongly resists a symmetrical view of the ethical encounter. "[T]he face speaks to me and thereby invites me into a relation commensurate with a power exercised" (*TI*, 198). The other commands me: I do not command the other.

However, the notion of correlativity, as I use it here, does not imply symmetry. There is a *logical* correlativity between duties and rights; if I have a duty toward another person, that person holds a right in respect of me. However, behind this logical relation lies the ultimate ground of normative discourse: the *ethical* and *ontological* priority of the subject's responsibility for the other. It is my primeval duty to acknowledge the other. The opening of rights discourse raises the prospect that I, too, may have rights. However, it is only through reference to the rights of the other that I can recognize *myself* as potentially a rights-bearing entity: the *type of thing*, thematically speaking, to which rights might belong.

It follows that rights are always, in the first place, the rights of the other: the formal correlativity of duty and right is only possible insofar as I acknowledge myself as subject to an unconditional ethical demand. I, too, may bear rights as a matter of theory; but my rights appear "arbitrary and violent" where they run up against my duties to other people (*TI*, 84). The challenge of rights discourse is therefore to prevent the primordial claims of the other from being submerged in the logical framework of rights and duties. As Levinas says, "The principal task . . . consists in thinking the Other-in-the-Same without thinking the Other as another Same" (*OGM*, 80).

The challenge outlined above represents the inherent danger of rights discourse. There are risks—as well as benefits—in ascribing rights to humans. On the one hand, rights discourse provides a rich and versatile conceptual framework for recognizing the social dimension of ethical life. On the other hand, the availability of rationalization as a technique of moral avoidance means that people may employ the language of rights in order to evade their responsibilities. Rights discourse may be used to acknowledge the other; it may also be used to place the other at a distance. People may assert the rights accorded as other precisely in order to keep the other at bay.

This approach to rights discourse invokes the conception of justice reflected in the objections mentioned at the start of this chapter. Justice, here, is distinct from ethics. It requires institutions, negotiation, and discourse. However, the proposition that animals cannot engage in discourse or hold moral duties is immaterial to the kind of small justice suggested by Levinas. The ethical encounter, for Levinas, is essentially asymmetrical: it starts from oneself and projects outward toward the other. The strangeness of the other prevents me from assuming a reciprocity of obligations. It is only where the other reveals herself by assuming responsibility for aspects of our common world that a form of reciprocity is created (*TI*, 214).

Moral discourse introduces a form of symmetry that is unthinkable in the ethical encounter. In this sense, it represents a barrier as well as an aid to justice. Levinas is keenly aware of the problem that rights discourse poses to just relations between humans. It arises because humans play double roles in moral discourse: both self and other, hostage and captor, potential holder of duties *and* rights. The same problem, however, does not arise when we ascribe rights to animals. There is no risk in animal rights, because animals cannot engage in ethical avoidance. We see this in Bobby's inability to shun the Jewish internees. The other animal, unlike our fellow human, cannot use rights discourse to evade its duties.

Nonhuman animals gaze at us from beyond the borders of the moral community, commanding but not commanded. There is no danger of entrenching their rights as a mode of cultural rationalization: animals cannot exploit their rights to keep the other at a distance. The rights of the other animal might therefore properly be regarded as a *model* for human rights—what Levinas describes as the rights of a "stranger" (*TI*, 77), extended unconditionally, without expecting or demanding anything in return. This is what it means to say that rights are always the rights of the other. The true economy of rights, like the economy of kindness, is therefore deeply radical. It is the economy of the pure ethical gift, without exchange or consideration. I acknowledge your rights, without any thought to my own.

Notes

1. Compare Jan Narveson, "Animal Rights," *Canadian Journal of Philosophy* 7 (1977): 161–78; Jan Narveson, "On a Case for Animal Rights," *The Monist* 70 (1987): 31–49; Brian Barry, *Culture and Equality: An Egalitarian Critique of Multiculturalism* (Cambridge, UK: Polity, 2011), 95.

2. Compare John Rawls, *A Theory of Justice* (Cambridge, MA: Belknap, 1999), 3–10.

3. Compare Robert Garner, *A Theory of Justice for Animals: Animal Rights in a Nonideal World* (Oxford, UK: Oxford University Press, 2013).

4. Friedrich Nietzsche, *Human, All Too Human*, trans. Marion Faber and Stephen Lehmann (London: Penguin, 1984), 48, §48.

5. Ibid., 71 [§101] (emphasis in the original).

6. Mark 12:31 (*ESV*).

7. Genesis 4:9 (*ESV*).

8. John 10:16 (*ESV*). See also John 11:52.

9. Luke 6:27 (*ESV*). See also Matthew 5:44; Proverbs 25:21.

10. John 13:34.

11. Nietzsche, *Human, All Too Human*, 71 [§102].

12. For further discussion, see Jonathan Crowe, "Levinasian Ethics and Animal Rights," Windsor Yearbook of Access to Justice 26 (2009): 313–28.

13. Compare Peter Singer, *Animal Liberation* (New York: Avon Books, 1975), 184–88; Tom Regan, *The Case for Animal Rights* (Berkeley: University of California Press, 1983), 337.

14. Compare Jonathan Crowe, "Levinas on Shared Ethical Judgments," *Journal of the British Society for Phenomenology* 42, no. 3 (2011): 233–42.

15. Compare Simon Critchley, "Five Problems in Levinas' View of Politics and a Sketch of a Solution to Them," in *Levinas, Law, Politics*, ed. Marinos Diamantides (New York: Routledge, 2007); William Paul Simmons, "The Third: Levinas' Theoretical Move from An-archical Ethics to the Realm of Justice and Politics," *Philosophy and Social Criticism* 25 (1999): 83–104.

16. Crowe, "Levinas on Shared Ethical Judgments," 233–35.

17. Diane Perpich, "A Singular Justice: Ethics and Politics in Levinas and Derrida," *Philosophy Today* 42 (1998): 59–70, 59.

18. Olivier Todd, *Albert Camus: A Life*, trans. Benjamin Ivry (New York: Carroll and Graf, 2000), 379.

CHAPTER 7

Ecce Animot

Levinas, Derrida, and the Other Animal

MATTHEW CALARCO

In recent years, there has been increasing interest in developing an animal ethics based on the writings of Emmanuel Levinas. Jacques Derrida's reflections
on the question of the animal have been important for this task, inasmuch as
Derrida's work on the issue has been heavily influenced by several key Levinasian concepts and themes. To date, however, there has been very little attention
given to Derrida's most sustained engagement with Levinas on animals in *The
Animal That Therefore I Am* (1997).[1] The aim of this paper is to provide a critically engaged overview of Derrida's reading of Levinas in that text, with an eye
toward both Derrida's earlier engagements with Levinas and some of Derrida's
subsequent writings on Levinas and animals in his final seminars. As I seek
to demonstrate here, despite borrowing many themes from the larger body of
Levinas's writings for his own work on animals, Derrida's analysis defends a
primarily negative and critical conclusion about the promise of Levinas's work
for the development of an animal ethics. Indeed, according to Derrida's reading,
Levinas's work constitutes a largely uncritical continuation of the humanism and
anthropocentrism of the Western philosophical tradition that we find in such
thinkers as René Descartes, Immanuel Kant, and Martin Heidegger. Derrida
argues that we need to move beyond the limits of Levinas's work if we wish to
contest the philosophical tradition that has disavowed the complexity of animals,
animal life, and animal modes of expression, relation, and responsivity. I close
the essay with some reflections and suggestions on what would be required to
think with and beyond Levinas in view of doing justice to animals beyond the
limitations of humanism and anthropocentrism.

Humanism, Anthropocentrism, and the
Sacrifice of the Animal Other

Derrida's main line of critical engagement with Levinas in *The Animal That Therefore I Am* is already present in germinal form in Derrida's 1964 essay "Violence and Metaphysics."[2] In discussing Levinas's conception of the face in this early piece, Derrida notes that Levinas's effort to delimit the face to the human and to describe it as resembling God in terms of being a substance[3] risks reproducing a kind of classical humanism and anthropocentrism.[4] Derrida's observation is confirmed with particular force by those passages in *Totality and Infinity* and elsewhere in which Levinas aims to render radical alterity exclusively human[5] and to limit the significance of theological concepts to human sociality.[6] These points about the humanist and anthropocentric limitations of Levinas's ethics are revisited by Derrida in a 1987 interview with Jean-Luc Nancy titled "'Eating Well,' or the Calculation of the Subject,"[7] a wide-ranging exchange in which Derrida takes up the question posed to him by Nancy: "Who comes after the subject?" As was the case in "Violence and Metaphysics" two decades earlier, Derrida here confirms the novelty and importance of Levinas's ethics as a means of challenging traditional notions of subjectivity based on humanist notions of agency, self-presence, and so on. If we wish to think about a "who"—that is, a singularity that comes after the deconstruction of humanist subjectivity—Levinas's ethics would seem to be an essential reference for such a project. But the same concerns are raised here by Derrida: Levinas's anthropocentric tendencies carry a sort of intellectual baggage that keeps his ethics firmly lodged within the metaphysical tradition[8] that gave rise to the classical notion of humanist subjectivity.

So, what precisely is the link between metaphysical humanism (understood as the tradition that gives us an image of human nature as having its foundations in autonomy, agency, and achieving full subjective and objective presence) and anthropocentrism (understood primarily as a discourse that limits the ethical to the human)? To answer this question, we need first to make more explicit the underlying logic of subjectivity at work in Levinas's ethics. On Derrida's analysis, Levinas's conception of ethical subjectivity is in part posthumanist inasmuch as it calls into question the hegemonic notion of ethics as having its ultimate origin in the autonomous self. By transferring the locus and point of departure of the ethical relation from the Same (the autonomous, humanist subject) to the Other (the one who arrives from outside the purview and the machinations of the enjoying I), Levinas opens a path of thought that helps to create the space for a thought of responsibility beyond the dominant tradition of humanist autonomy. Ethics, on this account, would thus not begin in the sovereign decision of the Same but would have its origin in a call received from the Other, a call that is often phrased by Levinas in terms of the Mosaic commandment, "Thou shalt not kill." But to whom does this imperative of not killing apply? And from whom is it received? It is in pursuing the answers to these questions about the scope and origin of the call of the Other that we begin to see the inner connections between the lingering humanism and anthropocentrism in Levinas's thought. What Derrida argues, in essence, is that Levinas's efforts to limit the origin and scope of the call to the *human* Other subtly reproduce the founding gestures of both humanism and anthropocentrism.

In order to make this connection between humanism and anthropocentrism clearer, consider first the way in which Levinas's understanding of "Thou shalt not kill" unsuspectingly brings back a certain form of humanism. As Derrida notes, "the 'Thou shalt not kill' is addressed to the other and presupposes him. It is destined to the very thing that it institutes, the other as man" (*EW*, 279). Derrida also suggests that Levinas, following the dominant Judeo-Christian tradition, does not give serious thought to the idea that the killing prohibition might be understood in a very broad sense as meaning "Thou shalt not put to death the living in general" (*EW*, 279).[9] At issue here is the point that, in trying to circumscribe in advance the scope of those beings to whom the imperative applies and from whom one might receive such an imperative ("man," instead of, say, the living in general), Levinas has unwittingly brought the call of the Other back within the purview of the subject and its desire for subjective and objective presence. If, in fact, we understand ethics as ultimately arriving from heteronomous sources, then it is impossible to determine in advance (either a priori based on concepts or a posteriori based on previous phenomenological experience) whether the ethical call will arrive solely from human sources. To delimit the scope and origin of ethics in this way is to allow the most classical, humanist epistemology of presence to reassert itself just at the point where the subject's finitude and nonknowledge should instead be underscored.

Consider next the way in which limiting both the face and the imperative not to kill to the human reinforces anthropocentrism. If we follow Levinas's analysis and grant ethical alterity and the ethical force of the face only to fellow human beings, then a zone is opened up in which nonhuman others can be removed from ethical consideration and harmed, or killed, with impunity. Now, it is no doubt true that leaving a given group of beings outside the scope of ethical consideration does not *necessitate* their being abused or killed; but to engage in such a gesture against the backdrop of a dominant culture that is grounded in a binary human/nonhuman ontology coupled with a hierarchical value system centered on human privilege is effectively to guarantee that one is reinforcing and providing ideological cover for violence inflicted on those who are excluded. Derrida considers this anthropocentric gesture in Levinas's work to be a serious shortcoming, one that he suggests Levinas shares with several philosophers in the Western philosophical tradition. For Derrida, what remains in place in Levinas and in much of this dominant philosophical tradition is an unwillingness to "*sacrifice sacrifice*" (*EW*, 279). In other words, Levinasian ethics conceives of ethics on a fundamentally anthropocentric model that belongs to "a world where sacrifice is possible and where it is not forbidden to make an attempt on life in general, but only on human life" (*EW*, 279). Levinasian ethics, then, participates in one of the founding gestures of the anthropocentric tradition, namely, that of maintaining a zone for killing with impunity, "for a noncriminal putting to death" (*EW*, 278) of animals and others deemed to be nonhuman.

Although Derrida doesn't put things in exactly these terms, we could say that Levinas's humanism (his efforts to determine in advance that radical alterity will arrive only from the human) is an outgrowth of his anthropocentrism (his unwillingness to extend ethics to animals and to challenge the idea that animals and nonhuman others can be killed with impunity). In other words, Levinas cannot shake off the lingering humanist tendencies in his work because they are a logically necessary, concomitant implication of his anthropocentric commitments; such commitments ensure in advance that exposure to the Other will not exceed the interhuman orbit and that the status quo with regard to human-animal and human-nonhuman interaction will not be fundamentally disturbed. This inner relation between humanism and anthropocentrism implies, then, that Levinas's thought is beholden to an anthropocentrism that is "older" and more basic than humanism; if that implication holds, then it would also be the case that the focus on the critical reworking of subjectivity that is so dominant in Levinasian and other postphenomenological circles needs to be supplemented by consideration of the anthropocentrism that first opens up the space in which humanist subjectivity is itself formed. Indeed, in a certain sense, one could read Derrida's entire intervention on the question of the animal as pointing up this connection and to draw those who are working in this tradition beyond the critique of humanism toward a critique of anthropocentrism. To gain some sense of how such a critique of anthropocentrism might proceed, let us turn more closely to Derrida's analysis of Levinas on the question of the animal in *The Animal That Therefore I Am*.

The Animal Face: From Disavowal to Nonknowledge

Now, as we move from these earlier, brief reflections to Derrida's later, more sustained engagement with Levinas, we should pause for a moment to consider whether Derrida has thus far offered a fair and charitable reading of Levinas in the texts we have examined. If we took into account only Levinas's published writings up to the time of the publication of Derrida's interview with Nancy, then one could say that Derrida's analysis provides a fairly accurate and even insightful critical reading of Levinas's humanism and anthropocentrism.[10] But in 1986, just prior to Derrida's interview with Nancy, Levinas had been pressed on the very issues of anthropocentrism and the ethical status of animals in the interview that has been retranscribed and retranslated for this volume as "The Animal Interview." And Levinas's responses in this interview certainly complicate the kind of critical reading that we have seen Derrida offer up to this point. However, the interview did not appear in print until 1988, a year after Derrida's "'Eating Well,'" making it impossible for Derrida to take it into account in the material we have examined thus far. So, when Derrida returns to the question of the animal in Levinas some ten years later, does "The Animal Interview" force Derrida to change his reading of Levinas in any substantial way?

At first glance, Derrida's overall judgment regarding Levinas's lingering humanism and anthropocentrism in *The Animal That Therefore I Am* would appear to be even more critical and categorical than in the earlier texts we have examined. Derrida states flatly at the outset of his reading that the most dominant aspects of Levinas's thought are clearly aimed at "putting the animal outside of the ethical circuit" (*ATT*, 106). Derrida couches this thesis in a kind of double surprise in regard to Levinas's ethics, one that (it seems to Derrida) *should* have made room for animals but, in a profoundly disappointing manner, fails to do so. With regard to the first surprise, Derrida maintains (reiterating the thesis from his earlier texts) that Levinas's critical displacement of the humanist subject by way of an ethics of radical alterity never leads him to consider the ways in which animals might make a claim on us, a possibility that the underlying logic of Levinas's ethics should have raised. As Derrida states, Levinas "fails to feel concerned or looked at . . . by the *animot*[11] and fails to recognize in it any of the traits attributed to the human face" (*ATT*, 106). In this anthropocentric gesture of exclusion, Levinas rejoins the humanist philosophers of subjectivity that his ethics had done so much to contest and reorient.[12]

In view of the second surprising aspect of Levinas's failure to take animals into account in his work, Derrida wonders how the primary theorist of an ethics of the Other could fail to notice the Other *animal*, or animal alterity. As Derrida suggests, animals would seem to constitute paradigm examples of the Other, to serve as examples of an Other that is even "more other" than the Other human. In Derrida's words, "If I am responsible for the other, and before the other, and in the place of the other, on behalf of the other, isn't the animal more other still, more radically other, if I might put it that way, than the other in whom I recognize my brother, than the other in whom I identify my fellow or my neighbor? If I have a duty—something owed before any debt, before any right—toward the other, wouldn't it then also be toward the animal, which is still more other than the other human, my brother or my neighbor?" (*ATT*, 107).[13] I will confess that I find this point rather to miss the mark with regard to Levinas's account of radical alterity, especially if it is read in the way that a Levinasian would likely read it.[14] For Levinas, radical alterity denotes the otherness of the Other's radical interiority, the Other's singular subjectivity and point of view, to which I have no access. What calls me out of myself, and what renders the Other *radically* Other and not *relatively* other to me, is that the Other announces her- or himself from a position and a point of view that I cannot fully cognize or conceptualize. In this sense, radical alterity does not come in degrees (*more or less* Other) and cannot be assigned predicates or content (animal, human, and so on). A given animal, then, is not "more other" than a given human being on this account of radical alterity; there are only different, singular modes of interiority here that exceed the machinations of my conceptual apparatus.

But what if we think about radical alterity less in terms of inaccessible interiority and more in terms of the expression of vulnerability? Here, I think, is where Derrida's point might begin to gain some traction. If the quintessential way in which the Other announces her- or himself is through an expression of the face, through a saying of vulnerability, then there might be a sense in which (some) animals are especially vulnerable and make a particularly strong claim on us. In view of the expression of vulnerability, alterity predicates and content *do* have an important role to play, for vulnerability betrays not only singularity and interiority but a fundamentally *situated* singularity and interiority in which specific contextual and historical factors inform both how vulnerability is expressed and what that expression comes to mean for the one who receives the call. Levinas's thoughts on these kinds of finer points concerning the situatedness of the expression of vulnerability are notoriously problematic, as many of his feminist and postcolonial critics have demonstrated. With regard to animal Others, as well, Levinas seems fundamentally inattentive to the specific ways in which animals might express their alterity and vulnerability and how those specific modes of expression might make even stronger claims on us in certain instances. This is, *perhaps*, one way of making some sense of Derrida's point here.

Thus, even though (according to Derrida) Levinas's ethics of radical alterity should have opened onto a more expansive notion of responsibility and should have made us more attentive to animal alterity, Derrida maintains that Levinas surprisingly neglects to pursue either path of thought. He states bluntly that, for Levinas, "The animal has no face" (*ATT*, 107). Now, as we know, in "The Animal Interview," Levinas is pushed precisely on this question of whether the animal has a face—and it is not entirely clear that Levinas categorically denies animals a face in the way that Derrida states. So, how does Derrida read Levinas's ambiguous remarks on animal faces in this interview?

Derrida's text here unfortunately bears the marks of being an unpolished lecture course. He does not seem to have direct access to the original English transcription and translation of the interview in question (published under the title "The Paradox of Morality") and reads it secondhand through excerpts from John Llewelyn's *The Middle Voice of Ecological Conscience*,[15] sometimes confusing Llewelyn's questions with those of the interviewers. Thus, the material in the interview doesn't receive the kind of full and careful consideration it likely would have had, had Derrida seen this lecture course through to publication. That said, Derrida did home in on several of the aspects of the interview that we would have expected him to, had he had such time, taking up first the issue of Levinas's attempt to grant a certain priority to the human face over that of the animal. Levinas's remarks along these lines[16] are read by Derrida as suggesting not simply that we analogically transpose the human face onto the animal and that it is through our familiarity with the human face that we come to recognize animal suffering (which is the more evident meaning of Levinas's statement). Instead, Derrida maintains that Levinas's transposition and privileging of the human face is subtly aimed at *evading* the gaze of the animal, of seeking not to be seen by the animal and instead directing his gaze *at* the animal through anthropogenic concepts and a humanist lens (*ATT*, 108–9). Although Derrida does not develop this point in any depth, it is one worth considering, inasmuch as Levinas's statements about the priority of the human face do seem to suggest that the animal is unable to present her- or himself to us without assistance. The face of the animal, if it has one, would seem to be in need of an intermediary, a concept and a borrowed sense, to come to presence—something that stands in stark contrast to the *kath' auto* manifestation of the human face. And if, in fact, we are able to grasp the animal face only after our interactions with human beings and on the basis of transferring the human face to an animal, then it could be suggested that, effectively, we have no experience of the animal face—or even, perhaps, that the animal has no face at all (that is, if we follow through with the logic of Levinas's remarks).

Examining Levinas's remarks from the interview more closely does little to clarify the issue here, as his responses on whether the animal even has a face are equivocal. He seems to suggest that animals do have a face, even if it is secondary to the human face ("The human face is an altogether different thing, and we rediscover [only] afterwards the face in the animal"; "I also think that quite clearly, . . . even if animals are not considered as human beings, the ethical extends to living beings. I really think so" [*AI*, 4]), while at the same time denying that animals have a face in the ethical sense ("[Even] if animals

do not have a face in the ethical sense, we have an obligation toward them"
[*AI*, 4]). Derrida picks up on this double-handed (indeed, ham-handed) gesture,
noting that Levinas grants a certain face to the animal with one hand while
taking the face away with the other. But it is the second hand, the one that
takes away the animal face, which says no to the alterity of the animal that,
according to Derrida, dominates in Levinas's thought. Derrida aligns Levinas's
negation of the animal face with the broader philosophical tradition exemplified
by Descartes that denies animals any responsivity, as well as with the anthropocentric tradition we analyzed above that places animals in a sacrificeable zone
from which paradigm instances of "the human" are exempted.

Now, what is perhaps more interesting than Levinas's contradictory remarks
on the face of the animal or his off-the-cuff remarks on animals and vegetarianism is his admission of *nonknowledge* concerning the animal face when first
pressed on the issue in the interview. When Levinas is initially asked, "Can
the face of an animal be considered also as the other who must be welcomed?
Or is the possibility of speech necessary in order to be a 'face' in the ethical
sense?" he answers, "I don't know. I cannot tell you at what moment you have
the right to be called 'face.'" And he also says, "I do not know whether one
finds it in the snake!" (*AI*, 4). This response, while perhaps disheartening to
proanimal readers of Levinas, actually strikes me as a much more promising line
of thought than even an outright affirmation that animals (or human beings,
for that matter) do have faces, for any such general affirmation presumes a kind
of epistemological confidence where it should be entirely lacking. The logic of
finitude at work in ethical experience should be understood as disallowing, in
principle, the ability to make confident claims about the precise nature and scope
of the face. So, even though one could reasonably maintain that something like
interiority and sentience are required to have a face in a way that is consistent
with the dominant logic of Levinas's writings, such claims are in no way consistent with the logic of finitude. To suggest that only beings with interiority
and a subjective point of view can make ethical claims constitutes little more
than an expansion of anthropocentrism and an attempt to find what "we" (that
is, those of us who recognize ourselves in such a description) consider to be
ethically relevant among a relatively narrow class of beings who are relatively
and relevantly similar to "us."

Derrida himself takes up Levinas's admission of nonknowledge concerning
the animal face, emphasizing that this admission has a number of unanticipated
consequences for the entirety of Levinas's ethics. Derrida aptly describes Levinas's
admission of nonknowledge as "dizzyingly risky, exposed" (*ATT*, 108). For, if
we follow Levinas's initial admission and accept that we don't know whether
an animal has a face, that we don't know at what moment one has a face, and

that we don't know whether a snake has a face, what we are acknowledging is that we don't really know where a face begins and ends. When Levinas opens up this line of thought that remains true to the logic of finitude, he is effectively undermining the dominant humanist and anthropocentric thrust of his own work. In Derrida's words,

> By admitting that he can't respond to the question of knowing what a face is . . . he can thus no longer answer for his whole discourse on the face. For declaring that he doesn't know where the right to be called 'face' begins means confessing that one doesn't know at bottom what a face is, what the word means, what governs its usage. . . . Doesn't that amount, as a result, to calling into question the whole legitimacy of the discourse and ethics of the 'face' of the other? (*ATT*, 109)

Although readers who are enamored of the received version of Levinas's discourse might wish to retreat from this possibility, I would suggest that it is important to recognize that this suggestion and question from Derrida speak to the intractable limits of finite subjectivity in ethical experience. These limitations of finitude are not to be jettisoned but should be acknowledged and endured. Even though in dealing with animals Levinas often takes leave of this risky zone for the safer and more comfortable terrain of humanism and anthropocentrism, if our desire is to think and live beyond the limits of anthropocentrism, then it is essential to stay with this other thread within Levinas's work (the thread committed to the logic of finitude) and continue to pull on it in order to unravel the larger fabric of anthropocentrism and humanism that dominates his work and the philosophical tradition more generally.

So what to make, then, of Levinas's other extended foray into animal issues, "The Name of a Dog, or Natural Rights"? With which hand—the more generous, exposed hand that risks a thought of animal alterity, or the hand that seeks to grasp animals and deny them a face—does Levinas read and encounter dogs, and Bobby in particular? Derrida's assessment of the potential of this piece for the question of the animal is almost entirely critical and negative, suggesting that Levinas is able to read and think only with the one, comprehending and negating hand. Derrida sets his analysis against those readers of Levinas who find hope in the Bobby essay for linking Levinasian ethics with an animal ethics. Derrida insists that in this essay Bobby is ultimately reduced to a figure within Levinas's narrative, an allegorical witness to the humanity of "man" and a metaphorical representation of the animal's general lack of responsivity and subjectivity (*ATT*, 114–17).

Beyond these critical points, Derrida also suggests that Levinas's "The Name of a Dog" can be read against the grain and that even this extremely anthropocentric text bears witness to the disruptive singularity of Bobby and other animals. Tracking the curiously high number of exclamations and exclamation points in Levinas's essay, Derrida notes how often these pitched statements take the form of a *disavowal* of animal alterity and transcendence. Derrida reads these "exclamatory disavowals" (*ATT*, 117) as suggesting the precise opposite of what Levinas means them to say. Where Levinas declares a "No! No!" concerning our responsibility to animals or the possibility of animal transcendence, Derrida senses the trace of a prior "Yes! Yes!," in which a certain obligation has already been received and where a certain transcendence has already been glimpsed. After all, why the need for the recurrent disavowals if animals are so clearly outside of the ethical circuit?

Ultimately, however, Derrida maintains that Levinas's disavowals function to point toward the conclusion that his dominant ethical discourse is insufficient for challenging the long-standing humanist and anthropocentric dogmas of the philosophical tradition. Despite moments of equivocation and even possibility in Levinas's discourse on animals, Derrida concludes that in the final analysis,

> the animal remains for Levinas what it will have been for the whole Cartesian-type tradition: a machine that doesn't speak, that doesn't have access to sense, that can at best imitate "signifiers without a signified" . . . , a sort of monkey with "monkey talk," precisely what the Nazis sought to reduce their Jewish prisoners to. (*ATT*, 117)

Although we could no doubt imagine more generous ways of reading Levinas, it is hard to deny this general critical conclusion when considering his writings as a whole. On questions concerning animals and nonhumans more generally, Levinas's discourse is deeply disappointing and suffers from a number of poorly articulated arguments and stubborn dogmas.

This negative conclusion should not, of course, be taken to suggest that there are no resources in Levinas's work for carrying through on the task of displacing the problematic humanism and anthropocentrism characteristic of so much of past and present philosophy. Derrida's own efforts to carry out this kind of critical contestation of humanism and anthropocentrism have undoubtedly gained much from Levinas's approach to ethics. So if Levinas's thought might be helpful but insufficient for the task at hand, how might we begin to build a more sufficient approach using his work and Derrida's critical analysis of it as our point of departure?

Facing beyond Anthropocentrism

Perhaps the first thing to be done is to return to Levinas's admission of non-knowledge concerning the face of other animals and the concomitant need to carry out "more specific analyses" (*AI*, 4) on this issue. Derrida describes this admission of the need for a more specific analysis as a "responsible, courageous, and humble" (*ATT*, 109) gesture on Levinas's part, for in doing so Levinas not only threatens to undercut many of his previous statements about animals but also opens up his thought to ethical possibilities it has hitherto sought to close off in advance. In view of the more specific analysis that is needed regarding animal faces, animal vulnerability, expression, and so on, one could fruitfully read Derrida's own, much-discussed encounter with "his"[17] cat as carrying out just this kind of analysis. Derrida demonstrates how several of the standard motifs in Levinas's ethics (nudity, the look and presence of the Other prior to my own initiative, the inaccessibility of the Other's interiority, the saying before the said, and several others) are at work, albeit in their own specific ways, in this encounter.

Also in view of this more specific analysis of animal faces, Derrida takes up Levinas's challenge of thinking more carefully about "whether the snake has a face" (*AI*, 4). Following the distinction that he develops in the first chapter of *The Animal That Therefore I Am*, Derrida turns to poets rather than philosophers to think about snake faces, inasmuch as philosophers have generally tended to disavow the notions that animals might have their own point of view and that human beings might sometimes find themselves *being seen by* animals (*ATT*, 13–14). His reading of Paul Valéry's "Silhouette of a Serpent" (*ATT*, 65–68) underscores the way in which the serpent in Valéry's poem speaks (or, rather, hisses) for and expresses itself—*kath' auto*, we might say.[18] And Derrida again returns to the question of the snake face some five years later in his The Beast and the Sovereign lecture course, where he dedicates a session to reflecting on Levinas's discourse on the snake in the context of a reading of D. H. Lawrence's brilliant poem "Snake."[19] The narrator of this poem encounters a snake at a water trough and notes how the snake arrived there to drink before him, presenting and announcing itself to him, the "second comer." The narrator then relates the inner voice he hears telling him that the snake (which has the markings of a poisonous snake) "must be killed" and how he ultimately comes to regret his (failed) efforts to kill the snake by throwing a log at him. After scaring the snake away with his actions, the narrator finds himself wishing that the snake "would come back," ashamed of himself for missing the chance for a more hospitable encounter with such a remarkable Other.[20] Derrida explores

how the narrator of Lawrence's poem is awakened to the ethics of hospitality
and to the "Thou shalt not kill" in relation to the snake, and poses a question
to seminar participants in view of this snake encounter: "Does an ethics or a
moral prescription obligate us only to those like us . . . or else does it obligate
us with respect to anyone at all, any living being at all, and therefore with
respect to the animal?" (BS, 247).

Perhaps as a gesture of generosity and hospitality to his students, Derrida declines to venture an answer to this question in that particular session.
But we know from his other writings on the ethics of hospitality—the bulk of
which are developed in relation to Levinas's discourse on ethics—that Derrida
believes the challenge is to open a thought and practice of hospitality as broadly
as it can go.[21] The logic of finitude that we have discussed here, the one that
seeks to take permanent leave of the humanist notion of subjectivity, exposes
the Same to others of all sorts—and the task of ethics for Derrida is to learn
to endure and negotiate that space in all of its complexity. Indeed, it is due to
the complexity of ethical experience that more specific analyses are needed, and
it is due to the finitude that opens this space that such analyses must always
be seen as risks, as humble experiments and practices, always falling short of
full knowledge and certainty.

Beyond the initial task of thinking about the specific and differentiated
modes of animal expression, it would also be necessary to take up the question
of animal transcendence (which is to say, responsivity to the Other manifesting
itself on the side of animals themselves), a question that Levinas raises but quickly
disavows. Derrida does little to pursue this line of thought in the context of his
analysis of Levinas, but it is clear that the majority of his texts on the question
of the animal are aimed at developing the sorts of "quasi-infrastructures" that
would expand notions of exposure, relation, and responsivity into zones that
include animals and that go "well beyond humanity" (EW, 274). Essential here, as
well, would be recognizing that the traces of transcendence that we find among
animals and other nonhumans are not supernatural instances of certain beings
leaving nature behind and joining "us," or somehow gaining privileged access
to the sphere of "the human." Rather, animal acts of transcendence need to be
reinscribed within the larger, natural, more-than-human story of the origins
and vicissitudes of responsivity. We have to risk the thought, against Levinas,
that more-than-human transcendence precedes the historical and evolutionary
arrival of human beings on the scene; such a stance would entail understanding
responsivity as being immanent to, emerging out of, and participating in natural
structures and systems of relation that exceed human beings in every direction.
And lest we be tempted to raise a skeptical eyebrow concerning these points
about animal transcendence, we need only cast a glance sideways at the count-

less instances of intra- and interspecies altruism and radical hospitality that we encounter in the present among beings of all sorts. It would, to say the least, strain credulity to believe that animals and other nonhuman beings waited for the historical arrival of human beings to engage in such acts.[22]

Finally, as we pursue a thought and practice of ethics beyond humanism and anthropocentrism, there is a need to give serious consideration to whether an ethics of the face in either an expanded Levinasian or Derridean form will be adequate to the task of thinking about ethics beyond individual human beings and animals. There are compelling reasons to believe that Levinas's ethics really does reach a breaking point as we start to consider ethical relations with beings that don't have interiority or a subjective point of view in any meaningful sense of the terms. While we might be tempted to conclude that such a lack of subjectivity on the part of others means we have arrived at the limits of ethics, such a conclusion should be avoided, for it proceeds from the same anthropocentric and humanist premises that first gave rise to Levinas's problematic discourse on animals. The task that we are called to today is, perhaps, to learn to think ethics *beyond* the transference of human premises (individuality, interiority, singularity, subjectivity, and so on) to the animal and nonhuman world and instead proceed in the opposite direction. What are the various and differentiated ways in which the world might *present itself* in ethical experience? How can we learn to think and respond to the world outside the strictures of individual singularity and subjectivity, to think with and respond to collectives, assemblages, and systems of various sorts? What might an ethics that proceeds from such premises look like? Would such an ethics require us to dismantle the face altogether?[23] These are some of the questions we encounter as we seek to take genuine leave of the confines of the human for a thought and practice of responsivity in relation to the more-than-human world.

Notes

1. Jacques Derrida, *The Animal That Therefore I Am*, ed. Marie-Louise Mallet, trans. David Wills (New York: Fordham University Press, 2008), 106. Hereafter cited as *ATT*. This text was originally delivered in 1997 and was published posthumously in 2006.

2. Jacques Derrida, "Violence and Metaphysics: An Essay on the Thought of Emmanuel Levinas," in *Writing and Difference*, trans. Alan Bass (Chicago, IL: University of Chicago Press, 1978), 79–153.

3. Derrida is referring here to two passages from Levinas: "The encounter with a face is not only a fact belonging to anthropology. It is absolutely a relationship with that which is. Perhaps man alone is substance, and therefore is a face" (*CPP*, 15–24); and "the Other, in his signification prior to my initiative, resembles God" (*TI*, 293).

4. "It is the analogy between the face and God's visage that, in the most classical fashion, distinguishes man from animal, and determines man's substantiality" (*VM*, 142).

5. For example, "The absolutely foreign alone can instruct us. And it is only man who could be absolutely foreign to me" (*TI*, 73).

6. For example, "It is our relations with men . . . that give to theological concepts the sole signification they admit of" (*TI*, 73).

7. Jacques Derrida (with Jean-Luc Nancy), "'Eating Well,' or the Calculation of the Subject," in *Points . . . Interviews, 1974–1994*, ed. Elizabeth Weber, trans. Peggy Kamuf (Stanford, CA: Stanford University Press, 1995), 255–87. Hereafter cited as *EW*.

8. I am using *metaphysical tradition* here in the more Heideggerian and Derridean sense of the term as denoting the philosophical-intellectual tradition associated with a metaphysics of subjectivity, presence, and humanism. For Levinas, of course, metaphysics and the terms associated with it by Heidegger and Derrida often have a very different meaning.

9. This passage should not be taken to imply that to displace the limit of responsibility from the human to the living in general would be sufficient to resolve the issue at hand. We will revisit this question of the extent of the ethical in more detail below.

10. There are exceptions to the dominant thrust of Levinas's humanism and anthropocentrism in his writings. See, for example, Levinas's remarkable but idiosyncratic 1937 essay on religious ritual in which he suggests that "the world never appears to the practicing Jew as a natural thing," and that Jewish religious ritual ensures that "nothing is entirely familiar, entirely profane." According to Levinas, the sheer existence of things becomes through ritual "infinitely surprising . . . a miracle," such that the practicing Jew "experiences wonder at every instant at the fact—so simple and yet so extraordinary—that the world is there." It is thus in ritual that one brackets "the racket of our everyday action," and is introduced into "the mystical resonance of things" and "the mystery of the world." Levinas goes so far here as to suggest that things have a face and that ritual "touches the sacred face of things." See "The Meaning of Religious Practice," trans. Peter Atterton, Matthew Calarco, and Joelle Hansel, *Modern Judaism* 25 (2005): 285–89; citations are from 288. The question of whether nonhuman beings can take on a face is raised elsewhere in Levinas's more mature philosophical works as well, most notably in "Is Ontology Fundamental?" (1951), where Levinas concludes his analysis of the face in the essay by querying, "Can things take on a face? Is not art an activity that lends faces to things? Does not the facade of a house regard us?" Levinas answers these questions provisionally by noting that his "analysis thus far does not suffice for an answer," but he hints at his anthropocentric reservations about extending the face beyond the human when he follows up this provisional response with the words: "We ask ourselves all the same if the impersonal but fascinating and magical march of rhythm does not, in art, substitute itself for sociality, for the face, for speech" (Emmanuel Levinas, "Is Ontology Fundamental?," trans. Peter Atterton, in *Emmanuel Levinas: Basic Philosophical Writings*, ed. Adriaan T. Peperzak, Simon Critchley, and Robert Bernasconi [Bloomington: Indiana University Press, 1996], 2–10; citations are from 10). Concerning the question of whether things might take on a face, see Silvia Benso's important book *The Face of Things: A Different Side of Ethics* (Albany, NY: State University of

New York Press, 2000). It should also be noted that Levinas does on occasion seek to *demonstrate*, both propositionally and phenomenologically, his theses on the restriction of ethics and the face to the human (see esp. *TI*, 73–77); thus, his anthropocentrism, while problematic, is not entirely dogmatic or unreflective. I engage critically with Levinas's arguments concerning human ethical specificity in *Zoographies: The Question of the Animal from Heidegger to Derrida* (New York: Columbia University Press, 2008), 55–78.

11. The term *animot* is a neologism meant to recall the complex relationships between animality and language (ani-*mot*) as well as the multiplicity and heterogeneity of animals themselves (when pronounced, *animot* sounds like *animaux*). The phrase *ecce animot* in the title of this chapter is used by Derrida as a play on Friedrich Nietzsche's autobiographical text *Ecce Homo*.

12. Significantly, Derrida notes here that consideration of a particular philosopher's position on the human/animal distinction and on the issue of where animals stand inside a philosopher's project are the key to understanding his overall system. (We should note that Derrida is deliberately targeting exclusively male philosophers here.) By paying close attention to the question of the animal in philosophy, we gain "access to a sort of secret 'architectonics' in the construction—and therefore in the deconstruction—of a discursive apparatus" (*ATT*, 106) that is shared by numerous philosophers in the Western tradition. What Derrida is pointing toward in this passage recalls the point we touched on earlier concerning the ways in which a very deep and subtle kind of anthropocentrism guides so much of philosophical and intellectual work, whether humanist or posthumanist. As Derrida's overall argument will go on to suggest, these anthropocentric architectonics cannot be seriously challenged simply by reworking traditional humanist ethics in the direction (following Levinas) of an ethics of radical alterity.

13. A similar claim about the relative degree of animal alterity is raised by Derrida in relation to the aporia of duty in *The Gift of Death*: "By preferring my work, simply by giving it my time and attention, by preferring my activity as a citizen or as a professorial and professional philosopher, writing and speaking here in a public language, French in my case, I am perhaps fulfilling my duty. But I am sacrificing and betraying at every moment all my other obligations: my obligations to the other others whom I know or don't know, the billions of my fellows (without mentioning the animals that are even more other others than my fellows), my fellows who are dying of starvation or sickness" (Jacques Derrida, *The Gift of Death*, trans. David Wills [Chicago, IL: University of Chicago Press, 1995], 71).

14. Here I have in mind the kind of reading offered by Peter Atterton in "Levinas and Our Moral Responsibility toward Other Animals," *Inquiry: An Interdisciplinary Journal of Philosophy* 54 (2011): 633–49. I will suggest a possible alternative approach to Derrida's claim in what follows.

15. John Llewelyn, *The Middle Voice of Ecological Conscience: A Chiasmic Reading of Responsibility in the Neighbourhood of Heidegger, Levinas, and Others* (London: Macmillan, 1991).

16. Derrida cites these two passages from the interview, which differ slightly from the version included in this volume: "I cannot say at what moment you have the right to be called 'face.' The human face is completely different and only afterward do

we discover the face of an animal. I do not know if a snake has a face. I can't answer that question. A more specific analysis is needed" (*ATT*, 108; cf. *PM*, 171–72); "We do not want to make an animal suffer needlessly and so on. But the prototype of this is human ethics. Vegetarianism, for example, arises from the transference to animals of the idea of suffering. The animal suffers. It is because we, as human, know what suffering is that we can have this obligation" (*ATT*, 108; cf. *PM*, 172).

17. "His" is in scare quotation marks here because the questions concerning the possession, domestication, and ownership of animals are all called into question by this encounter.

18. Concerning Valéry's poem, Derrida notes:

It interests me because the serpent from Genesis is speaking, and it says 'I,' naming thus, by designating itself, what will be for us one of the very forms of the question: ipseity, indeed *sui-referential egoity*, auto-affection and automotion, autokinesis, the autonomy that one recognizes in every animal: the very genesis of *zootobiography*. The serpent says 'I,' . . . Listen to it hiss, for Valéry has it say, insisting on it, 'I hiss':

Beast I am, but a sharp one,
Whose venom however vile
Can far out-vie the hemlock's wisdom (Valéry cited by Derrida, *ATT*, 65)

Although Derrida states he is unable to give a full analysis of the poem, he remarks that he would have liked to focus on the way in which, in the serpent's hiss, "an 'I' speaks . . . and presents itself" (*ATT*, 65). Derrida also briefly takes up this poem in view of the themes of hospitality and democracy in his *Rogues: Two Essays on Reason*, trans. Pascale-Anne Brault and Michael Naas (Stanford, CA: Stanford University Press, 2005), 5.

19. Jacques Derrida, *The Beast and the Sovereign*, ed. Michel Lisse, Marie Louise Mallet, and Ginette Michaud, trans. Geoffrey Bennington (Chicago, IL: University of Chicago Press, 2009), 1:236–49. Hereafter cited as *BS*. Lawrence's poem is reproduced in full in Derrida's text on *BS*, 247–49. My citations from Lawrence will be drawn from Derrida's reproduction.

20. "And so, I missed my chance with one of the lords / Of life. / And I have something to expiate; / A pettiness" (*BS*, 248–49).

21. "Let us say yes *to who or what turns up*, before any determination, before any anticipation, before any *identification*, whether or not it has to do with a foreigner, an immigrant, an invited guest, or an unexpected visitor, whether or not the new arrival is the citizen of another country, a human, animal, or divine creature, a living or dead thing, male or female" (Jacques Derrida, *Of Hospitality: Anne Dufourmantelle Invites Jacques Derrida to Respond*, trans. Rachel Bowlby [Stanford, CA: Stanford University Press, 2000], 77).

22. I am well aware that some readers will dismiss such acts on the part of animals as not being instances of genuine altruism and will see that behavior in more

reductive terms; however, such analyses cut both ways and can be used to explain away human altruism, as well, which would move the discussion to a different, extra-ethical register. I am here offering an immanent critique of Levinas (who presumes that radical altruism *is* in fact possible among human beings), so I will defer that extra-ethical discussion to another occasion.

23. "The face has a great future, but only if it is destroyed, dismantled" (Gilles Deleuze and Félix Guattari, *Capitalism and Schizophrenia: A Thousand Plateaus*, trans. Brian Massumi [New York: Continuum, 2004], 190).

CHAPTER 8

Facing Animal Research

Levinas and Technologies of Effacement

SOPHIA EFSTATHIOU

This chapter proposes that encountering the Other through the face can be conditioned by social and built technologies.[1] In "The Name of a Dog, or Natural Rights," Emmanuel Levinas relates his experience as a prisoner of war, held in a forced-labor camp in Nazi Germany. He contrasts being denied his humanity by other humans, "called free" (*DF*, 152), while being recognized as human—indeed as a friend—by a dog the prisoners named Bobby. The episode suggests that though the concept of the face applies to humans, the face is not enough for *facing*, at least not in the setting of the camp. By contrast, the prisoners seem able to face and be faced by Bobby, even if Levinas remains inconclusive about whether the face applies to animals elsewhere. It follows that the face is operating less like a property, and more like a capacity, a mode as Levinas calls it. But what conditions encountering an Other in this mode? If the face is neither sufficient for facing, nor prior to it, then what conditions facing (or effacing)? I propose that social structures, techniques, architectures, professional roles, and so on matter in coming to face (or efface) the Other. I conclude this from analyzing human-animal encounters in a scientific space of exception: the animal lab.[2]

Building on empirical accounts of animal research,[3] I propose that animal research is populated by what I call "technologies of effacement." These include: (1) built architectures; (2) entering and exit procedures; (3) protective garments and equipment; (4) identification and labeling techniques; and (5) experimental protocols. These technologies serve other manifest ends, but they operate to condition encounters between humans and animals in the lab: they help block the face of humans and animals.[4] Following Levinas in *Totality and Infinity*, I understand "face" to mean not only the ordinary "head-face," but an expressive, bodily or body-based surface that "exudes" or communicates the inner being of the Other. This includes visual, auditory, tactile, olfactory, or other sense-scapes that communicate the inner, "secret" being of the Other. Technology blocking the human and animal face is implicated in the distinctive normative challenges of animal research. Technologies of effacement sustain an ethos of the ordered at the expense of an ethics of the Other, notwithstanding that effacement is never total. This makes the ethics of the face and the ethos of analytic science crash head-on, begging for a response, practically and philosophically. A *humanimal* research ethics would go beyond simply butting human benefits against animal suffering, and would consider the particularities of human-animal relationships in the lab.

The chapter is structured as follows: I first outline key normative tensions arising from working with animals in research. I then describe a concept of the face and of the contingency of facing, following Levinas. The last section proposes that animal experimentation is structured through five types of technology that block the face during human-animal encounters. I conclude with an urge toward a humanimal research ethics.

Normative Tensions in Animal Research

Animal research is hard and it is hidden. It is hard epistemologically, as it involves getting inferences to cross "species" boundaries, aggravating epistemological problems by generalizing from observations based on tokens of a presumed type.[5] It is also hard because it requires the practical attention, skills, and social organization common to all large-scale experimental labor.[6] But animal research is hard in a further, special way: it involves working with, or rather against, the will of other animals. Consider this account, of the graduate student whom the science and technology studies scholar Nicole Nelson calls "Alex."

> The rats that I was microinjecting in the series of experiments that I've done so far, they just—I just couldn't take it. I was almost in tears over these guys, because they hate it . . . And you talk to people and they'll tell you, "Oh, you know, what you should do is wrap a towel around them so that you get a better grip and they don't fight as much." And it's like, well, it's not the fighting that's the problem with me or whether or not it's wrapped in a towel; it's the fact that

I know I'm causing these animals physical pain right now, and that just really bothers me. And it doesn't just bother me from a moral perspective—I don't know if this is what you had in mind—but it bothers me from [a perspective of] "Oh my God, I'm just creating so much stress in these animals right now and then I'm going to go and test them!" How can I realistically say that that super stress that I just gave it—I'm talking about a two-minute injection where they're squirming and squealing the whole time—and then I put them in the box and say, "Hey, show me what you've learned, but don't let stress affect you." It's just ridiculous.[7]

We can hear the frustration in Alex's voice. First, he is struggling emotionally. Alex relates that he was "almost in tears" over these (rat) guys because "they hate it." "[T]hey just—I just couldn't take it." The "squirming and squealing" of "these guys" made to take a microinjection that lasts for two minutes flow into Alex's own distress around administering that injection, and his frustration with having to pretend that stress does not matter. Why should Alex be doing this type of work? The obvious answer is for the research: to promote his and his team's scientific aims; for Society's ultimate benefit. However, at that point further tensions show up.

Leaving aside the moral and emotional difficulty of the work, there is the question of how to relate this problem to other colleagues. When "you talk to people" what "they tell you" in effect blocks the struggle communicated. Prefaced by a routine "Oh, you know," his colleagues propose to tell him what he should already know to do: "wrap a towel around them"—devise a cover, so that he gets "a better grip," and they "don't fight" as much. Alex rejects his colleagues' advice as beside the point: he "knows" he is "causing the animals physical pain right now." And that "just really bothers" him, not only from a moral perspective, but from an epistemological one. And this is a further aspect of the emotional and practical challenges of animal experimentation: their epistemological significance. How can one reasonably expect an intervention where the animals are visibly physically distressed for a whole two minutes not to affect their physiology and measured outcomes? Alex thinks it's "just ridiculous."

Crucial for my analysis is the communication of a perceived duplicitousness. Alex communicates what happens as a kind of farce. He and the animals first go through these distressing injections, and then he is to "put them in the box" and tell them, in a new (happy, teacherly) voice: "Hey, show me what you've learned, but don't let stress affect you" (MH, 9). The ridicule made of the researcher and his animals, the joke played on them is that they work in a frame expecting them to both suffer the stress, and pretend that it does not affect them. Indeed, after this exchange, Alex corrects his own reaction as exaggerated, since the rats' test results appeared "normal" (*MH*, 9). Perhaps the effects of animal stress are incorporated into existing baselines for normality.

As Vinciane Despret explains, human-animal relationships as well as the expectations of the researcher can affect research results with animals, not unlike the case of physician bias/placebo effects in the case of research with humans.[8] In the experimental setup she describes, rats presumed to be either "bright" or "dull" were tested in their abilities to figure out a maze. In fact, there was no difference among the rats. Researchers were just told that their rats were bright or dull; and went on to coach the animals and obtain results that fit their expectations. Despret claims that the human-animal relationship, researchers' and animals' responses to each other and to the situation can indeed steer results in an expected direction.

Another testimony of conflicting roles/identities around animal research engagements is offered by Mette Svendsen and Lene Koch's account of necrotic enterocolitis research in Denmark.[9] This infectious disease of the colon affects prematurely born babies and is studied using newborn piglets. The research involves inducing early labor, removing the piglets from their mother, infecting the piglets with the microbe and isolating them in heat chambers to observe the disease progression. The exchange below regards the piglets that had survived with this painful condition up to day five of the experiment and were to be sacrificed.

> As someone enters the room, Morten [a researcher] shouts: "Welcome to the slaughterhouse." A lab technician, Tina, comments, "You say 'slaughter.' Yesterday, I said to my friend: 'Tomorrow we are going to murder pigs,' and she answered: 'Can't you say that you put them down [*afliver dem*]?' 'No,' I said, 'we murder them [*dræber grise*].'" Laura [a lab technician], who is labeling pieces of intestine, interrupts: "No, you are wrong. What we do is that we put them down." While the three of them obviously disagree about how to describe the act that has just happened, they also laugh. Lone [a researcher] grabs a small container and jokingly begs Morten. "May I have my piece?" "You vulture!" comments Laura ironically. Lone gets her piece of intestine, puts the container in her pocket and leaves for the cell lab. [Professional roles added].[10]

What is, perhaps playfully, but actively broached here is an instability, a shakiness in the roles that humans and animals assume in the lab. The researcher called Morten, who is already in the sacrifice room, humorously, perhaps farcically, greets newcomers with a "Welcome to the slaughterhouse!" The lab technician, Tina, counters Morten. She relates what she told her friend (in anticipation): it is not slaughter but *murder* ("We are murdering pigs tomorrow"). The friend, perhaps feeling Tina's distress, asks whether she could not call it something different ("put them down?"). Tina insists: "No, we murder them." Another technician, Laura, disagrees with Tina ("What we do is that we put them down"). Another researcher, Lone, interrupts and requests from Morten her piece of scavenged kill. "You vulture!" Laura responds.

The episode demonstrates the vacillating relationships between humans, piglets, and piglet parts. Staff of different professional roles take on or assign each other the roles of farmers, of murderers, of pet owners, or of vultures and scavengers. The animals become respectively farm-reared animals to be slaughtered, ailing pets to be put down, people (unjustly) murdered, or kill, a quarry that will go to waste unless consumed. The ethical responsibilities of the pet owner, the farmer, the murderer, and vulture all come up in the attempt to pin down what the animal research team is responsible for doing. Humor operates to vent emotion while shielding team members from feelings of sadness and guilt.

What makes animal research especially vexed is that such tensions typically stay hidden. The work itself is often hidden geographically, happening in protected locales for fear of actions by animal rights activists, while within the institution and among its personnel, details about the work are communicated in specific ways with specific audiences. Tora Holmberg and Malin Ideland call the strategies used to control information flow between research contexts and different publics *technologies of secrets*.[11] On an institutional level Holmberg and Ideland note a tension between protecting personnel from activist interventions, while being transparent, informing the public, and inviting its support for animal research. Institutional technologies of secrets include keeping animal houses unmarked, in effect marking them by a lack of signs and windows (*SL*, 8; 13–14), or keeping ethics committees hard to reach. But other strategies are personal, for instance, telling white lies and withholding information from people one does not know very well, "because there are maniacs, you know" (*SL*, 8). Holmberg and Ideland see a tension in how informants relate their experiences—on a personal level characterizing themselves as open, welcoming discussion, having integrity—while also reporting their own shame and being shamed by others. In their book *The Sacrifice: How Scientific Experiments Transform Animals and People*, Lynda Birke, Arnold Arluke, and Mike Michael similarly report that people in animal research struggle with being considered "unprincipled or shameless" and feeling "stuck behind the barricades."[12]

Animal research staff can face pressures from lay publics. However, pressure also comes from scientists drawing sharp lines between "science" and "ethics" for fear of contaminating the former. Carrie Friese reports on a train journey she had with the professor she calls "Elspeth" who was traveling to a conference. A student in their compartment called out that he would not attend any "ethics" panel sessions because "all he cared about was the science";[13] his loud declaration embarrassed Elspeth. She had developed a new telemetric measurement device to be implanted in animals' bellies under anesthesia instead of a surgically inserted tether, a rubber tube that would be permanently attached to animals' backs and to a computer.[14] The technique improved the experience of the animals, who were markedly more active, but also enhanced what philosophers of science would call the "external validity" of experimental results, that is, their translation to clinical settings, as most humans do not go around attached to computers (at least not physically).

In sum, we find at least four types of interconnected, normative challenges around human-animal encounters in the lab, vexed by different levels of secrecy: first, how to feel; second, how to work; third, how to learn with/from animals; and fourth, how to talk about all of the above. These normative, emotional/moral, social/professional, epistemological, and communicative/political challenges affect how one learns from animals, and vice versa. These tensions escape current animal research ethics guidelines that contend with harm-benefit calculations, where harm goes to animals and benefits to society. The golden rule for animal research is often summed up in the so-called three Rs: reduce the number of animals in research; replace more with less "sentient" organisms; and refine the experimental setup, enriching it with toys or enhancing the animal's welfare, where possible.[15] Nowhere in these guidelines are the humans' encounters with animals in research considered ethically significant in themselves.

The next section uses the philosophical insights of Emanuel Levinas to bring forth these encounters as ethically relevant. The central analytic concept I use is that of the face.

Front, Habitus, and Face

Let me first define a face by what it is not. The sociologist Erving Goffman develops the concept of a *front* in *The Presentation of Self in Everyday Life*. He defines a front as follows:

> [O]ne may take the term 'personal front' to refer to the other items of expressive equipment, the items that we most intimately identify with the performer himself and that we naturally expect will follow the performer wherever he goes. As part of personal front we may include: insignia of office or rank; clothing; sex, age and racial char-

acteristics; size and looks; posture; speech patterns; facial expressions; bodily gestures; and the like. Some of these vehicles for conveying signs, such as racial characteristics, are relatively fixed and over a span of time do not vary for the individual from one situation to another. On the other, some of these sign vehicles are relatively mobile or transitory, such as facial expression, and can vary during a performance from one moment to the next.[16]

Goffman says that people have and develop "fronts" and that we meet others in our professional lives through a front (*PS*, 34–36). He specifically talks of medical doctors and nurses assuming different fronts vis-à-vis patients in the clinic, a more formal or informal manner, that are yet still both frontal in the same way (*PS*, 51–53).[17]

A related concept is that of *habitus*. Developed by Pierre Bourdieu, habitus conveys how one habitually inhabits and perceives the world through one's body. Habitus is shaped by physical and social—class, cultural—environments, and it in turn shapes how distinctions and classifications are made: it is "a structured and structuring structure."[18] Perhaps bridging the idea of a habitus with that of professional fronts is the proposal of Bourdieu that there is such a thing as *disciplinary* habitus, elaborated more recently as *epistemic habitus* to emphasize what epistemic methods and paradigms professionals are trained to trust.[19] These ideas are crucial for understanding the social constitution of embodied, profession-specific beliefs and practices, and how these in turn can be structuring social relations. They can help pick out the performed characters of a practice and its ethos. But the concepts of habitus and front differ from that of the face. Indeed, as I understand it, the face can crack through fronts and punctuate habitus.

Like habitus, the face is embodied, and, like a front, it is surface-like. What is special about the face, however, is that encountering it raises a moral question: *How are you doing?*[20] The face, unlike one's front or habitus, is expressive of a particular, unique, though undoubtedly multiply classifiable, being. Encountering the face comes with a kind of moral qualia grounded in a relational, communicative experience with the Other.[21] Psychologists and neurologists now study special responses to facial expressions, as well as humans' and animals' capacities to read faces as signs of empathy.[22] Emmanuel Levinas is one of the first philosophers known to credit faces with this type of power.

Levinasian Faces

Levinas's contribution to ethics is quite ingenious: According to him, what binds me ethically to the Other is not sameness or kinship—I do not have a responsibility to you because you are my child or friend—but rather radical Otherness. How can this radical difference be understood? Levinas calls it a "secrecy" or "inner life."

> The real must not only be determined in its historical objectivity, but also from interior intentions, from the *secrecy* that interrupts the continuity of historical time. Only on the basis of this secrecy is the pluralism of society possible. It attests this secrecy. We have always known that it is impossible to form an idea of the human totality, for men have an *inner life* closed to him who does, however, grasp the comprehensive movements of human groups. (*TI*, 57–58; emphasis added)

Now, if we accept that other living beings, apart from humans, can present us with such hidden, inner lives, then what Levinas calls secrecy means that there is something left over when we try to comprehend individuals as (just) part of a social whole.[23] If this type of secrecy is common among us, then why should we think of it as a point of difference? Though it might be a feature that we can think of as shared, the shared feature is the impossibility of *it* being shared. Furthermore, otherness is radical for Levinas: it does not admit of degrees. There can be no order according to how much "more Other" beings are.[24]

> The alterity of the other does not depend on any quality that would distinguish him from me, for a distinction of this nature would precisely imply between us that community of genus which already nullifies alterity. (*TI*, 194)

Though the concept of otherness implies a kind of other-than structure, that is, *something* to be other than, the basis of Otherness is radical (rooted, cutting deep), for each and all.

How can we tell whether someone is the Other? Levinas says that this is a matter not of epistemology, but of ethics. As Peter Atterton notes,[25] relating to the Other is not a matter of making a kind of inference, for example, based on noticing similarities, that here is some other person. Rather, what the ethical encounter consists of is a *direct experience of a self in the expressiveness of the Other*. This primary expressiveness Levinas calls "the face."

> The way in which the other presents himself, exceeding *the idea of the other in me*, we here name face. This *mode* does not consist in

figuring as a theme under my gaze, in spreading itself forth as a set of qualities forming an image. The face of the Other at each moment destroys and overflows the plastic image it leaves me, the idea existing to my own measure and to the measure of its *idea-tum*—the adequate idea. It does not manifest itself by these qualities, but *kath'auto* [i.e., in person, *per se*]. It expresses itself. (*TI*, 50–51)

So, Levinas defines the face as a mode in which the Other presents himself to me, which exceeds any one conception of the Other. How, then, is the face *expressed?* The face is "given" through "speech" (*parole*): "The face speaks. The manifestation of the face is already discourse" (*TI*, 66). However, the way the face speaks need not involve language: "Saying opens me to the other, before saying something said, before the said that is spoken in this sincerity forms a screen between me and other. It is a saying without words . . . silence speaks" (*TI*, 170). Thus, for Levinas speech is not necessary for encountering the Other, and it could even create "a screen," despite its sincerity. Expressing the face happens further through the eyes and body. As Levinas notes: "The eyes break through the mask—the language of the eyes, impossible to dissemble. The eye does not shine; it speaks" (*TI*, 66). And further: "In the face the existent par excellence presents itself. And the whole body—a hand or a curve of the shoulder—can express as the face" (*TI*, 262).

Levinas thus concedes that the following aspects express the face: eyes, as well as embodied movement. These modes are available to animal Others. In "The Animal Interview," when directly asked whether animals have a face, Levinas professes ignorance, though a conditional ignorance: "I do not know how to answer that question, since more specific analyses are needed" (*AI*, 4). Perhaps what Levinas is after, what a more specific analysis would offer, is what conditions *encountering* a face, that is, how a face is faced (or effaced). Levinas rejects the idea that the face applies to a flea: "It's an insect, which jumps, eh?" (*AI*, 4). Still, the specification of who the flea is through what Levinas proposes it does ("jumps, eh?") flags this as a matter for consideration. Were the flea trying to escape from a pool of water, or hide from a scratching claw, might one consider it differently? I turn to another essay for some guidance.

On Facing Animals: Emmanuel Meets Bobby

Levinas discusses the *expression* of the face in eyes, bodies, silence: this is how the face is given. But what is needed to "receive" the face? What is involved in *facing*, understood as encountering the Other through the face?

In the essay "The Name of a Dog, or Natural Rights," Levinas recounts his experience as a prisoner of war, protected from Nazi atrocities by his French uniform.

> [T]he other men, called free, who had dealings with us or who gave us work or orders or even a smile—and the children and the women who passed by and sometimes raised their eyes on us—stripped us of our human skin. We were subhuman, a gang of apes. (*DF*, 152–53)[26]

One imagines the force of those raised eyes, or the giving of orders or "even a smile" as "stripping" the prisoners "of their human skin." The torture of giving something (recognition, a smile) only to take it away. The pain and nakedness felt have nothing to do with physical violence—the uniform protected them against that. It is rather the denial of the prisoners' "secrecy" that Levinas communicates. Those people were perhaps seen, yet considered known; they were marked, they were prisoners and French; not German. They could be banded together in thought, as another kind of (human) animal. In this type of encounter both prisoners and captors become unfree.

Levinas notes the prisoners' thinking, pains, laughter, sickness, "the work of our hands and the anguish of our eyes," "all that passed between parentheses" (*DF*, 153). The parentheses were offered literally by the walls of the encampment, the construction of a space perceived as "nowhere" (*DF*, 153),[27] but also by their human captors: "[b]eings entrapped in their species; despite all their vocabulary, beings without language" (*DF*, 153). Both prisoners and those "called free" are seen to be constrained: shut "in a class," deprived of expression, condemned to "being 'signifiers without a signified,'" and from there to violence and fighting" (*DF*, 153). They are deprived not of the face understood as a property, as something had; if we follow Levinas, *all humans* (perhaps all living beings) have that. What gets denied is the face understood as a capacity and accomplishment: *the expression and encounter of the Other through the face.*[28] And what is it that brackets facing? Whatever it is, Bobby remains immune to it.

Levinas recounts that "a stray dog ["*un chien errant*"] entered our life." This "mistaken," errant dog diverged from the humans' behavior. Bobby appeared at the prisoners' morning assembly and when they returned from work. He jumped on them with joy and barked, happy to see them. For him they were (his) people. Levinas tries to make sense of this dog: the one they called "Bobby," giving him an exotic (singular) name "as one does with a cherished dog" (*DF*, 153).

The naming of the dog introduces the natural into the realm of rights, of reason and justice. However, that is subsequent to the human-animal encounter. What Emmanuel and his camp mates accomplish in the naming is an ethics of the face; and that is because the dog accomplishes that first, too. In that sense, and though Levinas purports to have been literal in this story, the dog is "Emmanuel" (Hebr. Immanuel): bearing the message of "god with us," he recognizes and holds the Other's "secret," the silence (or happy barking), the face. Bobby, like his ancestors, which Levinas sees in the dogs of Egypt, keeping silent while Jewish slaves escaped, helps these prisoners get free: free from their own namelessness in encampment.

Now I hope that we have not been carried too far away from the lab. The crux of Levinas's "entire" philosophy is that "with man, there is something more important than my life, and that is the life of the other. That is unreasonable. Man is an unreasonable animal" (*AI*, 5). Using animals to reason with, in the lab, faces this type of unreason; and systematically evades it.

I use *face* to denote the extended/expressive face, expressive through bodily or body-based surface that "exudes" or communicates the inner being of the Other. The face includes visual, auditory, tactile, olfactory, or other sense-scapes that communicate the inner, "secret" being of the Other.

Technologies of Effacement: How to Systematically Avoid Facing Others

I propose that the normative struggles that staff working with animals experience are partly due to a vacillating ethical stance: both facing and effacing animals. Facing animals need not bar killing them. Levinas discusses the face as in fact the only thing that might inspire murder, that is, total negation.

> Murder exercises a power over what escapes power. It is still a power, for the face expresses itself in the sensible, but already impotency, because the face rends the sensible. The alterity that is expressed in the face provides the unique "matter" possible for total negation. I can wish to kill only an existent absolutely independent, which exceeds my powers infinitely, and therefore does not oppose them but paralyzes the very power of power. The Other is the sole being I can wish to kill. (*TI*, 198)

The challenge is that in the case of animal research, it is not clear that anyone *wishes* to kill these animals. People certainly do kill animals, *but the act of killing seems to lack intention*. The episode in Svendsen and Koch, where staff consider the act of killing, as slaughter, murder, as euthanasia, or as someone else's doing communicates this kind of uncertainty. Without this wish for total negation, the act of murder becomes a problem.[29] But perhaps this missing wish to kill *each* animal indicates something further: killing, in this context, rides on a kind of negation, a blocking of the face, or what I call *effacement*.

Technologies of effacement are techniques, tools, and procedures manifestly developed to support rational, in this case epistemological, engagements with other animals. They also operate to sustain effacement: impeding the *direct experience* of the Other by modifying sensory-symbolic, visual, olfactory, tactile, auditory, or sonic features the Other presents with. Technologies of effacement help to script encounters with individual animals as tokens of a type. They are premised on an assumption common in experimental science that the particular can be made to speak of the general. That is the opposite of encountering the Other, the "secret" of Levinas: it is an encounter with the ordered, the "known" or "knowable." Though I am not making any claim about the epistemological superiority of either of the two stances, they imply different ethics.

What follows is based on my own engagement as an "embedded philosopher" with a biomedical research facility in a Scandinavian university, which included six months of following animal research experimentations, from animal training through sacrifices and subsequent processing of samples in the spring and fall of 2012. My informants withdrew their consent for me to share empirical material, including photos and interviews collected in that period, so my references remain vague. I discuss five types of what I understand as technologies blocking the human and animal face. These are: (1) built environments and architecture; (2) entering and exiting procedures; (3) personal protective clothing and equipment; (4) naming and identification techniques; and (5) experimental protocols. I propose that effacement does not always result in a missing face, but rather in a new, added face.

Architectures and Built Environments

As already mentioned, animal research facilities are characterized by secure locations. The animal house might be geographically secluded, located underground, and behind doors that are unmarked and require access codes to enter. The space of the laboratory is a clinical, surgical space: smooth, often metallic surfaces promote sanitization and sterilization, and pale and cold colors (white, light green, grays, and blues) evoke something ethereal canceling out the reds and pinks of flesh and blood. Animal houses are not designed as the homes of integral animals. They facilitate spotting, processing, and eliminating bodily fluids, microbes, contaminants, and so forth that might have a higher chance of being encountered here.

Animals are often in temperature- and light-controlled rooms, lacking windows. The natural waking cycle of laboratory rodents is the opposite of humans: they are nocturnal. Thus, rodent rooms will be kept dark during the day so that the animals are awake when experimenters want to work with them. Though labs are often dubbed "animal houses," one rarely sees or hears these animals except when inside experimental rooms. There are no windows, no displaying of animals for its own sake as in a zoo. Rather the staff encounters the animals in work situations during feeding, examining, training, or experimenting. Soundscapes here are, in general. muffled sounds absorbed rather than let out. One is more likely to hear doors opening and closing mechanically, the beeping of codes as they are punched in, and human conversation than hear the animals. When staff members bump into each other, there are standard greetings but little sustained conversation. Actions here are mostly oriented toward the work at hand, namely, experiments. The sacrificial situation is markedly different: teamwork is in train, and camaraderie, joking, "make-believe" singing or shouting out of organ names as they get passed out, weighed, and measured makes the sacrifices socially one of the liveliest phases in the research. But I'll say more about added faces later.

The built environment blocks the animal and human face by holding bodily movements, senses, and the gaze tied to the experimental situation and precluding viewing or hearing the Other until and unless one is working with her. I remember how relieved I was to discover a window, looking out to a river, in a common staff room within the animal house. It was a one-way window, but the sense of the outside, of a river—even if it was, atypically for Scandinavia, littered—made me realize that I had been holding my breath in these rooms. The blocking of perspective, of closed doors and corridors leading movements to experimental rooms that keep animals and researchers hidden, creates a sense of enclosure if not entrapment. Built space helps constitute another type of secrecy: this is manifestly driven by concerns of hygiene and security, as what is needed to extract the real "scientific" find from messy reality and politics, but it is also where the face is obstructed—constituted as irrelevant, if not polluting.

Entering and Exit Procedures and Special Garments

Entering and exiting these facilities involves special procedures for sanitizing the body. The populations of animals held in animal houses are often bred for specific conditions, frequently from genetically identical strains. Animals are highly standardized and sensitivities to pathogens can affect whole cohorts. Strict standards for hygiene are crucial for limiting the traffic of contaminants into and out of the lab. Entering and exiting the lab happens in liminal, in-between spaces. The function of these rooms is, on the one hand, to hold staff members' personal items, clothes, boots, umbrellas, and so on, and, on the other hand, to offer staff, once undressed and washed, clean laboratory uniforms, clogs, masks, hats, and gloves. This "personal protective equipment" (PPE) is not personalized. Items come in standard sizes that generally are a bit too loose or too tight. One tolerates that for a short while.

The effect of this preparation is dual. On the one hand, there is the purpose of hygiene, achieved via new, exterior cover for these interior spaces. On the other hand, there is the effect of having donned gear that expresses much less of one's style than one's personally chosen cool shirt, or jewelry, or favorite colors, streamlining instead exterior looks to match the known, expected professional uniform. Much like the uniforms that "protected" Levinas and his campmates, these uniforms function to protect people not only physically but symbolically. Their actions with/on animals in these locales are ones that would create intense reactions outside the lab ("What? You are touching a rat!"). Uniforms and equipment physically block the expressiveness of the face, hats hiding hair and haircuts, goggles shielding eyes, gloves sheathing fingers and touch, masks muffling the voice and mouth; a known, same look prevails. And yet, one does not thereby become unrecognizable. I remember feeling the gaze of a male technician, looking at me as if I were a woman. I was so startled— I thought this could not have happened while I had my lab clothes on. Of course, one's gender, race, and individuality do not disappear just because of a uniform. My reaction though showed that I was not preparing to be looked at like *that*. (Does one ever *prepare* for that? Probably, when making oneself look "attractive"; though that seems like another fiction of control.) Still, the liminal, in-between spaces and new garb create the opportunity not only for shielding built interiors from germs, but for shielding the moral integrity of staff working on animal experimentation, at least by dressing as professionals.

Uniformity also characterizes the animals' appearance, though not by means of uniform clothing. Common laboratory animals, like rats and mice, are typically bred from the same strain, and thus look similar to each other. Often laboratory animal strains will have uniformly colored fur, making individuals difficult to tell apart. It would seem silly to propose that there might be some identifying bows or clothes for the lab animals, and yet such garments are not unheard of for pets.

Identification and Labeling Techniques

Michael Lynch wrote a seminal paper on how a "naturalistic" animal gets rendered into an "analytic" animal through laboratory sacrifices.[30] The paper compares laboratory sacrifices to sacrifices in other, social-anthropological settings where they amount to transforming the profane into the sacred, using the animal as an intermediary between the human and the divine. Lynch argues that the scientific sacrifice has that same character of mediating between the profane or mundane, and the scientific. To turn the naturalistic animal into an analytic object, special identification and labeling techniques are used.

> The same inscription [the animal's identifying number] was previously written in a number of different places: on a tag affixed to each rat's cage while the animal was still alive, on the rat's tail (written with a marking pen) just prior to its sacrifice, on a jar of preservative fluid in which the decapitated head was placed, on a disk of plastic in which dissected fragments of the brain were embedded, and on the container in which electron micrographic sections were stored. Each of these sites marks a stage in the selection and processing of the animal's remains.[31]

Preferred ways of identifying laboratory animals include numbers and graphic signs, such as lines drawn on tails or holes punched in ears. Instead of "exotic" names, fit for "cherished" animals, laboratory animals are identified as items in an order of numbers or lines. They each get a unique number, though there is nothing about *that* number that fits *them*. Rather, what gives meaning to the number are practices of counting, of ordering items into predefined spaces, whether these be cages in the animal house, the experimental room, the spreadsheet holding information about the animal's performance on the test, or the vial holding his clavicle or aorta. *That* rat is already those samples, even before his body gets dismembered. Interestingly, naming animals is more common in fields of behavioral research with "higher" animals, such as primates. Perhaps this means of effacement is unwarranted when individual behavior is under study, indicating the type of relational attention that otherwise gets blocked. According to some studies, using proper names for laboratory animals affects how closely laboratory staff relates to an animal.[32] In human societies, proper names are usually reserved for people, pets, and—because they are respected for their power—storms.

To be sure, even when animals are identified numerically, one could get to know them. A number need not prevent a special relationship with some animals, especially those encountered regularly. The active one becomes "the athlete," the lazy one "the academic." Still, identification methods that use the logic of a series (of numbers, letters, lines, holes) help to efface each animal, making it a token of a known type instead of a radically other individual. For similar reasons, some species of animal may be preferred as experimental models because they are taken to all "look the same": for instance, mice, rats, or fish.[33] One rarely finds these animals as pets: their face then can get more easily blocked by a front, their presumed type or species.

Experimental Protocols

Human-animal engagements in the lab follow a protocol. Protocols are like recipes: they offer instructions for how, how often, using what techniques, and with what cohorts one should engage to test a hypothesis. Protocols carve out the time humans and animals spend together into tasks. The manifest aim of following a clear routine is to create a procedure that can be easier to track causally, to validate, and to replicate scientifically. In practice, however, experimental protocols operate to script engagements between humans and animals, streamlining them to the scientific task at hand; this means that often the same procedure will be followed with each animal, in either the test or the control groups, repeatedly. Further, engagements between humans and animals that are not dictated by the protocol could be seen as unnecessary: petting, massaging, or talking with the animals might be frowned on as "unprofessional," if not as confounding research results.

Crucially scripting human-animal engagements through a protocol might inhibit the kind of spontaneity that would occur when facing the Other. But also, specific techniques block the human and animal face in the lab. For instance, picking up a rat from the root of her tail is a technique that is preferred by researchers though distressing for the rats. One reason why it may be preferred by staff is that the technique helps block the animal face. Unlike holding a rat in one's palm, which the rat prefers, picking her up from her tail prevents you from feeling tiny clawed paws grasp back on your fingers. (They are warm and sharp!) The rat becomes like a teacup you hold by the tail, giving the impression (especially if you don't look at her swiveling) that she is disembodied, not there. Or recall the case of Alex. Wrapping the animal in a towel, as "people" say, functions not only as a material bondage, but also as a barrier between the animal and human face, shielding the Other's face from speaking against one's grip.

Ironically, even anesthesia affects the animal face: anaesthetized eyes lose their shine. The process aims for the animal to lose his sensibility to the painful procedures that ensue, but the limpness of the body and dullness of his eyes help convince the experimenter that the Other is not fully "there," enabling the experimenter to perform the procedures culminating in the cutting and delegated, distributed progressive killing of an animal during sacrifices.[34] Indeed it becomes hard to say when exactly the animal dies, as he gets progressively emptied of organs. Still, the face can speak through the body, the blood flowing, the heart beating even once it is excised.

While blocking the animal face is part of doing research, so is reading the face, first, to comply with regulations for minimizing animal suffering, and second to draw accurate inferences regarding how test procedures affect the animals. Perhaps not surprisingly, facing experimental animals has been subject to standardization and automation via the mouse and rat "grimace scales," implemented in Rodent Face Finder® software.[35] These scales have the stated aim of translating pain research results from rodents to humans, figuring out whether pain relief is achieved in the rodent or not. The scales use a standard set of markers on rodents' faces, for example, the scrunching of their noses, or narrowing of the eyes, the drawing back and flattening of ears or whiskers.[36] Now, an instrument such as a grimace scale has obvious benefits once it comes to the ethos of the ordered: it enhances measurability by codifying visual aspects of human-animal encounters into particular variables that can then be ordered in a series or scale, allowing for measurement, generalization from individuals to populations, and replication.

However, by now you know what I will say: the projection of a scale on the animal face is a prime example of a "frontal" encounter with the Other. What you are bound to find is expected, a grimace, fitting somewhere on a scale. Meeting the shiny eyes of the Other becomes, if actual, a problem. As we read in the description of the software developed to automate reading these face-frames, Rodent Face Finder® "successfully automates the most labor-intensive step in the process."[37] What is this arduous step? "Grabbing individual face-containing frames from digital video, which is hampered by uncooperative subjects (not looking directly at the camera) or otherwise poor optics due to motion blurring."[38] It is hard to reduce the animal to a "frame," or a front, when it is moving, or looking away. Photography holds the potential to mediate encounters with the face (a reason why some photographs are so haunting), yet what gets mediated here is what Michel Foucault has called the medical, ordering gaze.[38] This automation need not exclude an empathetic response—such as euthanizing an animal suffering "too much." Still, the labor saved is that of facing the Other. Facing is not equivalent to empathy: it involves meeting radical *otherness*, bringing a kind of groundlessness as an aspect of the encounter: an openness, a silence—what comes before empathy, or sorrow, or dread.

Laboratory procedures and instruments producing "inscriptions" operate in a similar manner. The ready-labeled containers, test tubes, vials, or spreadsheets help to funnel the unexpected singular animal into a context structured already by scientific assumptions about what matters.[40] The bench equipment provides, as does a built architecture, a material environment that guides the body and its movements, and orders the gaze to hold some aspects of the experience and name them, while discarding others. The flesh may be sticking to the bone, warm, but you just need to cut it out, and put it into the vial. Throw the rest of the animal in the trash.

Added Faces

Laboratory technologies are built structures, tools, techniques, and procedures enveloped in logos, in a rationale for their design and use. I have been describing how some of these technologies operate as technologies of effacement, blocking the human and/or animal face, and structuring encounters between humans and animals according to an ethos of the ordered. I see it perhaps as a symptom of such a process of effacement that what I call "added faces" may show up in these spaces. It is tempting to see these add-on faces as fronts—as surfaces hiding, or glossing over the Other's interiority in ways that align with some professional ethos. However, and perhaps to be a bit more precise about the kind of texture these add on, I would rather keep calling them *added faces*, in that they provide symbols of some inner, emotional, or moral being that humans and animals have or acquire in the lab and that do not immediately strike one as developed as part of a professional practice. Added faces are found across all the preparations I mentioned.

Once it comes to the built environment, added faces may take the shape of decorations. These could be posters, images of wildlife or of natural sur-roundings, aiming to counter the artificiality of the animal house and make it more home-like for animals. For instance, images of wild snow-bunnies were hanging in one of the animal houses I visited. These wild relatives of the cap-tives in the lab offered a kind of balm for the gaze, perhaps a reassurance of things being otherwise elsewhere, much like a window to an ideal landscape.

Adding faces to personal protective equipment could take the form of personalizing uniforms, or styling the wearing of the uniform. It might also involve expressions of humor, flirting, or joking as strategies that succeed in venting emotion and in performing personality, while at the same time evading hurtful or stressful encounters and building rapport with others on the team. Such behavior has been observed among medical staff working in acute situ-ations.[41] These behaviors can be seen as adding an alternative, happy face to oneself, enacting work as if it were fun, palatable, and natural. Faces can be added through other laboratory equipment. Especially evocative was a plastic (or polystyrene) foam block where rodents' paws would get pinned after anaes-thetization so that the first incision down the chest can be made. A smiley face was drawn on the plastic foam so that, once the animal's body is passed to the next person, the foam block smiles back. And so on.

Added faces may also be found in the form of cartoons. In her account of the development of the Jackson Lab experimental mouse, Karen Rader mentions that the lab director C. C. Little wrote to Walt Disney to ask him to produce some promotional imagery for the lab—unsuccessfully.[42] A blow-up photocopy of a smiling Disney character, *Ratatouille*, with holes drawn on the rat's ears was used to guide staff on how to punch holes in rodents' ears, how many holes to punch, and where in order to tell the animals apart. The imagery manages to add face to an invasive labeling procedure. Imagery used in scientific presentation slides will often include stock images of the strain of animal used in high definition; sometimes images of the animals under study appear as part of the evidence or methods presented. Rarely are animals presented for their own sake, as in the case of family vacation slides. Rather, cartoon characters of the animal in question, dressed in a lab coat may appear, saying something pleasant or funny to the scientific audience, like "Thank you for your attention!"

Staining and Remaining Faces

Levinas identifies something persistent about what is existent in the face.

> The primordial signifyingness of the existent, its presentation in person or its expression, its way of incessantly upsurging outside of its plastic image, is produced concretely as a temptation to total negation, and as the infinite resistance to murder, in the other qua other, in the hard resistance of these eyes without protection—what is softest and most uncovered. (*TI*, 262)

Effacement cannot be total for Levinas. Perhaps for him what resists negation is the divine: "In the face the Other expresses his eminence, the dimension of height and divinity from which he descends" (*TI*, 262). I doubt Levinas would find divinity in a rat, but I cannot forget a particular one. She tried to escape the experimenter's grip on her way to the anesthesia chamber, and in that instant I could not but hope with her. Her inability to escape that grip, and my inability to move, all became a message from her, facing me—both of us hoping in our hopelessness.

Caught in this vacillating, split gaze, from the fascia to the face, humans and animals in the lab cannot but get tangled up in what Donna Haraway calls "sharing suffering."[43]

Conclusion:
Toward Humanimal Research Ethics

The strangeness of the Other, his irreducibility to the I, to my
thoughts and my possessions, is precisely accomplished as a calling
into question of my spontaneity, as ethics. (*TI*, 43)

Within a Levinasian frame, ethics becomes an accomplishment: that of
breaking up one's habituated behavior, stumbling at the Other's face. Current
ethics guidelines call attention to aspects worthy of consideration in the experimental situation ("*Reduce, replace, refine!*"). However, the effect of such guidelines
is often to create new mnemonics that flow by without capturing the type of
silence that Levinasian ethics mandates.

A humanimal research ethics is an ethics of the human-animal relation
itself, premised on the possibility of humans and animals encountering each other
through the face.[44] Humanimal research ethics claims that harms and benefits
cannot be considered for one side alone, for just the animal or the researcher. In
that sense, the point is neither to develop professional ethics to help the humans
cope, nor to make animals more comfortable. Rather humanimal research ethics
involves stumbling on the particularities—good, bad, or visceral—of encountering
the Other through her face. It offers a frame where humans can share suffering
with the animals, irrespective of whether their research aims are achieved or
whether society approves or disapproves. A humanimal research ethics would
leave space for facing each other in research, as animals.

Smart and passionate philosophers have developed principled positions for
how to relate to animals (e.g., animal rights, utilitarianism, care ethics). These
approaches have power. But they can also become philosophical tropes that lack
a face. As Niklas Forsberg so eloquently asks,

Is it possible that we sometimes turn to arguments to hide our own
weaknesses? Do we at times turn to abstract theorizing in order not
to face reality? And, if so, how does that affect philosophy, how we
do philosophy? (These are questions, not answers. I'm asking, not
asserting.) This much seems to be true: philosophical clarity may
require a form of writing that enables us to absorb the intimate
details of our lives in language.[45]

So to finish, I present two texts about my encounters with animals, facing each other:

[My pet dog,] Pavlo has a small warm soft silky body. When I wake up I go to him, and I kneel on the floor by his pillow and I embrace him, I cover his body with mine, my head on the crook of his belly, his head in the crook of my neck, his face breathing into my heart. And we rest there happy to not be fully woken up.

I read somewhere that dogs do not like hugs. But mine seems to envelop me instead.

The orchestrated movement of humans, animals and organs within the sacrificial dance is impressive, timed, precise, and exhausting. The joking atmosphere, the calling out of organ names as they are repeatedly extracted, weighed and preserved, the carrying forward, singing (instead of crying or screaming) is no antidote to how heavy one feels. Afterward.

The red that takes over the white as rats get cut open, again and again—that is what I see. And the one who tried to escape.

Notes

1. A broader version of this argument that includes phenomenological approaches to the face/front distinction is published in German as Sophia Efstathiou, "Im Angesicht der Gesichter: *Technologien des Gesichtsverlusts* in der Tierforschung," in *Philosophie der Tierforschung, Vol. 3: Milieus und Akteure*, eds. Matthias Wunsch, Martin Böhnert, and Kristian Köchy; trans. Franz Mutschler (Freiburg/Munchen, Germany: Karl Alber Verlag, 2018), 375–419.

2. According to Giorgio Agamben, *Homo Sacer: Sovereign Power and Bare Life*, trans. Daniel Heller-Roazen (Stanford, CA: Stanford University Press, 1998), camps articulate a political exception by providing the physical spaces where the law is suspended. In this sense, and given that general laws for animal welfare are suspended in the space of the lab, these spaces might be thought of as examples of camps.

3. I will be working with Nicole C. Nelson, "Model Homes for Model Organisms: Intersections of Animal Welfare and Behavioral Neuroscience around the Environment of the Laboratory Mouse," *Biosocieties* 11, no. 46 (2016), doi10.1057/biosoc.2015.19; Mette Svendsen and Lene Koch, "Potentializing the Research Piglet in Experimental Neonatal Research," *Current Anthropology* 54, no. 57 (2013): 118–28; Carrie Friese, "Realizing Potential in Translational Medicine: The Uncanny Emergence of Care as Science," *Current Anthropology* 54, no. 7 (2013): 129–38; Tora Holmberg and Malin Ideland, "Secrets and Lies: 'Selective Openness' in the Apparatus of Animal Experimentation," *Public Understanding of Science* 21, no. 3 (2010), 354–68; Lynda Birke, Arnold B. Arluke, and Mike Michael, *The Sacrifice: How Scientific Experiments Transform Animals and People* (West Lafayette, IN: Purdue University Press, 2007).

4. For a discussion of the critical work done by noticing differences between manifest (defined) and operative (used) concepts of X, see Sally Haslanger, "What Are

We Talking About? The Semantics and Politics of Social Kinds," *Hypatia* 20, no. 4 (2005): 10–26.

5. For epistemological issues around model organism, see: Soraya De Chadarevian, "Of Worms and Programmes: *Caenorhabditis elegans* and the Study of Development," *Studies in History and Philosophy of Science* 29 (1998): 81–105; Robert Meunier, "Stages in the Development of a Model Organism as a Platform for Mechanistic Models in Developmental Biology: Zebrafish, 1970–2000," *Studies in History and Philosophy of Biological and Biomedical Sciences* 43 (2012): 522–31; Rachel A. Ankeny et al., "Making Organisms Model Humans: Situated Models in Alcohol Research," *Science in Context* 27 (2014): 485–509.

6. Consider the history of the Jackson lab, as described in Karen Rader, *Making Mice: Standardizing Animals for American Biomedical Research 1900–1955* (Princeton, NJ: Princeton University Press, 2004).

7. Nicole C. Nelson, "Model Homes for Model Organisms: Intersections of Animal Welfare and Behavioral Neuroscience around the Environment of the Laboratory Mouse," *Biosocieties* 11, no. 46 (2016), doi10.1057/biosoc.2015.19: 8–9. Hereafter cited as *MH*.

8. Vinciane Despret, "The Body We Care For: Figures of Anthropo-zoo-genesis," *Body and Society* 10, no's. 2–3 (2004): 111–34.

9. Mette Svendsen and Lene Koch, "Potentializing the Research Piglet in Experimental Neonatal Research," *Current Anthropology* 54, no. 57 (2013): 118–28.

10. Ibid. 125–26. Note that because of Denmark's tradition of pig farming, cultural and historical relationships to piglets may be distinctive in this context.

11. Tora Holmberg and Malin Ideland, "Secrets and Lies: 'Selective Openness' in the Apparatus of Animal Experimentation," *Public Understanding of Science* 21, no. 3 (2010): 354–68. Hereafter cited as *SL*.

12. Lynda Birke, Arnold B. Arluke, and Mike Michael, *The Sacrifice: How Scientific Experiments Transform Animals and People* (West Lafayette, IN: Purdue University Press, 2007), 154–55.

13. Carrie Friese, "Realizing Potential in Translational Medicine: The Uncanny Emergence of Care as Science," *Current Anthropology* 54, no. 7 (2013): 129–38. The episode I discuss is described on p. 134.

14. Ibid., 131–32.

15. William M. S. Russell and Rex L. Burch, *The Principles of Humane Experimental Technique* (1959). Available at: http://altweb.jhsph.edu/pubs/books/humane_exp/het-toc. Last accessed: 05.09.17.

16. Erving Goffman, *The Presentation of Self in Everyday Life* (Garden City, NY: Anchor Books, 1959), 34. Hereafter cited as *PS*.

17. For more on "fronts" and "frontality," see David Morris, "Faces and the Invisible of the Visible: Toward an Animal Ontology," *PhaenEx* 2, no. 2: 124–69, and Elizabeth Behnke, "From Merleau-Ponty's Concept of Nature to an Interspecies Practice of Peace," in *Animal Others: On Ethics, Ontology and Animal Life*, ed. H. Peter Steeves (Albany: State University of New York Press, 1999), 93–116. Morris contrasts the "logic of the face" to what he calls a "frontal logic," which reduces things to fronts for other things, as lacking inner depth or life. Articulating Behnke's notion of "frontality," Morris

identifies it as "an attitude in which nature, being, space, duration, and so on are posited as objects, over-against a subject who surveys them from above or the outside, and in which nature is posited as a totality of things that are spread out outside of one another, with no internal relations" (145)—a logic that infuses the ontologies of modern science.

18. Pierre Bourdieu, *Distinction: A Social Critique of the Judgment of Taste* (New York and London: Routledge, 1984), 170 (see also the figure on 171).

19. Mathieu Albert, Susanne Laberge, and Brian David Hodges, "Who Wants to Collaborate with Social Scientists? Biomedical and Clinical Scientists' Perception of Social Science," in *Collaboration across Health Research and Medical Care: Healthy Collaboration*, eds. Bart Penders, Niki Vermeulen, and John N. Parker (London: Ashgate, 2015), 59–80.

20. David Morris, "Faces and the Invisible of the Visible: Toward an Animal Ontology," *PhaenEx* 2, no. 2 (2007): 124–69.

21. Facing could be understood more broadly as the type of process enabling the experience of normative qualia, that is, values that are understood as intrinsically experienced. This would make *value-ing* instances primary to determining a valued value.

22. The literature here is vast, but I offer some suggestions. British neurophysiologist Jonathan Cole argues that the face is crucial for interpersonal relatedness, and that empathy requires the embodied expressiveness of the face, though he primarily considers humans; see "Empathy Needs a Face," *Journal of Consciousness Studies* 8, no's. 5–7 (2001), 51'68; also *About Face* (Cambridge, MA: MIT Press, 1998). Work on primates suggests that the face has a role in communication and empathy, for example, mother-to-infant communication parallels human mother and infants via exaggerated facial expressions, that are then mimicked by the infant, as reported in Pier Francisco Ferrari et al., "Reciprocal Face-to-Face Communication between Rhesus Macaque Mothers and Their Newborn Infants," *Current Biology* 19, no. 20 (November 3, 2009): 1768–72. See also Marina Davila Ross et al., "Rapid Facial Mimicry in Orangutan Play," *Biological Letters* 4, no. 1 (February 23, 2008): 27–30. Even more fascinatingly, some recent work suggests that facial recognition need not exclude invertebrates, even ones lacking neocortex-like cells, such as fish. See Cait Newport et al., "Discrimination of Human Faces by Archerfish (*Toxotes chatareus*)," *Nature Scientific Reports* 6 (2016) (article number 27523).

23. Note that a similar idea, of the real making itself known to perception in part through its hiddenness, is an idea that we find in Husserl, with whom Levinas studied in Freiburg in 1928. A typical example is of an object, such as a cup, which makes itself apparent to our perception only by showing part of its surface, what painters call perspective (see Morris, "Faces and the Invisible of the Visible").

24. Thus, as Peter Atterton argues in "Levinas and Our Moral Responsibility toward Other Animals," *Inquiry* 54, no. 6 (2011): 633–49, Derrida is wrong to claim that animals are "more" Other than humans (634–36).

25. Ibid., 637.

26. Atterton (this volume) notes that Levinas gestures to the animals, the band of apes, in what appears to be a derogatory manner, as "less" than human, though he may just be communicating a common perception that being treated as if they were apes by these people meant being treated as less than human, since most people think that apes are quasi-human.

27. Levinas here echoes the exclusionary thinking of racism: of considering the camp as a no place, with no people, not mattering. Reversely in the recognition (even of a dog) the prisoners can find a home—that is, having a home is implicated in having a friend.

28. From an epistemological perspective, one might say that encountering "proves" the having of a face. I would thus be tempted to claim that facing is epistemologically prior to the face, even if we accept with Levinas that the face is not known epistemically, that its mode of expression is ethics.

29. See also Tora Holmberg's auto-ethnography of taking an animal research training course in "A Feeling for the Animal: On Becoming an Experimentalist," *Society and Animals* 16 (2008): 316–35. Holmberg justifies her killing an animal, delegating murder, by stating that someone else would have killed the animal if she hadn't. Lynda Birke, Arnold B. Arluke, and Mike Michael also note this kind of stance among science students, and characterize it as a case of denial or distancing in *The Sacrifice: How Scientific Experiments Transform Animals and People* (West Lafayette, IN: Purdue University Press, 2007). I here attribute this type of denial to, in part, the systematic effacement of humans and animals involved in the research.

30. Michael Lynch, "Sacrifice and the Transformation of the Animal Body into a Scientific Object: Laboratory Culture and Ritual Practice in the Neurosciences," *Social Studies of Science* 18, no. 2 (1988): 265–89.

31. Ibid., 271. I have been thinking of the transfiguration of the everyday into the scientific as *found science*, by analogy to found art. See Sophia Efstathiou, *The Use of "Race" as a Variable in Biomedical Research*, PhD thesis (University of California, San Diego, 2009). Found science arises through what I think of as a two-part process of finding and founding entities in scientific contexts of space and interest. In my vocabulary, the rat thus becomes a found model, by being founded in a context of modeling spaces and interests.

32. Hal Herzog, "Ethical Aspects of Relationships between Humans and Research Animals," *ILAR Journal* 43, no. 1 (2002): 27–32.

33. Arnold B. Arluke and Frederic Hafferty, "From Apprehension to Fascination with 'Dog Lab': The Use of Absolutions by Medical Students," *Journal of Contemporary Ethnography* 25, no. 2 (1996): 201–25, discusses the training of medical students using dogs, and the challenges of encountering dogs.

34. See ibid.

35. D. J. Langford et al. "Coding of Facial Expressions of Pain in the Laboratory Mouse," *Nature Methods* 7, no. 6 (2010): 447–49; S. G. Sotocinal et al., "The Rat Grimace Scale: A Partially Automated Method for Quantifying Pain in the Laboratory Rat via Facial Expressions," *Molecular Pain* 7, no. 55 (2011), doi: 10.1186/1744-8069-7-55.

36. These types of images are also used to train personnel to recognize when and what care is needed for animals, for example, how big a tumor should be allowed to get, what types of behaviors like scratching or biting may be signals of distress, and so on.

37. Sotocinal et al., "The Rat Grimace Scale: A Partially Automated Method for Quantifying Pain in the Laboratory Rat via Facial Expressions," *Molecular Pain* 7, no. 55 (2011), doi: 10.1186/1744-8069-7-55: 1 of 10.

38. Ibid., 2 of 10.

39. Michel Foucault, *The Birth of the Clinic: An Archaeology of Medical Perception*, trans. Alan Mark Sheridan Smith (New York: Vintage Books, 1994).

40. I have elsewhere called this type of equipment "founding tools" because they are used to establish or institute a nonscientific thing as part of science; see Efstathiou, *The Use of 'Race' as a Variable in Biomedical Research*, PhD thesis (University of California, San Diego, 2009). Here I am interested in the loss of the face incurred during such a founding process.

41. See Kate Watson, "Gallows Humor in Medicine," *The Hastings Center Report* 41, no. 5 (2011): 37–45; Gitte Koksvik, *Blurry Lines and Spaces of Tension. Clinical-Ethical and Existential Issues in Intensive Care: A Study of Three European Intensive Care Units*, PhD thesis (Norwegian University of Science and Technology, 2016). See also Erving Goffman, *The Presentation of Self in Everyday Life* (Garden City, NY: Anchor Books, 1959), on "disruptions" of a projected definition of a situation that may include jokes and humor (25).

42. Karen Rader, *Making Mice: Standardizing Animals for American Biomedical Research, 1900–1955* (Princeton, NJ: Princeton University Press, 2004).

43. Donna Haraway, *When Species Meet* (Minneapolis, MN: University of Minnesota Press, 2008), 69–94.

44. Thank you to Robert Meunier for stressing this point.

45. Niklas Forsberg, "Different Forms of Forms of Life: A Philosophical Introduction," in *Language, Ethics and Animal Life: Wittgenstein and Beyond*, eds. Niklas Forsberg, Mikel Burley, and Nora Hämäläinen (London: Bloomsbury, 2012), 1–15.

PART IV

TRADITIONS:
GREEK/HEBREW/ASIAN

CHAPTER 9

Homo Homini Lupus

Levinas and the Animal Within

KATHARINE LOEVY

Levinas's assertion that the human being is the radical exception to the rest of being is startling. In order to make sense of it, we must understand that Levinas's human being is complex in a way that cannot be accounted for in terms of a synthesis of components or a collection of capacities. For while we are indeed included among living and nonliving things as a part of nature, Levinas identifies our humanity with our ethicality, and locates our ethicality outside of any evolutionary continuum through which human beings and nonhuman animals would be related. We see this, for example, in "The Animal Interview" when Levinas states, "It is a widespread thesis saying ultimately the human is but the culmination of the animal. I myself say, on the contrary, that in relation to the animal, humanity is a new phenomenon" (*AI*, 4). The human being is biologically and therefore ontologically related to nonhuman animals, but we are also the occasion of a certain transcendence that is other than and different from the ontological. To be human rather than animal, therefore, is not simply to be a different kind of organism, but to be different from or other than nature.

For Levinas, this transcendence of the human being is identified with ethics as a possibility within a human life, and hence with the occasioning of the ethical within a life that is also immanent to nature and related to nonhuman animals and to the rest of being. To be human and not animal, therefore, is to be ethical, hence ethics has no part in nature or in the constitutive ontology of nonhuman animals.

At the same time, Levinas uses the figure of the animal to identify a part of the human that must be suspended or overcome in order for the humanity of the human to be manifest. Consequently, the figurative divide that separates humans from nonhuman animals circumscribes the human being, but also traverses its center. As human beings, we are both immanence and transcendence, animality and ethicality, and hence the kind of beings who are forever engaged in an internal struggle against our animal selves.

What are the implications of Levinas's positioning of the animal both within and beyond the human? How does this ambiguity and ambivalence affect the meaning of the human and of the animal in Levinas's philosophy? More to the point, in what way does this constellation of identification and antagonism impact the degree to which nonhuman animals can be accorded the position of the ethically summoning Other? And how can an analysis of this constellation enable us to interpret differently moments in Levinas's philosophy when he speaks most directly about nonhuman animals?

We are both animal and not-animal. It is a doubled and conflicted identification, and its significance is founded on Levinas's particular rendering of the human/animal binary and on the relation of this binary to an entire series of binaries that are quintessentially Levinasian. Totality/infinity, same/other, said/saying, Greek/Hebrew—each in its own way functions so as to distinguish the human being from the rest of being, and to describe or to refer to the tensions and conflicts that Levinas identifies as internal to human subjectivity and human politics. This web of related binaries links the figure of the animal with the rest of Levinas's philosophy, and traverses the divide between kinds of thinking and kinds of being. And while one side of this oppositional vision is associated with the animal side of the human/animal binary, it is the other side—the "human" side—that introduces ways of thinking and of being that hold the most promise for nonhuman animals.

What follows is a discussion of Levinas's figure of the animal insofar as it is located both within and beyond the human being, and insofar as this ambiguous positioning is implicated in a series of other critical binaries that constitute the heart of Levinas's philosophy. The essay is oriented by the contention that Levinas's rhetorical deployment of animal imagery is relevant to the question of ethics, and that it has serious implications for whether nonhuman animals are beneficiaries of robust ethical consideration. There are consequences, in other words, to Levinas's double positioning of the figure of the animal. By locating the animal both within and beyond the human being, Levinas symbolically blocks nonhuman animals from occupying the position of the ethically summoning Other.

Historical Precedents

Levinas is not the first thinker in the history of philosophy to identify the animal as a contrary element located within the human being. Aristotle in the *Politics* defines the human being as a "political animal" (ζῷον πολιτικὸν) (1253a3), about which Derrida in *The Beast and the Sovereign* states the following:

> [T]he double and contradictory figuration of political man as *on the one hand* superior, in his very sovereignty, to the beast that he masters, enslaves, dominates, domesticates, or kills, so that his sovereignty consists in raising himself above the animal and appropriating it, having its life at his disposal, but *on the other hand* (contradictorily) a figuration of the political man, and especially of the sovereign state *as animality*, or even as bestiality, . . . either a normal bestiality or a monstrous bestiality itself mythological or fabulous. Political man as superior to animality and political man as animality.[1]

If Derrida is right, then a pernicious ambiguity attends to Aristotle's identification of the human being as both human and animal. Instead of signaling an embrace of animality or an alliance with nonhuman animals, the identification asserts human superiority at the same time that it sets the terms of the human project as one of overcoming contamination by an endemic animality. This is only one of several definitions of the human being developed by Aristotle. At *Metaphysics* Zeta, for example, Aristotle defines the human being through the conjoining of "animal" and "two-footed" (ζῷον δίπουν) (1037b) as a part of his complex discussion of the meaning and function of definitions. But in the legacy of the notion of the political animal, we find a dynamic whereby the animal names the viciousness at the heart of human politics and the viciousness at the heart of the human self over which political and social life triumphs.

Another, more prevalent definition of the human being, but one that bears this same basic structure, is that the human being is a rational animal. Drawn from Aristotle's theories of the human soul, it is referenced from the Hellenistic period to the early twenty-first century by a wide variety of thinkers. One relatively early philosopher to embrace this notion is Aquinas. In his *Summa Theologica*, Aquinas writes that "in the idea of a man we understand animal and rational,"[2] and "there is sensible nature by reason of which he is called animal, and the rational nature by reason of which he is called man."[3]

Like the notion of the political animal, the rational animal has ambivalent and largely derisive implications for nonhuman animals. Within the context of a discussion of Rousseau's use of the phrase, Kelly Oliver writes,

> Man's status as the "rational animal" puts him at the same time in an ambiguous space as animal but not animal. In the history of philosophy, bodies and passions threaten *regression* to animality, which is associated with man's abject animal ancestors.[4]

Endemic to the formulation is thus its manner of highlighting rationality as unique to human beings. Animality is what we are left with when we fail to be rational. It is our animality that comes to the fore if our rationality, and hence our humanness, has somehow lapsed.

Levinas makes explicit reference to the idea of the "rational animal" in a variety of places. In two essays, "The Ego and the Totality" (*CPP*, 27) and "Humanism and Anarchy" (*CPP*, 131), Levinas takes over the formulation so as to variously critique and to embrace it, and uses it to introduce his notion that the human being is simultaneously a being of immanence and transcendence. The latter essay begins,

> The unburied dead in wars and extermination camps make one believe the idea of a death without a morning after and render tragic-comic the concern for oneself and illusory the pretension of the rational animal to have a privileged place in the cosmos and the power to dominate and integrate the totality of being in a self-consciousness. (*CPP*, 127)

The "pretension" at issue is the pretention to human superiority vis-à-vis nonhuman animals, which Levinas is calling into question given the horrors of human history. One of Lacan's statements on human exceptionalism comes to mind. Citing a fable by Balthazar Gracián, Lacan writes that "the ferocity of man with respect to his fellow goes beyond anything that animals can do, and . . . faced with the threat that this ferocity poses to the whole of nature, even the carnivores recoil in horror." He continues: "[T]his very cruelty implies humanity."[5] For Levinas, human history likewise threatens to reveal that the "privileged place" we accord ourselves as rational animal is completely unfounded. But while Lacan identifies our excesses with regard to viciousness as the mark of our humanity, Levinas will ultimately cite our susceptibility to the ethical imperative as that which can interrupt the egoism and violence of human history, and as what ultimately marks the difference between our humanity and the inhumanity of human history.

At other moments in his work, Levinas redetermines the traditional formulation, and defines the human being as an irrational or unreasonable animal. In "The Animal Interview," Levinas states that "with the appearance of the human—here is my entire philosophy—that is with man, there is something more important than my life, and that is the life of the other. That is unreasonable. Man is an unreasonable animal" (*AI*, 5). Levinas says something similar in the interview from 1989 published under the title "Being-for-the-Other."

> But by understanding the vocation of being-for-the-other, which must be thought in all its acuity, that which is human in man has also put into question the *conatus essendi*. In this possibility of disinterestedness, in this goodness, the awakening to biblical humanity is produced: to respond to the other, to the priority of the other, the asymmetry between me and the other, him always *before* me, man as an irrational animal, or rational according to a new reason. (*IR*, 119–20)

In both instances, Levinas mobilizes the idea of the "irrational" or "unreasonable" in order to indicate that ethics is a break with nature. From the perspective of the human being's survival and flourishing, ethics can be detrimental, and hence irrational or unreasonable. What Levinas has done is thus to enact a dramatic subversion of the association of the human being with rationality. Levinas positions rationality on the animal side of human nature, and identifies human ethicality as other than and as operating beyond a naturalized and self-interested reason.

Of course, among the many figures in the history of philosophy that locate an animal dimension within the human, not all regard the animal as something to overcome. We find a different conclusion, for example, in the writings of Niccolò Machiavelli when he states,

> A ruler, in particular, needs to know how to be both an animal and a man. The classical writers, without saying it explicitly, taught rulers to behave like this. They described how Achilles, and many other rulers in ancient times, were given to Chiron the centaur to be raised, so he could bring them up as he thought best. What they intended to convey, with this story of rulers' being educated by someone who was half beast and half man, was that it is necessary

for a ruler to know when to act like an animal and when to act like
a man; and if he relies on just one or the other mode of behavior
he cannot hope to survive.[6]

For Machiavelli, it is necessary for the ruler to know when to act like a
man and when to act like a beast—practical know-how that Machiavelli considers necessary for political survival. We must be both man and animal, says
Machiavelli, and for him this means that we must be able to wield the violence
and the ruthlessness for which his political theory is famous, and which is here
identified with the figure of the animal. Thinking as well of Machiavelli's reference to the lion and the fox, the ruler must be sly (fox) and cruelly powerful
(lion), depending on what the situation requires. Through such animal imagery,
therefore, Machiavelli argues that it is rational to always maximize one's own
position in regard to others.

If for Machiavelli the human being is most effective when human and
animal aspects of a person's mixed ontology are properly integrated, for Levinas, the human being is the site of a perpetual struggle between animality and
humanness. Levinas is a preeminent thinker of human subjectivity as determined
by an internal and irresolvable agon. We find a description of this agon in
Totality and Infinity. Levinas writes,

> [T]he acute experience of the human in the twentieth century teaches
> that the thoughts of men are borne by needs which explain society
> and history, that hunger and fear can prevail over every human
> resistance and every freedom! There is no question of doubting this
> human misery, this dominion the things and the wicked exercise
> over man, this animality. (*TI*, 35)

In opposition to Machiavelli's ruler and his image of the centaur, Levinas's
conception of the human being determines the animal within as the nonhuman
player in a perpetual struggle between two forces internal to human subjectivity—self-preservation and promotion versus ethical behavior toward others. We
are humans and not animals, but we are also the site of the struggle between
humanity and animality. We are distinct from the rest of beings because we
are claimed by an ethical vocation, but we are also expressions, like everything
else, of the egoist law of being.

Levinas calls this the "insurmountable ambiguity" of the human—that the
human being can be claimed by the ethical and also affirmed in its being "as an
animal in its *conatus* and its joy" (*OB*, 79). The "shattering of indifference" with
regard to others that determines the human side of this human/animal conflict

is significant for Levinas, "even if indifference is statistically dominant" (*EN*, xii). Such are the marks of the human, and such are the aspects of human life that do the work of circumscribing human difference from nonhuman animals and from the rest of being within these determinations of human subjectivity. As Levinas writes, "But to know or to be conscious is to have time to avoid and forestall the instant of inhumanity. It is this perpetual postponing of the hour of treason—infinitesimal difference between man and non-man—that implies the disinterestedness of goodness" (*TI*, 35).[7]

At war with ourselves, we are also unique insofar as we are the beings who are at war with war. For Levinas, the otherwise-than-being that emerges through us is the one thing that can interrupt the egoism of both the individual and history. Levinas will sometimes call this possibility Messianic, by which he means an interruption of history, and hence of political violence, as a result of undergoing the ethical imperative vis-à-vis the vulnerability, suffering, or distress of others. Catherine Chalier explains, as follows:

> The messianic rupture is identified, therefore, with the advent of the human I in worldly violence. It is indeed a question of a rupture since this I, which opens itself without limits to human distress in order to console it and carry it, this I, knowing itself the obligee of that suffering, creates space in itself, in its most profound intimacy, for the other than itself and must immediately interrupt the interested movement of its perseverance in being.[8]

The Messiah enters history through us, and emerges from within us, without being reducible to our egoism, and yet it arrives precisely through the welling up of ethical conscience in the interiority of the I. Messianism is thus one way of talking about Levinas's conception of human subjectivity as fundamentally heterogeneous. We harbor the other within ourselves, and it is this internal presence of the other that moves us against our own egoism.

Homo homini lupus—"man is a wolf to man." The earliest known attestation and likely the origin of the phrase is found in the *Asinaria* of Plautus from the second century BCE. And just as we saw with the idea of "rational animal," the phrase transcends historical periodization. It occurs, for example, in Erasmus's *Adagia* from the early sixteenth century, and in Montaigne, Rabelais, Bacon, and Hobbes in the sixteenth and seventeenth centuries. We find it in Rousseau in the eighteenth century, and in both Freud's *Civilization and Its Discontents* and Lacan's *Écrits* in the twentieth century. A politics of the wolf is thus evident in the history of philosophy, or, as Derrida notes, and with Rousseau in mind, the wolf, sometimes as werewolf, is a privileged figure: "It is always a matter of the law and of placing the other outside the law. The law (*nomos*) is always determined from the place of some wolf" (*BS*, 96).

Plato's *Republic*, teeming with animals, shows us, moreover, that a lupine political philosophy has been underway since philosophy's beginnings. Socrates in the *Republic* states the following in his discussion of the ruler-turned-tyrant. Such a ruler,

> does not hold back from shedding the blood of his tribe but unjustly brings charges against a man—which is exactly what they usually do—and, bringing him before the court, murders him, and, doing away with a man's life, tastes of kindred blood with unholy tongue and mouth, and banishes, and kills, and hints at cancellations of debts and redistributions of land; isn't it also necessarily fated, I say, that after this such a man either be slain by his enemies or be a tyrant and turn from a human being into a wolf. (Book VIII: 565e–66a)

To behave unjustly from a position of political power—to be or become a tyrant—is thus to devour other human beings, and Socrates represents this with the image of a human being becoming a wolf. One cannot help but think of Socrates as a victim of such animal transformation. Who else, if not Socrates, is devoured by kinsmen through the issuing of unjust accusations followed by trial and execution? Who else but those Athenians complicit in the death of Socrates ought to be compared to the one who "does not hold back from shedding the blood of his tribe" and who "tastes of kindred blood"?

In deploying the image of the man becoming wolf, Socrates cites the ancient story of King Lycaon, mythic founder of the cult of Zeus in Arcadia, whom Zeus turned into a wolf for surreptitiously mixing human sacrificial flesh with animal flesh in order to test Zeus's claims to omniscience. Socrates references it in his comments on tyranny when he states that "the man who tastes of the single morsel of human inwards cut up with those of other sacrificial victims must necessarily become a wolf" (Book VIII: 565d–65e). To mix human flesh and animal flesh thus warrants being turned into a human/animal hybrid, and yet the implication is that Lycaon is already a hybrid, since his actions are too terrible, so it seems, to be committed by a human being. Lycaon—the name itself echoes with the secret of his destiny (λύκος = "wolf")—is thus one of the original literary lycanthropes: the wolf man or the werewolf.

In its original rendering in Plautus, the phrase reads: "*Lupus est homo homini, non homo, quom qualis sit non novit*"—"A wolf is a man for a man, and not a man, when one does not know which [man or wolf] he is."[9] The reference is to the stranger, since its meaning is that a man is taken to be a wolf by other men so long as he is not known or recognized. Plautus's statement suggests that human beings respond to strangers as if strangers were wolves, which is to say that we respond to strangers with fear. A similar view is put forth in Plato's *Republic*, here through the figure of the dog. Socrates in the *Republic* states, "[T]he disposition of noble dogs is to be as gentle as can be with their familiars and people they know, and the opposite with those they don't know" (Book II: 375e). The dog—companion and guardian of human beings, and cousin to the wolf—becomes fierce when face to face with a human being who is a stranger.

Where would we place the philosophy of Levinas with regard to such a wolf-turned-dog-turned-wolf? Levinas proposes that the measure of our ethics is the extent to which we can risk ourselves through displacing self-defensiveness and egoist indifference with hospitality and welcome. And Levinas, after all, is the preeminent thinker of ethics vis-à-vis the stranger. Central to Levinas's philosophical project is an ever-deepening questioning into ethics as an overcoming of the fear that makes us either violent or indifferent toward others, and especially toward those human beings who find themselves outside of the protective sphere of the human community.

Insofar as the stranger is the one whom I would otherwise regard with fear or indifference, the break with my natural egoism that Levinas has in mind could open critical reflection on the categories of neighbors versus strangers. And if this is the case, then we may want to ask whether such a break could occasion a rethinking of anthropocentrism or of any position that finds nonhuman animals to be nothing beyond their value as exploitable or consumable. All of these sites of engagement are potentially entailed in Levinas's notion of the break with being that initiates the welcome of the stranger, and yet it remains the case within his philosophy that this break is figured as a break with the animal.

What, then, is Levinas's explicit relationship to the *homo homini lupus*? Levinas's references suggest that the predecessor he has in mind is Hobbes, who includes *homo homini lupus* in the dedication of his *De Cive*. Hobbes writes, "There are two maxims which are surely both true: *Man is a God to man*, and *man is a wolf to man*. The former is true of the relation of citizens with each other, the latter of the relations between commonwealths."[10] Hobbes understands the condition between commonwealths to be a condition of perpetual war, which is the same condition that we find in Hobbes's state of nature between individuals—a condition Hobbes famously describes as "nasty, brutish [animal], and short."[11]

Levinas cites *homo homini lupus* in his essay "Ideology and Idealism." He writes, "[I]t is very important to know whether the state, society, law, and power are required because man is a beast to his neighbor (*homo homini lupus*) or because I am responsible for my fellow. It is very important to know whether the political order defines man's responsibility or merely restricts his bestiality" (*LR*, 247–48).[12] If we are ultimately only creatures of self-interest, then human society and politics are merely the expressions of a veiled, individualized egoism that seeks the cessation of war simply from the position of its own self-interest. But if political peace is not simply a peace brought about through rationalized egoism, and hence merely the illusion of peace, then the origins of human sociality and community might be found rather in an originary ethics.

One place in which Levinas evaluates a Hobbesian account of politics according to the figure of the animal is in his essay "Secularization and Hunger." Levinas writes,

> Yet the practical sense of men who, in a world at rest, think positively starting from being and bring all signification back to position, that is, to the *positivity* of the world in which one finds the given for taking, the daily bread, goods to accumulate, to store as reserves, or to display as merchandise—does this universal wisdom of the nations reduce to the effects of the empirical circumstances of man's needy organism, to the contingent apparition of a reasonable animality? *Is not the animal realm of the human also the bursting of the "gesture" of being* which carries all beings with it?[13]

Countless human phenomena have at their center the needs of the human being as a biological organism, and an entire world arises out of our conative effort to persist in being. As a result, these phenomena and this world are expressions of our animality no matter how sophisticated, rationalized, or scientifically advanced they become. The animal within produces the animal dimension of the human world around us—a world that is fundamentally marked by human beings' investment in their own persistence in being, and such that this investment has the potential to triumph over all other human commitments.

But what if our egoism is not at the center of the human world around us? In support of this possibility, Levinas writes of the liberal state as one that is "always concerned about its delay in meeting the requirement of the face of the other," and as one that "recognizes, beyond its institutions, the legitimacy—though it be a trans-political one—of the search for and defense of the rights of man" (*EN*, 203). We are indeed wolves to one another, but we are also human, and if our humanity founds human society, then the state and its institutions operating in the name of justice may indeed be oriented by concern for others, and hence by a justice worthy of the name. The image of the human being as both human and animal would then entail that there are two kinds of politics and two kinds of statehood: one driven by the egoist desire for survival and described by Machiavelli and Hobbes, and one by the humanity of the human being as we prevail over our animality.

How does the fate of nonhuman animals play out in this regard? In stark contrast to his predecessors, Levinas identifies the animal with our rationality (namely, our rationally calculating self-interestedness), and understands our rationality to be alienated from our humanity. Human society can be built on concern for others, but this is only because human beings can behave in ways that confirm our independence from nature. One consequence of this is that Levinas's image of human society oriented to justice can have no analogues in animal sociality, and this implies that even social animals are to be regarded as essentially egoist. As Bob Plant rightly states, "[T]he problem with Levinas's anti-naturalism is that it makes any other-oriented acts seem like a miracle."[14] In this way, Levinas's antinaturalism as applied to questions of politics and sociality entails that the only just society is an unnatural one, a notion that effectively removes nonhuman animals from the ethical relation.

Animal Greek, Human Hebrew

Levinas's positioning of the figure of the animal within the human being has further implications for nonhuman animals. These concern the way in which Levinas's opposition between the human and the animal is connected to a series of binaries that, like the figure of the animal itself, cross the divide between the within and the beyond vis-à-vis the human being. Some examples of those binaries that stand alongside animal/human are totality/infinity, said/saying, politics/ethics, Greek/Hebrew, and being/otherwise-than-being; while they do not each describe the same contrasting sets of ideas, each binary resonates with every other, with the result that the significance of any one binary is deepened when considered in light of the others.

The figure of the animal is positioned on the side of a kind of thinking that Levinas sometimes refers to as "Greek," and with ways of thinking and of being that Levinas associates with totality and with the said. The figure of the human, by contrast, is located on the side of the thinking that Levinas sometimes refers to as "Hebrew," and that is connected to Levinas's notions of infinity and of the saying. To think "Greek" is to think in a manner commensurate with totality, with the said, and in such a way that reflects the animal egoism at the heart of the human being, while to think "Hebrew" is to think in the mode of infinity, of the saying, and in such a way that reflects the humanness of the human being in its fulfillment of the human ethical vocation.

Given the associative network in which "Greek" and "Hebrew" modes of thinking are thus positioned, what is specifically entailed in a style of thinking that is more Hebrew than Greek, and hence that operates in the mode of infinity rather than of totality? Having introduced "Hebrew" and "Greek" alongside Levinas's other essential binaries, Oona Eisenstadt describes the "Hebrew" mode of thinking as the effort "to particularize universals, to break synthesis, to live in ruptured totalities, to call the judgment of history into question."[15] She notes, moreover, that the stakes involved in whether there can be such thinking are high, both for Levinas and for us.

> For, one could argue, if no one lives this way, Judaism will in the end be lost, meaning both the real Judaism will get lost in the imposition of global political totality, and also that Levinas's Hebrew—the way of thinking that respects alterity—will get lost in reciprocity. It may even be that Levinas's whole thought is at stake in this issue, since when particulars are subsumed by universals and asymmetry by identity, Levinasian ethics becomes an unheard echo.[16]

What we see, therefore, is that the kind of thinking that would resist the subsumption of particulars into universals has both epistemological and material consequences. A thinking that refuses the reduction of human beings to governing universals is one that can resist those institutions whose fundamental structures demand the expulsion of the nonidentical, and it is a thinking that makes room for alterity and difference.

Greek thinking, in these terms, is thus a totalizing form of thinking that subjects the other to conceptual mastery, while Hebrew thinking is on the side of infinity that encounters the other as always in excess of the categories to which this other is normally subjected. In reference to the kind of thinking characteristic of the latter, Levinas writes of "a relationship between terms such as are united neither by the synthesis of the understanding nor by a relationship between subject or object, and yet where the one weighs or concerns or is meaningful to the other, where they are bound by a plot which knowing can neither exhaust nor unravel" (CPP, 116n6). It is this alternative kind of thinking and the comportment toward others that it engenders that Derrida has in mind when he states, "Something of this call of the other must remain nonreappropriable, nonsubjectiveable, and in a certain way nonidentifiable, a sheer supposition, so as to remain other, a singular call to response or to responsibility."[17] This is the thinking on the side of the saying, and the implication of the saying is that the goal of conceptual mastery is displaced by an orientation toward the other founded in ethical responsiveness. Simply put, to think Greek is to regard the other as a thing to be known, while to think Hebrew is to regard the other as a being to whom I am ethically beholden.

These two forms of thinking extend into the sphere of politics, and are a potential basis for two kinds of communities and two kinds of political life. It is thinking on the side of totality, for example, that Nelson Maldonado-Torres discusses in his engagement with Levinas and decoloniality. Maldonado-Torres writes,

> He [Levinas] knows that while some people may be concerned with the future of ethics, others may be more interested in the achievement of lucidity. He is aware that there are many who are fully prepared to abandon ethics at the expense of even small advances in the search for knowledge. A civilization with this sense of priorities commits violence with good conscience.[18]

As Maldonado-Torres makes clear, the significance of Levinas's reflections on kinds of thinking extends to the structuring of the human world around us. There are consequences for those whose position vis-à-vis thinking in the mode of totality renders them violable or vulnerable to a suffering without redress. And where the conceptual, practical, or scientific appropriation of the world is more important than an ethical attunement that would intervene in order to end or prevent suffering, the most vulnerable among us—human or otherwise—are endangered by the rhetoric of advancement.

What Levinas struggles to achieve, therefore, is a different kind of writing—one that holds open the possibility of an encounter with alterity, and that is sufficiently suspicious of the philosophical pretension to having grasped and ordered the world into a comprehensive totality. Such thinking requires a different kind of writing, a turn toward styles of thinking and writing that resist rather than achieve mastery of their subject. To be capable of this may require reaching beyond the strictly philosophical and into other modes of textuality, or as Matthieu Dubost writes,

> He [Levinas] must therefore find something that allows him to be a philosopher, to commence with a classical and comprehensible language, without at the same time betraying his thought. For this, Levinas takes on the project of language in a manner that approaches the literary.[19]

A similar interpretation is offered by Elena Arseneva, who writes, "Levinas has us discover foreign horizons, a language irreducible to its thesis."[20] The betrayal of the singular other endemic to thinking Greek calls into question conceptual thought itself, and suggests that we must hear our philosophizing differently. In our relationship to the creative, productive side of philosophy, we will need to shelter the possibility of interruption in the mode of critique.

What do these reflections on Greek versus Hebrew modes of thinking imply for nonhuman animals in Levinas's philosophy? To take just one example, Levinas in "The Animal Interview" states, "We do not want to make an animal suffer needlessly" (*AI*, 4), and "But the prototype of this is human ethics" (4). In circumscribing the ethical to the domain of the interhuman, one wonders whether Levinas has not opted for totality rather than for an interruption of totality that might cede ground to an undefined infinity. If this is the case, then Levinas's position as it now stands would need to be understood on his terms as a moment of animal thinking pitted against animals.

On the other hand, in beginning with the statement that we do not want to make an animal needlessly suffer—in referring to *suffering*—Levinas interrupts his own conceptual figuration of the animal with a gesture toward animals in their existential concreteness. This brings to us an image of animals, not so much as things to be known and to be grasped conceptually, but as beings who can be caught in the throes of something into which we might intervene ethically. In this instance, we are seeing the predominance of infinity over totality and of Hebrew over Greek, and hence of human thinking over animal thinking, but for the sake of animals.

Yet, are we sure that the sentence "We do not want to make an animal suffer needlessly" announces the singularity of nonhuman animals through the acknowledgment of suffering? Or does it perpetuate a notion of human exceptionalism through its intimating that some animal suffering is necessary, and hence that some forms of suffering are positioned beyond the reach of ethical intervention constitutively and permanently? If so, then does this suggest that nonhuman animals remain forever vulnerable in Levinas's philosophy to human ends—a paradigm so strenuously in place, therefore, that even the acknowledgment of suffering cannot quite interrupt it? And does the persistence of this paradigm thus signal the victory of Greek thinking over Hebrew, which is to say of the human/animal conceptual binary over the disruptive force of suffering, and hence of animal thinking over human thinking to the detriment of animals?

Animal thinking against animals, or human thinking against animal thinking for the sake of animals–either way, the fate of the nonhuman animal appears impossibly ambiguous. Levinas's handling of nonhuman animals remains ambivalent, ambiguous, and hence precarious despite moments of opening onto more comprehensively ethical and just possibilities. We are caught in the tangle of an ethics of alterity that has conceptually circumscribed that alterity in a gesture that is nothing other than one of totality, and in a rhetoric that has committed to this circumscription from the outset.

Conclusion

For Levinas, the animal is a figure for the deprivation of human ethics. The animal is constituted in opposition to the human, and yet is located within human subjectivity as a figure for the egoism and the indifference to others that Levinas identifies with nature and with all nonhuman living things. Simultaneously a figure for the other-than-human and for an essential and irrevocable dimension of human subjectivity, the animal is the site of a complex and contradictory mix of identification and rejection on Levinas's terms. As a result, to be human is to be not-animal, but also to be forever confronting one's animality.

To engage in the work of unhinging the conceptual totalities that stand in the way of ethics is to be human rather than to be animal, hence we must ask to what extent such unhinging can include the liberation of nonhuman animals from their confinement within the terms set by Levinas's human/animal binary. It is this difficulty that our analysis of "The Animal Interview" attempted to diagnose. Despite forging an account of the meaning of ethics oriented by the alterity of the concrete other, and despite addressing himself explicitly to the question of animals and ethics, Levinas's liberatory potential vis-à-vis nonhuman animals is here marred by his committed anthropocentrism and by his deployment of the human/animal binary. And insofar as Levinas states in a variety of places and in myriad ways that the catastrophes of human history result from a *failure to not be animal*, the erasure of an ethically significant other has taken place, and calls for a rethinking of both the human and the animal.

Locating the animal within the human entails that Levinas's human being is fated to two ways of being, to two destinies, and to two ways of thinking. And while one of these ways of thinking reentrenches the human/animal binary of Levinas's rhetoric, the other holds the promise of its interruption, and it does so perhaps even despite having originated within a semantic framework complicit with the binary itself. Such an interruption would introduce the possibility of a break with the binary's conceptual tyranny over the singularity of animal others, and could provoke a rethinking of the human/animal binary itself. Does this not thereby announce an ethical opening toward nonhuman animals, even in the face of everything in Levinas's philosophy that serves to stave this off as a sustained possibility? And what could such a way of thinking mean for nonhuman animals, after all, if not the mobilization of Levinas's best insights against one of his more prominent shortcomings?

Notes

1. Jacques Derrida, *The Beast and the Sovereign: Vol. I*, eds. Michel Lisse, Marie-Louise Mallet, and Ginette Michaud, trans. Geoffrey Bennington (Chicago, IL: University of Chicago Press, 2009), *26*. Hereafter cited as *BS*.

2. Aquinas, *Summa Theologica: Vol. 1*, trans. Fathers of the English Dominican Province (Notre Dame, IN: Christian Classics, 1981), 57.

3. Ibid., 71. A more contemporary citation is that of Oscar Wilde, who makes humorous reference to it when his character Gilbert says to Ernest, "[M]an is a rational animal who always loses his temper when he is called upon to act in accordance with the dictates of reason." Oscar Wilde, "The Critic as Artist," *Intentions* (London: Methuen, 1934), 182.

4. Kelly Oliver, *Animal Lessons: How They Teach Us to Be Human* (New York: Columbia University Press, 2013), 71. Rousseau himself treats the formulation "rational animal" in order to critique it, highlighting instead capacities such as pity as most significant to the humanness of the human being. See, for example, Rousseau's *Second Discourse*, and specifically his polemic against Hobbes.

5. Jacques Lacan, "A Theoretical Introduction to the Functions of Psychoanalysis in Criminology," in *Écrits*, trans. Bruce Fink, in collaboration with Héloïse Fink and Russell Grigg (New York: W. W. Norton and Company, 2006), *120*.

6. Niccolò Machiavelli, *The Prince*, ed. and trans. David Wootton (Cambridge, MA: Hackett Publishing Company, 1995), 54.

7. The rhetoric of the animal within also filters into the scholarly literature on Levinas. As Jean-François Rey writes: "Tout se passe comme si l'animalité était une possibilité de l'humain, comme si la vie pouvait prendre deux directions opposées: celle du désintéressement ou celle de l'animalité. Avec Levinas, il y a intégration de l'animalité dans l'humanité, mais seul l'humain désintéressé, l'humain advenu à lui-même, est débarrassé de l'animalité" (*La Mesure de l'homme:* L'Idée *d'humanité dans la philosophie d'Emmanuel Levinas* [Paris: Éditions Michalon, 2001], 198). ("Everything takes place as if animality were a possibility of the human, as if life could take two opposite directions: that of disinterestedness or that of animality. With Levinas, there is the integration of animality in humanity, but only the disinterested human, the human having arrived to himself, is released of animality.")

8. Catherine Chalier, "The Messianic Utopia," trans. Andrew Slade, in *Graduate Faculty Philosophy Journal* 20/21, no. 1/2 (1998): 281–96. As Chalier notes, Levinas is explicitly following Rabbi Nachman in the tractate *Sanhedrin* (98b–99a), where Nachman locates the coming of the Messiah with the human I that fulfills its humanity.

9. Titus Maccius Plautus, *Asinaria,* line 495; personal translation.

10. Thomas Hobbes, *On the Citizen*, eds. Richard Tuck and Michael Silverthorne (Cambridge, UK: Cambridge University Press, 1998), 3–4.

11. Thomas Hobbes, *Leviathan*, ed. Edwin Curley (Indianapolis, IN: Hackett Publishing Company, 1994), 76.

12. See also *IR*, 68; 230.

13. Emmanuel Levinas, "Secularization and Hunger," in *Graduate Faculty Philosophy Journal* 20/21, 2/1 (1998): 10. Levinas will often use the animal as a figure for the violence in politics, but not exclusively. In the Talmudic essay "Damages Due to Fire," Levinas writes, "But perhaps the elemental force of fire is already the intervention of the uncontrollable, of war" (*NT*, 185). Annabel Herzog states in this regard: "Like Camus who, in *The Plague*, used the metaphor of the bubonic plague to personify Nazism, Levinas associates a natural process with human calamity" ("Dogs and Fire: The Ethics and Politics of Nature in Levinas," *Political Theory* 41, no. 3 [2013]: 364).

14. Bob Plant, *Wittgenstein and Levinas: Ethical and Religious Thought* (New York: Routledge, 2005), 229n136.

15. Oona Eisenstadt, "Levinas versus Levinas: Hebrew, Greek, and Linguistic Justice," *Philosophy and Rhetoric* 38, no. 2 (2005): 147–48.

16. Ibid., 148.

17. Jacques Derrida, "'Eating Well,' or the Calculation of the Subject: An Interview with Jacques Derrida," in *Who Comes after the Subject?*, eds. Eduardo Cadava, Peter Connor, and Jean-Luc Nancy (New York and London: Routledge, 1991), 110–11.

18. Nelson Maldonado-Torres, *Against War: Views from the Underside of Modernity* (Durham, NC, and London: Duke University Press, 2008), 51.

19. "Il faut donc trouver quelque chose qui lui permette d'être philosophe, de commencer par un langage classique et compréhensible, sans pour autant trahir sa pensée. Pour cela, E. Lévinas s'oblige à un travail du langage qui est proche d'une exigence littéraire." Matthieu Dubost, "Emmanuel Lévinas et la littérature: De l'herméneutique éthique à la langue originelle," *Revue Philosophique de Louvain* 104, no. 2 (2006): 302; personal translation.

20. "E. Levinas nous fait découvrir des horizon *étrangers*, une langue irréductible à sa thèse." Elena Arseneva, "Lévinas et le jeu des langues: La Russie à Auteuil," in *Revue Philosophique de Louvain* 100, no. 1 (2002): 65; personal translation.

CHAPTER 10

What Is the Trace of the Original Face?

Levinas, Buddhism, and the Mystery of Animality

BRIAN SHŪDŌ SCHROEDER

The paradox of the Zen *kōan*[1] resists in a significantly different way what Emmanuel Levinas identifies as the totalizing "way of the same" (*TI*, 38–39). Zen Buddhism provides a critical insight into faciality that goes beyond Levinas's fundamentally anthropocentric view and undercuts his refusal of "paganism," thereby providing the ground for a deeper realization of the ethical relationship between humans and animals. The question at hand is whether there exists a fundamental experience of the "original face" (Jp. *honrai no memmoku*)[2] of the animal, which is possible only by way of a direct face-to-face encounter.[3] After making initial observations regarding the relation between the face of the animal and Buddha-nature, I explore what is often an overlooked aspect of Levinas's philosophy when it comes to applying his philosophy to environmental ethics, namely, the status of the trace (*la trace*) and its relation to ethical transcendence. After a brief reflection on the difference between asymmetry and symmetry, and the relation of this difference to ethical transcendence, I contrast Levinas's position with the paganism that he critiques. Considering Buddhism as somewhat analogous to paganism, the tension between those perspectives highlights what is at stake in understanding our relation to the nonhuman animal in order to think the metaphysical-ontological dimension of the ethics of that relationship. I conclude by taking up the concept of mystery and consider how this standpoint possibly serves as a way to address the relation between ethical responsibility and transcendence that avoids the fundamentally anthropocentric dimension of the Levinasian interpretation of the trace. Rather than castigating the concept of mystery, as Levinas does, I propose that mystery is a necessary and funda-mental dimension of establishing an ethical relationship with the nonhuman animal. It is at this juncture that Levinas and Zen Buddhism are brought into proximity through their respective understanding of the role that teaching plays in the self-other relationship.

Animal Faces and Buddha-Nature

There is a famous Zen *kōan* usually stated as the following question: "What was your original face before your parents were born?"[4] Here a distinction is posed between the original and the phenomenal face. A typically Western prejudgment would be to construe this in terms of a transhistorical or metaphysical reality as opposed to a historical or phenomenal one. This misses, however, the point of the *kōan*. Buddhism eschews such metaphysical speculation and dualistic frameworks as ultimately meaningless. From its standpoint, emptiness (Sk. *śūnyatā*; Jp. *kū*)[5] and phenomenality (Sk. *tathātā*) indicate a state of originary interdependence or dependent origination (Sk. *prat tyasamutpāda*).[6] In other words, something simply is before it is identified as being this or that. There is nothing that arises in existence independently and stands alone. All beings and *dharmas* (or things) are interconnected. Realizing this fundamental nature of existence constitutes wisdom (Sk. *prajñā*) and allows compassion (Sk. *karu ā*) to emerge. This is the two-pillared heart of Buddhist ethics.

Zen Buddhism has maintained since the time when the historical Buddha, Siddhartha Gautama or Śākyamuni,[7] silently passed along his teaching to his follower and immediate successor, Kāshyapa, that the "face-to-face" relation-ship is the locus of Dharma[8] transmission. Similarly, according to Levinas, the face-to-face relationship is the modality of intersubjective existence that conveys the absolute passive demand of the ethical relation, which is a teaching that goes forth from the Other (*Autrui*),[9] as though from a height (*hauteur*), to the self. Levinas's interpretation of the face-to-face relationship parallels the Zen recognition of the necessity of the master in transmitting the Buddha-dharma to the student. The thirteenth-century Japanese Zen master Eihei Dōgen writes: "Masters and disciples always see one another when transmitting and inheriting the Dharma. This is the realization of the way, face-to-face transmission of the ancestral source. . . . Even without knowing one word or understanding half a phrase, the teacher sees the student within himself, and the student lowers the top of his head; this is the correct face-to-face transmission."[10]

Is this true also of the relationship between humans and animals? Is Dharma transmission possible between humans and animals? Another well-known *kōan*, which is the first case in the *Wumenkuan* (Jp. *Mumonkan*), asks, "Does a dog have Buddha-nature?," to which the Chan (Zen) master Zhaozhou (Jp. Jōshū) responds with an emphatic "No!" (Ch. *wu*; Jp. *mu*). Although one might at first think that this simple answer would have closed the matter, it actually inspired considerable commentary through the ages. However, the matter is made even more complicated by the fact that there are several versions of this *kōan*. In one of those, Zhaozhou gives conflicting answers.

> A monk asked Chao-chou [Zhaozhou]: "Does a dog have the Buddha-nature or not?" Chao-chou said: "Yes." The monk said, "If it does, then why does the Buddha-nature push into such a (lowly) bag of skin?" Chao-chou said: "Because it does it knowingly, deliberating transgressing." Then another monk asked: "Does a dog have the Buddha-nature?" Chao-chou said: "No." The monk said: "All sentient beings without exception have the Buddha-nature. For what reason then does a dog not have it?" Chao-chou said: "Because it exists in karmic consciousness."[11]

Zhaozhou's answer goes beyond mere ambivalence or paradox. The term *wu/mu* means "no," but it also signifies "not," "nothing," "non-being," or "have not." It is the opposite in meaning of *u*, which means "yes," but also "is," "being," or "have." In the everyday context, *mu* and *u* are relative terms. Zhaozhou's *wu/mu*, however, was not a relative answer but rather an absolute reply. The inquiring monk was not only asking about the particular dog but whether all sentient beings possess Buddha-nature. Zhaozhou's response was an attempt to sever all attachment the monk had to the very concept of Buddha-nature.

To say that Buddha-nature is either this or that, or neither this nor that, is to adopt a standpoint that invariably falls into either a substantializing or essentializing ontology, or what Levinas refers to as the totalizing logic of *theōria*, the imperialistic way of the same. Zhaozhou understood that all attempts logically to construe the meaning of Buddha-nature invariably fall into paradoxical absurdity. The absolute *wu* or *u* indicates the impossibility of all intellection to thoroughly comprehend the Dharma-nature of reality. Buddha-nature must be *experienced*. Only after the experience is it perhaps possible to render linguistically its meaning, but such language will be nonsensical to those who are not personally experienced, that is, who have not at least partially awakened to the truth of the karmically interdependent character of Buddha-nature.

To ask whether a dog has Buddha-nature is tantamount to asking whether all animals have Buddha-nature. Before that question can be *philosophically* answered, one needs also to inquire about the nature of Buddha-nature. To even make that very inquiry is to risk ontologizing Buddha-nature, that is, rendering it either as a conceptual object or something that exists. Buddha-nature is neither. And yet Śākyamuni Buddha himself speaks of Buddha-nature as that which must be affirmed. But if Buddha-nature is beyond predication, then how can it possibly be affirmed? Here Buddhism and Levinas stand in close proximity. The Other is affirmed as other, and conversely the absolutely other is affirmed as the Other, precisely by refusing to associate affirmation with an ultimate naming, identification, or classification. In other words, by not total-izing otherness under the hegemony of self-same Reason.

If we try to unpack the meaning of the *kōan* further, we engage the Buddhist concept of *karma*, which means literally act or deed, but also conveys the interconnectedness of all beings as well as the idea that Buddha-nature is, in some sense, only actual if it is realized in consciousness. Here, this does not refer to whether a dog (or any other nonhuman animal) is cognizant or not of Buddha-nature, but rather whether we are capable of moving beyond an anthropocentic standpoint such that we can simultaneously affirm both the presence and nonpresence of Buddha-nature in the nonhuman animal. In other words, this signifies a movement beyond a simple dualistic standpoint and points toward a realization that Buddha-nature is fundamentally ineffable and, moreover, to use Levinas's language, "otherwise than"—not being or essence—what can be known absolutely by rational thinking. This is the breakthrough that the *kōan* points toward, but which is only fully realized when one truly lets go of such thinking and experiences the emptiness—not nothingness—of all things, human *and* nonhuman, which is to say, the fundamental interconnectedness of impermanent beings and things. According to Dōgen, the "face-to-face" relationship is the locus of Dharma transmission in the Zen tradition.[12] "If you can understand the real movement," he states, "you will understand true enlightenment and awakening. If we can understand 'Buddha,' we can understand 'nature,' since they penetrate each other."[13] Here one begins to have a glimpse of insight into what the "original face" of Buddha-nature really is. Transmis-sion of what the Buddha terms the "treasury of the true Dharma eye" refers to when the fundamental unity between the seer and the seen, Buddha and nature, human and nonhuman, is established. This is "going beyond Buddha, [which] is neither causality nor fruition. However, there is realization-through-the-body and complete attainment of 'you don't hear it' at the moment of talking."[14] The significance of the face resonates throughout one's being, both body and mind, leading one to identify-in-difference-all-beings. This is the basis of an ethical relationship with animals in Zen Buddhist thought.

"One cannot entirely refuse the face of the dog," writes Levinas. "It is in terms of the face [that one understands] the dog. . . . The parentage of this phenomenon of the face is not at all in the dog. . . . It is not because you recognize the human face that you see the face of the dog" (*AI*, 3). Perhaps this is a vital clue for determining whether animals possess Buddha-nature, and whether that realization is transmittable. If the Buddha-face can be "brought forth," as Dōgen claims, it is because it is already "there," that is, originally existing. Dependent origination precludes the possibility of something arising out of nothing, since such a thing would be independent. The original face is the Buddha-face, which is to say, Buddha-nature. Yet there is a relational priority that exists in terms of realizing this. For Levinas, "the human face is completely different and only afterwards do we discover the face of an animal."[15] The face of one who is awakened is different from that of one who is not. So it is with the relationship between master and disciple, teacher and student. The Buddha-nature of the animal is what makes possible the realization of the interconnectedness between the human and the nonhuman animal. This is only recognized by one who has seen the "face" of the other being in a *nondual* perspective. Grasping the relation between Buddha-nature and animality necessitates a fundamental experience of the original face of the animal, which in turn is possible only by way of a direct face-to-face encounter. Buddha-nature is not something that can be cognitively known; it must be *actualized*, which is to say, transmitted between two beings fully present and aware of each other in the moment of transmission.

One of the defining features of Zen that distinguishes it from other approaches in Buddhism is that awakening is understood as a simultaneously occurring activity between the one who attains realization and the one who acknowledges it. While the relationship between the disciple and the master in this regard is unquestioned in the Zen Buddhist tradition, it also occurs, though admittedly far less frequently, in the relationship between humans and animals. Buddhism extends the teaching relationship that for Levinas constitutes the essence of the ethical beyond the merely human face to face to include the animal. Stated otherwise, animals are also teachers of the Dharma, and therefore beings worthy of full ethical consideration.[16]

Although not the principal focus of the present essay, I would be remiss not to address, however briefly, the relation between the full ethical consideration of animals and the practice of eating meat. This is not a consideration for Levinas, whose own tradition allows for the consumption of meat, albeit in its strictest form under *kashrut*, the set of Jewish dietary laws. Buddhism, on the other hand, has since its inception held a different perspective. Although the concept of "law" is foreign to it, Buddhism does adhere to "precepts," that is, to general guidelines to help regulate both thought and action. Theravāda, or early, Buddhism formulated numerous precepts for those following the monastic path, but at the top of the list for both monastics and laity is the precept against taking the life of other living beings, both human and nonhuman. This prohibition was also adopted by the later Mahāyāna and Vajrayāna forms of Buddhism and stands as the first of the essential or great precepts. Levinas establishes the commandment against murder as the first word that inaugurates the ethical relationship. Buddhism, along with Hinduism and Jainism, extends this notion of killing to include the animal, founding it on the general ethical principal of doing no injury or harm (Sk. *ahimsā*) to others. Some forms of Mahāyāna Buddhism, which includes Zen, with its expanded focus on the bodhisattva[17] as the highest ideal, developed what are sometimes referred to as the three pure precepts—to do no evil, to do good, and to liberate all beings—which go hand in hand with the practice of *ahimsā* and a plant-based diet. Seen from this perspective (the Christian sacrament of Eucharist aside), the practice of devouring one's Dharma teacher would indeed seem strange if not repulsive.

Transcendence and the Trace

Levinas associates the elemental and the pagan with the concepts of immanence, mystery, and enchantment, which he rejects on the grounds of their coercive, violent tendency to render the subject susceptible both to domination and to exercising the power of dominating. Yet most attempts to derive a nonhuman ethics from Levinas's philosophy basically try to paganize his distinctively Jewish-based philosophy. In doing so, they arguably commit a violence against Levinas's own text since all violence on the field of ethical relationships occurs first in thought, according to Levinas. A critical dimension that is often overlooked when considering the application of Levinas's conception of ethics to nonhuman animals is the notion of the *trace*.[18] In Levinas's hermeneutic, the trace is a disturbance, a disruption that produces interiority by causing the same to recognize and respond, even if negatively or apathetically, to the exteriority of the other. The face of the Other is the trace of the passing of a remote, never present, immemorial, heteronomous past;[19] a "*signification without a context*" (*TI*, 23), the "already said" (*OB*, 183). It is not simply because the Other is other than the self that the Other has an ethical priority. According to Levinas, the first ethical teaching of the Other—the prohibition against murder—is found in the "face" (*visage*) of the Other, which is the trace of what is "otherwise than being," an absolute, infinite other that Levinas does not hesitate to name repeatedly in both his philosophical and religious, or confessional, writings as "God." The height that both summons and commands is for Levinas nothing other than divinity, the source of all signification and the locus of all ethical movement revealed in the trace. And yet, the trace of the absolutely other, revealed in and as the face of the other person, exposes the meaning of transcendence as *sociality*, as the interpersonal relationship with the Other: "The absolutely other is the Other" (*TI*, 39). Levinasian transcendence is ethical because it *is* ethics.

A primary approach of many who have tried to employ Levinas in the service of constructing an animal ethics has been either to extend the concept of the face to include those of the nonhuman other, sentient or nonsentient (for example, the face of a mountain), or to ignore altogether the distinctive metaphysical dimension of transcendence, subsequently effecting a reduction to an ontological transcendence, a critical difference posed primarily in *Totality and Infinity*. "Transcendence," writes Levinas,

> designates a relation with a reality infinitely distant from my own reality, yet without this distance destroying this relation and without this relation destroying this distance, as would happen with relations within the same. . . . We have called this relation metaphysical. . . . It is prior to the negative or affirmative proposition; it first institutes language, where neither the no nor the yes is the first word. (*TI*, 41–42)

In this passage, Levinas is both removed from and yet close to the Zen understanding of the Buddha-dharma. Unlike the Levinasian understanding of the infinite distance between the same and the other, Buddha-nature collapses this difference into what it would consider to be a nontotalizing unity or whole while at the same time, like Levinas, maintaining that the Buddha-nature is beyond positive or negative proposition.

Despite Levinas's own retention and subsequent redefinition of the term *transcendence*, at least in his earlier work, this is a discussion also occurring in some circles of Levinas scholarship, centered on the question of whether Levinas is principally a secular or a religious thinker. It seems, to me at any rate, that the majority of those who want to extend Levinas's thinking into the domain of environmental ethics tend to situate him in the former category. Yet, despite his turn toward a deeper consideration of immanence, or at least of those aspects of being generally associated with immanence, Levinas's interpretation of the ethical is predicated on the possibility of being able to leave the Earth—that is, to break the hold of the totality of being—in order to be exposed to the transcendence of the radically other, in other words, to that which is otherwise than being.

An interesting and innovative approach is to take recourse to a deconstructive move that locates an element of undecidability that opens ethical transcendence to the nonhuman dimension; however, this falls short in its assertive assumption that transcendence necessarily signifies ethics. A case in point rests with an example that is often cited by those wishing to read Levinas with an eye toward a nonhuman conception of ethics. In his essay titled "The Name of a Dog, or Natural Rights," Levinas remarks, after considering the biblical passage in Exodus that notes the role dogs played in liberating Israel during the slaying of the firstborn by the Egyptians, "a transcendence in the animal!" (*DF*, 152). He then describes his experience with a dog while he was a prisoner of war, ironically referring to the dog as "the last Kantian in Nazi Germany" (*DF*, 153). This is a significant passage for those who want to argue that the basis for an ethical relation with animals exists in the framework of Levinas's philosophy. This rather idiosyncratic account disrupts the coherency of Levinas's otherwise consistent position regarding ethics as a matter solely concerning the interhuman relationship. Because the dog represents an interruption in Levinas's thinking about ethics, it could be argued that this allows for a space to extend the concept of transcendence to include the ethical relation to the nonhuman animal. An interruption, however, is not necessarily an ethical signal, nor is the desire to incorporate certain terminology a justification for reading into Levinas a dimension that simply is not present in his thinking, and not present for very strong and committed religious reasons.

Why should the other be granted some higher ethical status than the self? All animal and environmental ethics entail a sense of obligation to nature, even if the precise ground or nature of this obligation is contestable. Yet it is indeed the very ground of ethical responsibility that Levinas insists on. Levinasian ethics centers on the concern about and sense of responsibility for the Other in her or his exposure and vulnerability. The face of the other human is prioritized by Levinas because of its capacity for speech and appeal. Whether it is possible to extend this dimension to include the nonhuman animal face is the crux of the matter. From one perspective, animals are certainly vulnerable and many species, such as dogs, display what can easily be construed as emotion and needs, and are able to communicate these feelings accordingly. From another perspective, the vulnerability and relative weakness of animals, compared to the technologically superior human being, serves as the basis for an argument against any feeling of ethical responsibility toward the nonhuman and instead suggest rather a relation of domination by the human over the animal. This latter view is certainly not shared by Buddhist thinking, nor is it supported by Levinas's philosophy, even if he does draw a distinction between the human and nonhuman in terms of the extent of responsibility.

The status of ethical responsibility in Levinas is inseparable from the origin of responsibility. A difficulty for many readers of Levinas is that the relation between responsibility and the trace invariably forces one to address the question of God. In his philosophical (as opposed to his confessional) writings, Levinas draws inspiration and support for his use of the terms *transcendence* and *God* most notably from Plato's idea of the Good as *epekeina tēs ousias* and Descartes's *idée de l'infini*, elucidated in his "Third Meditation," as the thought that is overflowed by its *ideatum*. Yet this does not mean that Levinas affirms the Cartesian conception of the subject as the inheritance of the medieval concept of substance. While this may indeed be true for Descartes, this is decidedly not Levinas's conception of God, since it reduces God (even understood as infinite substance, as it is for Descartes) to being. The force of Levinas's argument regarding the ethical primacy of the Other and the irreversibility of the self's responsibility, not only for itself but for the other as well, rests precisely on the inability of thought to conceive God, thereby signaling our incapacity to approach the Other as simply another self. This question of God is important because God is the "wholly otherwise,"[20] signified in the trace that is present as an absolute passivity in the face of the Other. It is to the face as the trace of the absolutely other that the self responds in the ethical relationship; that is, to the realization that the other always stands outside comprehension, or to put it otherwise, outside the ontological scope of theory or philosophy. In this sense, ethics precedes ontology.

The Other is ethically significant because the face of the other (*l'autre*) is the trace of an absolute alterity, a movement that indicates what is otherwise than being. The concept of the trace, which Levinas expressly connects in numerous places in his writing to the thought of God, is precisely what needs to be addressed, if one is to avoid merely falling back into the simplistic claim that there is an inherent or intrinsic value to nature that ultimately must be acknowledged and respected. Would this not ground, however, a Levinasian animal and environmental ethics in some sense not of the sacred (*sacré*) but instead of the holy (*saint*)?[21] Levinas would of course reject this move, as would many others for understandable and philosophically justifiable reasons, even if they do not follow Levinas here. It is incumbent on them, however, to explain why the notion of the trace, which is so fundamental to Levinas's project, can or should be ignored or transformed, and if so then what supplies the content to the formalism of the ethical relation between the self and the Other.

Asymmetry and Symmetry

The notion of the trace refers back to the radical difference of the other (human and nonhuman), and the asymmetrical, nonreciprocal demand or obligation of responsibility that the other imposes on the self. This is the crucial dimension of Levinas's thinking on which his entire conception of ethics is based. If the face is considered without reference to the trace, as is often the case in numerous nonreligious interpretations of Levinas, the ethical is stripped of its very force. But is it possible to retain a sense of ethical transcendence that is not predicated on a radical asymmetry? From a Buddhist perspective, it is.

David Wood is a pioneering voice in the area of environmental philosophy and animal ethics. Although not a Buddhist, he offers a similar analysis that supports a symmetrical conception of the ethical relation. Wood is also a thinker of immanence, and in this respect he shares similar ground with Buddhist thinking. He takes up the challenge that Levinas poses regarding the relation between the ethical and the ontological, but what is noticeably absent in his analysis of Levinas is the importance of the role of transcendence. While I am not prone to follow Wood to the point of declaring "Where Levinas Went Wrong" (I might phrase it "Where Levinas Goes Otherwise"), the title of the third chapter of his *The Step Back*, I am sympathetic to the concerns he raises, particularly with regard to his charge that Levinas's construal of the history of metaphysics as ontology and his, at least early, opposition of ethics and ontology, is problematic in its reductionism. For Wood, this opposition of ethics and ontology reveals itself principally in what he terms the "dangerous" opposition between the asymmetrical and the symmetrical. He writes,

> If we understand the ethical relation to the other as purely asymmetrical, we are establishing this relation on the same grounds, with a reversed valence, as those that allow the greatest violence. Asymmetry is just what characterizes the relation between overwhelming power and victimhood. And what worries me here is that focusing on the relation of asymmetry will distract us from thinking about those *complex forms of mutual dependency and interaction* that would block a simple reversal of the valency of the relation . . . how the asymmetrical relation of obligation can be productively conjoined with symmetrical relations (of friendship, cooperation, negotiation, etc.).[22]

Wood's reading rests on the question of whether it is possible, much less meaningful, to separate ontology from ethics, since for him the actualization of ethics, as well as social and political relations, "demands of us . . . that we focus on the theoretical and practical tasks . . . that open up ever more complex symmetries, and mixed forms of symmetry and asymmetry."[23] What is implied in asymmetry is not only the notion of height, to which Wood correctly directs our attention elsewhere in his book, but equally the irreversibility, to which he alludes in the passage cited above, of the ethical relation that obligates the self to assume an infinite responsibility for the Other without expectation of reciprocity. Indeed, this is the heart of the ethical relation, namely, the face-to-face relationship, which is always and primordially dyadic in character. This is precisely where Levinas is most problematic for many philosophers, as this is where he leaves the climate of philosophy, despite his declared identity as a phenomenologist with regard to method, and moves to the dimension of religion, albeit understood as the relation with the other person and not with a transcendent God per se. As Wood adroitly draws to our attention though, the question of God cannot be simply ignored or bypassed. It is here that one may contest Wood's reading, which suggests that Levinas remains confined to the strictures of ontotheology or traditional metaphysics.

Wood's concerns might perhaps be addressed by reading Levinas alongside of Jean-Luc Nancy. One finds expressed in Nancy a conception of community that not only allows for difference but is also predicated on it, "the inoperative community" (*la communauté désoeuvrée*)[24] that neither opposes universality and difference nor collapses them into an ontologically comprehensible unity. Such a conception of community inverts Levinas's stance on separated being as that which makes being-in-common possible, an inversion that subsequently radicalizes the idea of transcendence as a fully *immanent* transcendence. Nancy's notion of transcendence parallels Levinas's, insofar as it is also primarily a movement toward the other, though not compelled by a metaphysical desire (either *désir* or *Begierde*).[25] And while for Nancy "community is the community of *others*,"[26] transcendence is radical exposure to the limit of existence, which is finitude itself. In this shared space of finite being, singularities are able to form community though their mutual exposure, producing perhaps the very event that Wood calls for and that Buddhism identifies as dependent origination.

Dōgen provides helpful insight here. He affirms that the "mountains, rivers, and the great earth are all the ocean of Buddha-nature" insofar as they "all depend on Buddha-nature."[27] This dependency surpasses all understanding, yet it is all around us. "If this is so, to see mountains and rivers is to see Buddha-nature."[28] By extension, to see animals is also to see Buddha-nature, and when this occurs we also see into our own true nature. In a radical move, Dōgen rejects the limitation of those positions to only sentient beings and expands the concept of Buddha-nature, in accordance with his expansion of the concept of mind, to include both sentient and nonsentient beings, as well as ever-changing phenomena and states of consciousness. "Buddha-nature is always *whole being*."[29] In other words, Buddha-nature is self-creating and this self-creation is a perpetual re-creation, which is the meaning of dependent origination.

Paganism and Mystery

Despite numerous provocative and interesting attempts to assign ethical significance to the elemental or *il y a*, or to broaden the concept of the face to include the natural world and nonhuman others, Levinas's own treatment of the ethical is delimited, due to the very nature of its approach, by the question of the interpersonal face-to-face relationship. Certainly, there are indicators in his work that seem not to preclude entirely the possibility of broadening his conception of ethics to include at least some dimension of our relation with nonhuman entities, such as animals. Nevertheless, the task of formulating a Levinasian ground for an environmental or animal ethics is problematic, especially when considering his interpretation of paganism and by extension the natural world.

Levinas's construal of paganism is determined largely by his Judaic background and his reaction to the *Blut und Boden* ideology of Nazism. Via a polemic against Hegel, Heidegger, and practically the entire history of Western ontology, including Christianity, he associates the elemental with a retention and promotion of the concept of mystery. "Here we have," he writes, "the eternal seduction of paganism, beyond the infantilism of idolatry, which long ago was surpassed. *The sacred filtering into the world*—Judaism is perhaps no more than the negation of all that. To destroy the sacred groves—we understand now the purity of this apparent vandalism. The mystery of things is the source of cruelty towards [humankind]" (*DF*, 232). Elsewhere, in a discussion on the image, Levinas castigates the "mystery of being" (*CPP*, 3) (and by extension paganism) along the same lines as "magic, song, music, and poetry" (*CPP*, 7), because they enchant, that is, indicate "a hold over us" (*CPP*, 3), thus rendering us susceptible to domination. Conversely, a subject capable of being so dominated is a subject capable of domination. According to Levinas, the natural enjoyment of the elemental can easily slide into or lend itself to a perspective that is either blind to or refuses the dimension of transcendence that makes all ethical sensibility possible. In other words, in this natural enjoyment (*jouissance*), the absolute alterity of goodness is eschewed in favor of the elemental anonymity of the earth, wherein all ethical subjectivity is mysteriously dissolved into the *ekstasis* of a primordial feeling of unity or wholeness, and the critical conjunction of human freedom and ethical responsibility subjugated or subsumed by a sense of destiny. Here the concept of power comes to the fore, not only as the elemental powers of nature, but also with respect to the powers of technology, through which the world itself and its very meaning is shaped.

Good modernist that he is at times, Levinas rejects all semblances of mystery on the grounds of its coercive, tyrannical, violent possibilities, and also because mystery is inseparable from paganism, which is to say, radical immanence or the purely elemental. Does Levinas's interpretation of paganism, however, constitute a sufficient ground for rejecting the element of mystery as constitutive for an ethical conception of the Earth, and for our purposes here, of an ethical relationship to the nonhuman animal? Stated differently, is mystery a necessary aspect to formulating an ethical relation to the Earth and to all its inhabitants? And is the dimension of mystery retained, even if unacknowledged as such, in Levinas's own construal of alterity as the element of *surprise* that resists the totalizing tendency of a purely rational consciousness to completely comprehend the world and thus the other—the very mark of intersubjective violence, according to him?

Buddhism arguably retains a dimension of mystery in the idea of Buddha-nature. This is part of what is expressed in the very nonlogical structure of the *kōan*. The face-to-face transmission of the Buddha-dharma is both a transcendence and a mystery, while at the same time being a wholly ordinary event, just as the phenomenal encounter with the face of the Other is for Levinas. And what is the trace if not a mystery, even if it is not tied to a pagan conception? Surely, for many the "otherwise than being" that the trace signifies or points toward is indeed mysterious!

Levinas wants to avoid either divinizing the natural world or romanticizing nature, which is why, for him, a nonhuman ethics is perhaps an impossibility. It is, of course, possible to extend certain ideas, such as the face, speculatively to include the elemental or nature, but such a move necessarily invokes a certain type of paganism and marks a significant departure from Levinas's Judaic ground. For Levinas, the Other is ethically meaningful not simply because the Other is other or different, but rather because the face is the trace of absolute alterity, of *illeity*, which for Levinas refers to the otherness of God arising from a conception of the beyond expressed in terms of the third (*le tiers*). There is a similar logic at play in the different but proximate notion of the third person (*la troisième personne*) wherein the self's relation to others occurs insofar as the self stands in relation to the Other whose face is the trace of illeity. This is what preserves transcendence and refuses the full immanence of community. "*Beyond being is a third person,*" claims Levinas, emphasizing these words, "which is not definable by the oneself, by ipseity. . . . The *illeity* of the third person is the condition for the irreversibility."[30] Elsewhere he writes: "The presence of the face, the infinity of the other, is a destituteness, a presence of the third party (that is, of the whole of humanity that looks at us)" (*TI*, 213). The meaning of the trace, in Levinas's reformulation of it, is ethical, and ethics is transcendence actualized.

The status of the multiple third to which illeity points is the crux of the matter. By grounding community in the neutrality of divinity or God (that is, in the *il* of illeity), animals, mountains, rivers, the elemental forces of wind, fire, and rain, for Levinas, do not present a face in the same manner as another person, precisely because they are not faces that "speak." Yet, while such natural phenomena express and give meaning to the self, do they necessarily invoke or produce the idea of infinity and the correlative ideas of difference and distance in the same qualitative sense as does the human other? And if not, is the transcendence that many associate with such phenomena necessarily ethical? It seems to me that this is precisely the tipping point of trying to apply the formal framework of Levinasian ethics, which is undeniably an interhuman ethics, to environmental and animal ethics. Can one do this if the crucial concept of the *trace* is not fully taken into account? And if it is not, then what is the basis for Levinas's claim that the face, the presence, of the Other calls the freedom of the self-same into question and thereby marks the asymmetry of the ethical relationship? Is a Levinasian ground for a nonhuman ethics able fully to escape or evade the aspect of mystery, which paganism knows as transcendence in immanence, if this grounding follows Levinas's distinction between the other and the elemental?

Let us imagine another scenario framed not by assertions of what is real, true, commanding, or sacred, but rather by a series of questions addressing the general concern of how to think the concept of ethical transcendence with respect to the Earth: Why not assert rather the mystery of the Earth as that which stands over and against the onslaught of technological ravage that has produced much of the current environmental crisis and the almost unimaginable slaughter of countless animals? Why not this other difference, a difference other than that of the Other, as that which prevents us from assuming a sovereign stance based on some rational identification with the Earth? Can we think of having an ethical relation with the Earth itself and *all* its nonhuman inhabitants, or must that relation always and necessarily be political because the Earth is always the third for us? Is the concept of mystery, understood as transcendence, a necessary standpoint to formulate an ethical relation to the Earth? Does Levinas's own construal of alterity border on such a standpoint insofar as it is the destabilizing dimension of surprise that resists the totalizing tendency of a sovereign human, all too human, consciousness?

The principal difference here between the philosophies of Levinas and Zen Buddhism concerns the status of the *beyond*. Both recognize that the attempt to comprehend the other rationally—whether it is the other person, the absolutely other, or Buddha-nature—invariably results in misunderstanding the ethical relationship, and promotes violence and delusion. Levinas's own inability to answer whether an ethical relationship is possible with animals finds company with Zhaozhou's conflicting response about whether a dog has Buddha-nature. Both Levinas and Zen affirm the primacy of the face-to-face relationship and the teaching that is conveyed through it. It is perhaps impossible to determine absolutely whether an animal ethics stands on the same ground as interpersonal ethics, but Buddhism's metaphysics of a nondual whole that refuses to take a firm position regarding transcendence, in the sense of relating to an otherwise than being, bypasses epistemological problems and potentially coercive tendencies that haunt Levinas's conception of ethics. The nonhuman animal has always been a mystery to the human animal, and its very difference from the human has more often than not been used to justify its cruel and inhumane treatment. The view that all sentient and nonsentient beings are Buddha-nature calls the individual self and its freedom into question in just as powerful a way as does the Levinasian Other.

Levinas teaches that the revelation of the face in its very nudity and defenselessness is the appeal of the Other to the self to respond, to assume responsibility not only for itself, but for all others as well. This impossible infinite demand is the primordial teaching, in which "in its non-violent transitivity the very epiphany of the face is produced" (*TI*, 51). It opens the possibility of discourse and therefore the possibility of forming new relationships and new bridges of understanding. The face of the animal conveys that very same vulnerability, and perhaps even more so because it cannot participate at the same level of communication. Despite Levinas's ambivalence about this, even a snake has a face and deserves the dignity of life. Levinas tells us that the Other "is manifested in a Mastery that does not conquer, but teaches" and that "this voice coming from another shore teaches transcendence itself" (*TI*, 171). Buddhism also teaches that there is an "other shore," but here it is not a Mastery but rather a Mystery that teaches. Yet this is a mystery devoid of magic or sorcery, a mystery in which the distinction that Levinas draws between the pagan "sacred" and the ethical or religious "holy" collapses, or "falls away," as various Zen masters have described what happens to the dual structure of mind/body in the moment of awakening or enlightenment (Jp. *satori*). This is the *prajñāpāramitā*, the "perfection of wisdom" in which all dualisms are revealed as "empty" (Sk. *śūnya*) and without "form." This "mystery" calls on the self to relinquish its sovereign conception of ego-identity and see that all beings and things are interconnected without hierarchy.

Notes

1. *Kōan* is a Japanese term for a narrative, question, or statement that challenges conventional thinking because of its generally paradoxical nature. It is used in Zen practice to help the practitioner break through the strictures of purely rational thinking in order to free the mind of conceptual attachments. It helps to produce what in Zen is referred to as the Great Doubt, which is a stage toward reaching enlightenment or awakening.

2. The following abbreviations will be used to designate the etymological origin of various important Asian terms: Ch. = Chinese, Jp. = Japanese, Sk. = Sanskrit.

3. I have developed this position elsewhere, bringing into dialogue Levinas and the Japanese philosopher Eihei Dōgen. See my "Zen Eye Hunter, Zen Eye Hunted: Revealing the Animal Face of Buddha-Nature," in David Jones, ed., *Buddha Nature and Animality* (San Francisco: Jain Publishers, 2007), 149–63.

4. This question is a transformation of the question asked by the sixth Chan ancestor Huineng (Jp. Eno) in case 23 of the famous collection of *kōans* titled the *Wumenkuan* (Jp. *Mumonkan*), or *The Gateless Barrier*: "Think neither of good nor evil. At such a moment, what is the true self [original self] of monk Myo?" See Zenkei Shibayama, *The Gateless Barrier: Zen Comments on the Mumonkan*, trans. Sumiko Kudo (Boston: Shambhala, 2000), 23; translation modified. The term *original face* (or "original nature") is first found in the writings of Huang Po. See Huang Po, "The Wan Ling Record," in *The Teaching of Huang Po: On the Transmission of Mind*, trans. John Blofeld (New York: Grove Press, 1958), 129.

5. This is a key Mahāyāna, especially Mādhyamika, Buddhist term. The various forms of Buddhism that flowered in East Asia, particularly Chan/Zen, in large measure resulted from interaction between Indian Mahayana and Chinese Daoism. The standpoint of absolute nothingness reflects the movement of *Dao*: "doing non-doing" or "acting non-acting" (Ch. *wei wuwei*), the spontaneous, unconditioned way of natural existence. The simultaneous unity and difference of all entities, absolute nothingness or emptiness, does not mean "nonbeing" in the sense of the conceptual opposite of "being." There is neither a temporal nor spatial disjunction expressed in the difference between absolute nothingness and being, nor between absolute nothingness and the relative nothingness of nonbeing.

6. Dependent origination is a fundamental metaphysical concept common to all schools of Buddhism. Along with the concept of *karma*, it forms the Buddhist conception of causality, stating that all phenomena arise together in a mutually interdependent nexus of cause and effect. Because all phenomena are thus conditioned and transient or impermanent, they have no real independent identity and thus no permanent, substantial existence, even if to the ordinary mind this is not apparent. All phenomena are therefore fundamentally empty or boundless.

7. Literally, "Sage of the Śākya clan."

8. In the Buddhist context, *Dharma* means something akin to a cosmic law and order and also to the teachings of the Buddha as found in the sutras and commentaries. In the Zen of Dōgen, its meaning is extended to include the teaching that can be found in the natural world of phenomena (which is also an early meaning of the term).

9. The convention established, with Levinas's approval, in translating *autrui/Autrui* (the personal other/s) as "Other" with a capitalized "O" and *autre/Autre* (otherness in general; alterity) as "other" will be followed.

10. Dōgen, "Face-to-Face Transmission," trans. Reb Anderson and Kazuaki Tanahashi, in *Treasury of the True Dharma Eye: Zen Master Dogen's Shobo Genzo*, vol. 2, ed. Kazuaki Tanahashi (Boston and London: Shambhala, 2010), 572.

11. Cited in "Dōgen's *Shōbōgenzō* Buddha-nature (Part 3)," trans. Norman Waddell and Abe Masao, *The Eastern Buddhist* New Series IX, no. 2 (October 1976): 80.

12. See esp. Dōgen, "Face-to-Face Transmission," in *Treasury of the True Dharma Eye*, 569–78.

13. Dōgen Zenji, "Buddha-nature," in *Shōbōgenzō: The Eye and Treasury of the True Law*, vol. 4, trans. Kōsen Nishiyama and John Stevens (Tokyo: Nakayama Shobo, 1983), 122.

14. See Dōgen, "Going beyond Buddha," trans. Mel Weitsman and Kazuaki Tanahashi, in *Treasury of the True Dharma Eye*, 315.

15. Ibid., 172.

16. I address this teaching dimension in Levinas's philosophy in my "Breaking the Closed Circle: Levinas and Platonic *Paideia*," *Dialogue and Universalism* 8, no. 10 (1998): 97–106; reprinted in Claire Katz and Lara Trout, eds., *Emmanuel Levinas: Critical Assessments*, vol. II: *Levinas and the History of Philosophy* (London and New York: Routledge, 2005), 285–95; see also my "There's More than Meets the Eye: A Glance at Casey and Levinas," *The Pluralist* 1, no. 1 (Spring 2006): 98–103. With regard to the relation between the animal and teaching, see my "Zen Eye Hunter, Zen Eye Hunted: Revealing the Animal Face of Buddha-Nature."

17. Meaning literally from the Sanskrit "enlightened (*bodhi*) existence (*sattva*)," this term refers to an awakened being (*buddha*) that compassionately refuses to enter *nirvāna* in order to continue to assist with the awakening or enlightenment of other beings.

18. The notion of the trace is pivotal for Levinas and recurs throughout his writings. For a sustained discussion, see Emmanuel Levinas, "The Trace of the Other," trans. Alphonso Lingis, in Mark C. Taylor, ed., *Deconstruction in Context: Literature and Philosophy* (Chicago: University of Chicago Press, 1986), 345–59; Emmanuel Levinas, "Meaning and Sense," in *CPP*, 102–7. For secondary sources see Robert Bernasconi, "The Trace of Levinas in Derrida," in David Wood and Robert Bernasconi, eds., *Derrida and Difference* (Coventry: Parousia Press, 1985), 17–44; and Edward S. Casey, "Levinas on Memory and the Trace," in John Sallis, Giuseppina Moneta, and Jacques Taminiaux, eds., *The Collegium Phaenomenologicum* (Dordrecht: Kluwer, 1989), 241–55.

19. See Emmanuel Levinas, "Diachrony and Representation," in *TO*, 111–14. Put differently, the "subordination" of the ethical Saying (*le Dire*) to the ontological Said (*le Dit*) is a reduction whereby the Saying goes beyond the Said, being prior to the Said, and is yet paradoxically "absorbed and died in the Said [*s'absorbait et mourait dans le Dit*]" (*OB*, 36).

20. See Emmanuel Levinas, "Wholly Otherwise," trans. Simon Critchley, in Robert Bernasconi and Simon Critchley, eds., *Re-Reading Levinas* (Bloomington: Indiana University Press, 1991), 3–10.

21. The distinction between the sacred and the holy is fundamental for Levinas. The former denotes an elevation of the natural or earthly to the level of divinity based on the epistemic limitation of comprehending the divine. Although eschewing mystery, the holy signifies the incomprehensibility of divinity *and* the Other that opens up the reception of transcendence in the ethical relationship. Levinas writes: "The comprehension of God taken as participation in his sacred life, an allegedly direct comprehension, is impossible, because participation is a denial of the divine, and because nothing is

more direct than the face to face, which is straightforwardness" (*TI*, 78). For a view that interprets Levinas as rejecting only a particular metaphysical view of the sacred, see N. H. Smith, "Levinas's Modern Sacred," *Law Text Culture* 5 (2000) [http://ro.uow.edu.au/ltc/vol5/iss1/8].

22. David Wood, *The Step Back: Ethics and Politics after Deconstruction* (Albany: State University of New York Press, 2005), 67–68.

23. Ibid., 68.

24. Jean-Luc Nancy, *The Inoperative Community*, trans. Peter Connor (Minneapolis: University of Minnesota Press, 1991).

25. On the relation between Levinas and Nancy on transcendence, see my "Politics and Transcendence," in Marinos Diamantides, ed., *Levinas, Law, Politics* (London: Routledge Cavendish, 2007), 127–41.

26. Jean-Luc Nancy, *The Birth to Presence*, trans. Brian Holmes (Stanford: Stanford University Press, 1993), 155.

27. Dōgen, "Buddha-nature," in *Shōbōgenzō*, 123.

28. Ibid. For a developed treatment of this understanding of Buddha-nature in Dōgen, see my "Walking in Wild Emptiness: A Zen Phenomenology," in Ron Scapp and Brian Seitz, eds., *Philosophy, Place, and Travel: Being in Transit* (New York and London: Palgrave Macmillan, 2018).

29. Dōgen quoted in Heinrich Dumoulin, *Zen Buddhism: A History*, vol. 2: Japan, trans. James W. Heisig and Paul Knitter (New York and London: Macmillan Publishing, 1990), 81.

30. Levinas, "The Trace of the Other," 356.

CHAPTER 11

"Now We're Talking Pedagogy"

Levinas, Animal Ethics, and Jewish Education

TAMRA WRIGHT

What is the difference between humans and other animals, according to Levinas's thought? In "The Animal Interview," the discussion is framed mainly by the question of whether nonhuman animals have faces in the Levinasian sense, and hence whether people have ethical obligations toward them. Additionally, Levinas presents the key teaching of his philosophy as the claim that what distinguishes humanity from the rest of nature is the capacity to value the life of another person above one's own.

> However, with the appearance of the human—here is my entire philosophy—that is, with man, there is something more important than my life, and that is the life of the other. That is unreasonable. Man is an unreasonable animal. (*AI*, 5)

Critics of Levinas, including contributors to this volume, have taken issue with Levinas's anthropocentric stance on both these points, arguing that his refusal to acknowledge ethically significant alterity in the faces of nonhuman animals is decidedly un-Levinasian, and that the claim that morally significant self-sacrifice is a uniquely human capacity is unfounded. In what follows, I will largely steer clear of these debates and focus on a different set of questions: To what extent is Levinas's approach to animal ethics consistent with, and possibly influenced by, Jewish tradition, and what scope is there, within this approach, for improvement to the treatment of animals?

Although there is no sustained discussion of animal ethics in Levinas's corpus, I will argue that his remarks in "The Animal Interview" suggest an approach that is broadly consistent with his Lithuanian Jewish heritage. However, as Levinas himself frequently reminds us in his confessional writings, the Bible and other Jewish texts have given rise to a multiplicity of readings and interpretations. In examining the extent to which his approach to animal ethics is consistent with Jewish thought, I will also mention alternative understandings, without attempting to adjudicate between them. The primary focus of this essay will be on the second question raised above: I will attempt to sketch the outlines of a Jewish animal ethics for the twenty-first century, one inspired by Levinas's conception of ethical subjectivity and grounded in Jewish law and tradition. Doing so will require us not only to look at Levinas's "confessional" writings, but also to focus specifically on an area that until recently has received relatively little scholarly attention, his essays on Jewish education.

Jewish Education and Ethical Subjectivity

To begin with the fundamental distinction that Levinas draws between humans and all other beings, on which his "entire philosophy" rests, it will be worth looking at the much more elaborate discussion of this topic in the Talmudic commentary "And God Created Woman." Here the meaning of the uniquely human is not understood simply on the basis of the capacity for "saintliness" or self-sacrifice, but as an inescapable duality within the human condition. The textual peg for the discussion of this duality, within the Talmudic text itself as well as in Levinas's commentary, is a variant spelling of the word וצר (read *vayyitzer*, "formed") as וייצר, with two *yods*, in the verse "The Lord God formed man" (Genesis 2:7).[1] The first interpretation offered within the Talmudic text is that it means that God created the first human with two inclinations (vocalized as *yetzer*), the good and the bad; but an objection is raised, namely that the same word is used, but spelled with a single *yod*, to refer to the creation of animals, who also appear to have both a good and an evil inclination. Levinas writes,

> The argument must be filled out on the basis of what the commentators have given us. An animal can bite and kick, but it can also obey and provide labor. The animal, then, would already have consciousness and choice. Is it therefore possible to say that consciousness and reason define human being? Here is another possible reading of the above objection which goes further. If man is a reasonable animal— reason can in fact pin itself onto animality—there is no unbridgeable

distance, no incompatibility between animality and reason. Reason can put itself at the service of bestiality and the instincts. . . . But must we not look elsewhere than to consciousness for the dividing line between what is human and the rest? (*NTR*, 165)

Following this objection in the Talmudic text, a new interpretation is offered: "Rav Simeon ben Pazzi said: Woe is me because of my Creator, woe is me because of my own evil inclination" (*NTR*, 165). This interpretation takes the word *vayyitzer* and breaks it down into two sections, "*vay*" ("woe," or "alas") and יצר (which could be vocalized as *yotzer*, "creator"). Levinas understands this interpretation to mean that "the specifically human would be to be caught between my Creator, that is, the Law that he gave me, and existence: the healthy desires of a creature that hungers" (*NTR*, 166). Hence, Levinas says, following this interpretation, it is not freedom but obedience that defines the human being. However, such obedience is not a source of contentment because the human being is always torn between obedience and desire.

A third interpretation in the Talmudic text introduces the idea that the two yods referred to God creating the first human with two faces. The proof text, Psalm 139:5, is "You hedge me before and behind; You lay your Hand upon me." The overarching theme of the Psalm is that it is impossible to flee from God's presence. Levinas explains the connection between this theme and the image of a being with two faces. A being with a single face has a space, the back of the head, for hidden thoughts, but to have a second face in the place of the occiput is to have nowhere to hide, no possibility of separating oneself from God, no possibility of avoiding responsibility. Levinas points out that within the context of Psalm 139, this impossibility of being separated from God is presented in a very positive light.

The Talmudic text goes on to quote Rav Ammi who interprets the Psalm as referring to the order of punishment. "For Rav Ammi said: 'behind' means 'the last one created,' 'before' means 'the first one to be punished.'" Within the biblical narrative, humans are the last beings to be created before God rests on the seventh day. Levinas reads Rav Ammi's statement as a comment on the existential situation of the human being.

This world is therefore not what man would have planned or wanted. It is not even what man has seen the beginning of. It has not come about as a result of man's creative freedom. Man has come into an already made universe. Man is the first to receive punishment. It is he who answers for what he has not done. Man is responsible for the universe, the hostage of the creature. Beyond the realm attributable to his freedom, he is pressed from his front and rear: he is asked to account for things which he did not will and which were not born from his freedom. (*NTR*, 170)

The last part of this Talmudic text that is significant for our purposes continues the theme of honors and punishments and the order in which they are distributed. The details need not concern us except to note that one of the verses cited relates to the flood (Genesis 7:23): "God wiped out all the creatures on the face of the earth, both man and cattle." Levinas argues that humanity's punishment is cited before that of the animals in this verse because people are held responsible for all ethical evil.

Rabbinic tradition and the Biblical text agree: the causes for the Flood were injustice and the sexual perversion of men and animals. Ethical evil from which the other person suffers. But also confusion of what is human and what is animal. Evil gnawing at the creature in this confusion of human and animal. For this perverted universe, man answers first. This humanity is defined, not by liberty—do we know whether Evil began with man?—but by a responsibility prior to all initiative. Man answers for more than his freely chosen acts. He is the hostage of the universe. (*NTR*, 171)

The language that Levinas uses in these sections of the commentary is strikingly similar to his descriptions of ethical subjectivity in *Otherwise Than Being or Beyond Essence*: humanity, or the ethical subject, is a "hostage," responsible for the whole universe, and such responsibility is neither contracted nor chosen, but is prior to the subject's freedom or initiative. Significantly for our purposes, in the same passage Levinas takes great pains to emphasize the Rabbis' concern about confusing what is "human" and what is "animal." We will return to this theme in the discussion below.

The relationship between Levinas's ethical philosophy and his Jewish or "confessional" writings has been the subject of much discussion in the secondary literature. Claire Katz's recent work on Levinas and education adds a new dimension to this discussion and has implications that are relevant to our discussion of animal ethics in Levinas's thought. In *Levinas and the Crisis of Humanism*, she notes that nearly every major Western philosopher from Plato to Hegel wrote at length about the philosophy of education. Although they had very different approaches from one another, they also had a shared understanding that "a subject develops in relationship to the larger society in which the subject is situated, and moral education is a fundamental component in this development." Plato, Aristotle, Rousseau, Kant, and Hegel (among others) all wrote an educational philosophy showing how the political or ethical end elaborated in their philosophy could be achieved.[2] Levinas, like many other twentieth-century philosophers, did not produce such a philosophy of education within his philosophical corpus, but he did develop a philosophical approach to *Jewish* education in his confessional writings.

Levinas's focus on Jewish education should not be understood as merely parochial. Throughout his essays on Judaism and Jewish education, he frequently underscores the universalism of Judaism as he understands it. As Katz points out, Levinas's critique of Western humanism is presented in similar terms in both his philosophical writings and his essays on Judaism; he argues that "the humanism modernity produced, one which leads us to believe we are each free, autonomous, and hold a privileged place in the sun, led to the cascade of inhumanities we experienced in the 20th century" (*LC*, 11). Levinas's philosophical work presents us with an alternative subjectivity, on which a different sort of humanism can be based. In place of Western humanism's self-centered ego, Levinas proposes a new humanism, at the heart of which we find a "subjectivity defined by ceding the egocentric status for the Other" (*LC*, 6). In his Jewish writings, however, Levinas shows that such a humanism is not really new, it is a biblical or "Jewish humanism . . . of the other man" (*NTR*, 98). More significantly for Katz, Levinas's writings on Jewish education do not simply elaborate this subjectivity and this humanism; they explore how such a subjectivity, "responsible for the universe," is shaped via Jewish education.

Although a detailed discussion of how Levinas understands Jewish education's role in shaping ethical subjectivity is beyond the scope of this article, two passages from the essay "An Adult Religion" are particularly relevant. In the first, Levinas offers an argument that not only the ethical commandments of Judaism (traditionally categorized as *mitzvot ben adam l'chavero*, interpersonal commandments), but also the ritual commandments (*mitzvot ben adam lamakom*, commandments between a person and God), serve to prepare a person for ethical responsibility.

> Jewish ritual law constitutes a severe discipline which leads to justice. Only the one who has been able to impose a severe rule on his own nature can recognize the face of the other. (*DF*, 18; translation modified)[3]

The second passage suggests that not any and every regime of discipline will have the effect of molding an ethical subjectivity.

> The way that leads to God therefore leads *ipso facto*—and not in addition—to man; and the way that leads to man draws us back

to ritual discipline and self-education. Its greatness lies in its daily
regularity. Here is a passage in which three opinions are given: the
second indicates the way in which the first is true, and the third
indicates the practical conditions for the second. Ben Zoma said: 'I
have found a verse that contains the whole of the Torah: "Listen O
Israel, the Lord is our God, the Lord is One."' Ben Nanus said: 'I
have found a verse that contains the whole of the Torah: "You will
love your neighbour as yourself."' Ben Pazi said: 'I have found a verse
that contains the whole of the Torah: "You will sacrifice a lamb in
the morning and another at dusk."' And Rabbi, their master, stood
up and decided: 'The law is according to Ben Pazi.' (DF, 18–19)[4]

Leaving aside the ethical issues regarding animal sacrifice, this passage
illustrates that the daily regularity of ritual practice is enmeshed within a web
of moral and religious teaching. The commandment to "love your neighbor as
yourself" might sound more obviously Levinasian to readers of his philosophical
work. Yet Levinas's comment on the whole text points out that the third opinion,
which cites twice-daily ritual obligations, "indicates the practical conditions" for
the fulfillment of the ethical commandment to love the neighbor.

In the Talmudic commentary "Toward the Other," Levinas again explores
the theme of the interrelation between ethics, ritual commandments, and religious
teachings in Judaism, suggesting that the ritual commandments and theological
teachings are somehow required for the successful transmission of ethical values
across the generations.

Are we to think that the sense of justice dwelling in the Jewish
conscience—that wonder of wonders—is due to the fact that for
centuries Jews fasted on Yom Kippur, observed the Sabbath and the
food prohibitions, waited for the Messiah, and understood the love
one's neighbor as a duty of piety?
  Should one go so far as to think that contempt for the *mitzvah*
compromises the mysterious Jewish sense of justice in us? If we Jews,
without ritual life and without piety, are still borne by a previously
acquired momentum toward unconditional justice, what guarantees
do we have that we will be so moved for long? (NTR, 17–18)

In his essays on humanism in *Difficult Freedom*, Levinas contrasts this
Jewish way of conveying and transmitting moral teachings with what he perceives as the failings of Western humanism. Drawing on Mendelssohn, Spinoza,
and Maimonides, Levinas asserts that Judaism is not a revealed religion but a

revealed law, that its truths are universal, and that its rules and moral institutions are designed to protect its truths from corruption. He argues that the truths of Western humanism have primarily been transmitted as pure abstractions, and that as such they have always run the risk of being forgotten or distorted.

> The naked intellect rises to the summits, but does not maintain itself there. Reason, sovereign and subject of the true, succumbs to the idolatry of the myths which tempt it, betray it and chain it up.[5] (*DF*, 382)

This understanding of the capacity of Jewish education to shape an ethical subjectivity and to transmit moral values gives rise to an obvious question for Levinas: Is there a non-Jewish analogue to the "severe discipline" of Jewish ritual law, or some other means by which non-Jews might cultivate ethical awareness and prepare to respond positively to the needs of the Other?

In "The Paradox of Morality," Levinas was asked, but didn't directly answer, a question along similar lines. Indeed, when asked, "How can [atheists] learn to welcome the face?" (*PM*, 177), his initial response, which does not appear in the published interview, was to exclaim, "*Là nous sommes dans la pedagogie!*" ("Now we're talking pedagogy!") As is apparent from the published interview, Levinas declined the opportunity to engage in a discussion of "pedagogy," and focused instead on clarifying his use of biblical quotations in his philosophical texts.

> I do not preach for the Jewish religion. I always speak of the Bible, not the Jewish religion. The Bible, including the Old Testament, is for me a human fact, of the human order, and entirely universal. What I have said about ethics, about the universality of the commandment in the face, of the commandment which is valid even if it doesn't bring salvation, even if there is no reward, is valid independently of any religion. (*PM*, 177)

The theme of morality without reward, and his moral reservations about "preaching" either religion or morality, were introduced into the discussion earlier in the interview. Echoing remarks in his 1982 essay "Useless Suffering" about the need for a "new modality" of religion and morality in the twentieth century,[6] Levinas said,

> If there is an explicitly Jewish moment in my thought, it is the reference to Auschwitz, where God let the Nazis do what they wanted. Consequently, what remains? Either this means that there

is no reason for morality and hence it can be concluded that everyone should act like the Nazis, or the moral law maintains its authority. . . . Before the twentieth century, all religion begins with the promise. It begins with the "Happy End." It is the promise of heaven. Well then, doesn't a phenomenon like Auschwitz invite you, on the contrary, to think the moral law independently of the Happy End? That is the question. *I would even ask whether we are not faced with an order that one cannot preach.* Does one have the right to preach to the other a piety without reward? That is what I ask myself. It is easier to tell myself to believe without promise than it is to ask it of the other. That is the idea of asymmetry. I can demand of myself that which I cannot demand of the other. (*PM*, 175–76; emphasis added)

Levinas's reservations about preaching, and his focus on the "asymmetry" of ethics, add an important caveat to our discussion of Jewish pedagogy. His writings on Jewish education, which significantly predate the remarks in this interview, span several decades, from the 1950s to the 1970s. "An Adult Religion," from which I have quoted above, was first published in 1957. I have argued elsewhere that Levinas's Jewish thought undergoes significant development from his early essays such as "Loving the Torah More Than God" and "An Adult Religion," to the 1980s texts quoted above.[7] While the earlier essays seem to suggest that a post-Holocaust Judaism need not be radically different from what has preceded it, "Useless Suffering" presents a radical critique of theodicy and, as previously discussed, explicitly calls for a new modality of religion and morality. Given these developments, and the concerns about "preaching" expressed in the interview, it is reasonable to wonder whether Levinas might have adopted a different tone or approach if he had written his essays about Jewish education in the 1980s rather than two or three decades earlier.

In a sense, then, the remainder of this paper draws on the "early Levinas" and is therefore potentially subject to critique from the perspective of Levinas's later writings.

Levinas and Jewish Animal Ethics

Levinas's responses to questions about animal ethics in "The Animal Interview" do not purport to represent the Jewish tradition, but it is reasonable to suppose that his knowledge of the Bible and Talmud may have influenced his thinking on the subject. In this section I will argue that key points that arise in his comments on animal ethics are consistent with Jewish tradition. In addition, building on the discussion of Jewish pedagogy as the endeavor to shape an ethical subjectivity, I will try to show that there are resources within the Jewish legal tradition that can be drawn on to shape an increasingly responsible and compassionate approach to animal ethics.

As discussed elsewhere in this volume, key features of Levinas's remarks in "The Animal Interview" include an emphasis on a purportedly clear binary distinction between humans and nonhuman animals (which contributes to the charge of "anthropocentrism"), acknowledgment of a concern not to make animals suffer unnecessarily, and the suggestion that this concern for the suffering of animals is based on an analogy between human and animal suffering.

The anthropocentrism that has been identified in Levinas's thought is a common feature in Jewish texts, beginning with the account of creation in the book of Genesis, which grants a special status to the human being compared with nonhuman animals and the rest of creation. This is implicit in the narration of the creation of birds, fish, cattle, wild beasts, and "creeping things" on the fifth and sixth days of creation, all of which are "brought forth by the waters" (fifth day) and the Earth (sixth day) compared with the creation of the human being, at the end of the sixth day, via a direct act of God. It is also made explicit when God announces his intention to create humans, in the divine image, to "rule over the fish of the sea, the birds of the sky, the cattle, the whole earth, and all the creeping things that creep on earth" (Genesis 1:24), and this formulation is repeated verbatim two versus later when God blesses the human he has created (Genesis 1:28). It is worth noting that, at this stage, "ruling over" nature does not extend to eating one's fellow creatures; neither humans nor other animals are given permission to eat animal flesh. Instead, human food is "every seed bearing plant" and "every tree that has seed bearing fruit," and the birds and animals are to restrict themselves to eating "green plants" (Genesis 1:29–30). (Levinas's remark in "The Name of a Dog" that "There is enough here to make you a vegetarian again" presumably refers to this Edenic existence.) We will return both to the question of vegetarianism in the Jewish tradition, and to a discussion of the extent of human dominion over nature.

Although it seems clear from the biblical texts we have looked at so far that the human being is fundamentally and significantly different from the rest of creation, one of the underlying themes of the early stories in the book of Genesis, particularly when interpreted in the light of rabbinic tradition, seems to be that humans struggle to recognize and live up to this distinction. For example, rabbinic tradition interprets the account of the creation of woman in a way that suggests that the difference between humans and other animals was not obvious to the first human. Chapter 2 of Genesis includes the well-known story of the creation of Eve from Adam's "rib."[8] Yet, between the announcement of the divine intention to create a "helpmate" for Adam, and the narration of that act of surgery and creation, the text interpolates the story of God presenting Adam with each of the animals in turn and Adam giving names to them. "And the man gave names to the cattle and to the birds of the sky and to all the wild beasts; but for Adam no fitting helper was found" (Genesis 2:20). Rabbinic tradition does not hesitate to pick up on the sexual implications of the positioning of this story of naming: Rashi suggests that the main point of the exercise was for Adam to realize that none of the animals were suitable mates for him, and Nachmanides explicitly cites one tradition of interpretation that Adam desired the animals but could not find a mate among them. When he awakens from his sleep and sees the woman, Adam says, "This one at last is bone of my bones and flesh of my flesh. This one shall be called woman, for from man was she taken" (Genesis: 2:23; JPS translation).

Another, lesser known rabbinic tradition that emphasizes the difficulty human beings have in living up to the ethical standard required of them, as opposed to those imposed on nonhuman animals, concerns the punishment and eventual death of Cain, the first murderer. When asked by God to account for Abel's whereabouts, Cain counters with the infamous and profoundly un-Levinasian rhetorical question: "Am I my brother's keeper?" (Genesis 4:9). According to rabbinic tradition, his crime leads not only to the punishment that is explicitly stated in the biblical text, but also to a confusion of the human and the animal in his appearance.[9] Poetic justice is served when this ultimately results in Cain being killed by a hunter who mistakes him for a wild animal. Rashi's commentary on Genesis 4:24 draws on a Midrashic tradition that the "mark of Cain" was a horn.

> Lemech was a seventh generation descendant of Cain. He was blind, and he would go out hunting with his son, [Tuval-Kayin]. [His son] would lead him by the hand, and when he would see an animal, he would inform his father, [who would proceed to hunt it]. One day, [Tuval Kayin] cried out to his father: "I see something like an animal over there." Lemech pulled back on his bow and shot. . . . The child peered from afar at the dead body . . . and said to Lemech: "What we killed bears the figure of a man, but it has a horn protruding from its forehead." Lemech then exclaimed in anguish: "Woe unto me! It is my ancestor, Cain!" (*Midrash Tanchuma, Bereshit* 11)

Contemporary educator Rabbi David Fohrman points out the thematic links between this story and the punishment of the snake in Genesis 3:14. The mythical talking snake who had enticed Eve to eat the forbidden fruit was punished by becoming more clearly animal like: instead of walking upright, it would crawl on the ground; it would eat dust (food unfit for human consumption); and there would be a natural enmity between snakes and future generations of humans. These changes emphasize the divide between human and nonhuman animals; and the story of Cain's horn reinforces this theme in the opposite direction, by showing the consequences of humans allowing themselves to behave "like animals." For Fohrman, using theological language, the key difference lies in how humans and other animals are meant to discern the divine will: animals are permitted to follow their instincts and desires ("the voice of God within"), whereas humans are expected to follow verbal divine commandments. In Fohrman's reading, whatever the cause of the quarrel between the two brothers, when Cain resorts to killing his brother, he has allowed his own desire, rather than the external divine/moral law, to reign supreme, and in so doing, has descended to the moral status of a nonhuman animal.

This insistence on a clear distinction between humans and all other animals is one facet of what Levinas has described as the way in which Judaism disenchants and demythologizes the world. In his wide-ranging study *Animal Life in Jewish Tradition*, Elijah Schochet looks specifically at how the Hebrew Bible radically demythologizes the animal kingdom. Within the biblical worldview, he argues, not only God but also humans are, in an important way, outside of nature, whereas nonhuman animals function "in a perfunctory and natural role as an animal, either bearing the burdens of domestication or moving about freely in the wild." Whether wild or domesticated, the animal "has no intimate or mystical relationship with either man or the cosmos. It is simply an animal."[10]

Schochet points out that although totemism was "an all-pervasive force" in the ancient world, Scripture is almost entirely free of totemistic elements. For the pagans of the ancient Near East, there was "no such thing as an inanimate world." They worshiped the gods of nature, and specific entities, including animals, were considered sacred (*AL*, 22). For example, In Egypt and elsewhere in the ancient Near East, the serpent was worshiped as a fertility god; and although, as we have seen, the figure of the serpent plays an important role in the early chapters of Genesis, Schochet argues that the biblical text is careful to give the serpent no special status—it is neither a demon, nor endowed with any supernatural powers, but is "merely one of the many animals God has created, nothing more" (*AL*, 29).

Although Schochet concedes that there is a certain amount of anthropomorphic re-mythologization of animals in rabbinic thought, he concludes his overview of the portrayal of animals in rabbinic literature with the suggestion that this is a "poetic re-mythologization of bird and beast," which was not intended to be taken literally, and therefore could be safely tolerated (*AL*, 109). His more detailed exploration of the themes of reward and punishment for animals in rabbinic literature, including cases where animals are "tried" for purported crimes, also concludes with a similarly rationalistic and anthropocentric interpretation.

> The animal is undeniably "humanized" in folklore and is featured
> by the fabulist in human-like roles. Yet both its prominence and its
> similarity to humans should be suspect. For in the main, it is not the
> animal per se that really matters, but what the animal represents to
> man. Thus if animals manifest authentic religious sensitivity toward
> their Creator, surely man should! If God rewards and punishes the
> beast, how much more so will man be requited for his deeds! There
> is, undeniably much that man can learn from the animal kingdom
> in the pages of rabbinic folklore, but on most occasions the animal
> is merely an object lesson used to make a point. (AL, 143)

However, some recent scholarship has looked to rabbinic texts and the medieval commentators to develop the case that "Judaism's teachings are in fact quite compatible with a broader and deeper understanding of beastly morality."[11] The scholars who put forth this view are more inclined to literal understandings of Talmudic and midrashic stories about animals receiving rewards or punishments (including in the afterlife) for religiously or morally significant behavior. Marc Goldfeder draws on Nachmanides's assertion that animals have some form of free will, together with Gaonic responsa that maintained that animals are rewarded in the afterlife for their worldly afflictions and good deeds, to support the legitimacy, if not necessity, of such interpretations (NAD, 73).

Nevertheless, even among these scholars, their work is seen as identifying "countercurrents" or countertraditions within the dominant tradition (NAD, 73), thus lending weight to the view that Levinas's anthropocentrism is consistent with the dominant tradition of Jewish thought on the matter, particularly within the rationalist, Lithuanian approach with which he identified.

The second feature of his remarks in "The Animal Interview," the idea of avoiding causing unnecessary suffering to animals, is also a key teaching of the Jewish tradition, the importance of which is sometimes overlooked. There are a number of commandments in the Torah that seem to enjoin compassionate treatment of animals, including the positive obligation to allow domestic animals to rest on the Sabbath (Exodus 20:8),[12] and the prohibitions of cooking a kid in its mother's milk, taking eggs or chicks from a nest when the mother bird is present (Deuteronomy 22:6), muzzling an ox when it is threshing (Deuteronomy 22:10), and plowing a field with animals of different strengths—an ox and a donkey—tethered together (Deuteronomy 22:10).

Although the rationale for these commandments is subject to the debate, Jewish law ultimately enshrines something like a general principle—the prohibition of *tza'ar ba'aley chayyim* (literally "suffering of a living being")—as a commandment with the status of biblical law (*Baba Metzia* 32b; *Shabbat* 128b).[13] Although the phrase *tza'ar ba'aley chayyim* does not appear in the Bible, it is relatively common in rabbinic literature. The Talmud records some level of debate among the sages as to whether the prohibition has the status of biblical law, even though it is not explicitly stated in the Torah, and reaches the conclusion that it does. The prohibition is assumed to have this status by subsequent generations of *halakhists* (Jewish legal scholars); where there are disagreements among *halakhists*, these tend to focus on the application of the law, often including a judgment as to whether the animal's suffering is outweighed by the human need that is satisfied in a particular case.

Another indication of the importance the rabbis attributed to proper treatment of animals is that the biblical commandment prohibiting the consumption of *ever min ha'chai*, flesh taken from a live animal (Genesis 9:4), is held to be one of the Seven Laws of Noah, the basic moral code that is understood to be incumbent on all of humanity.[14] According to some authorities, this specific commandment should be understood as a heading that represents the general obligation of compassionate treatment of animals; whether or not one agrees with this opinion, it is striking to note that a reference to animal welfare features in the universal Noahide code.

In addition to the prohibition of cruelty to animals, the rabbinic sages ruled that Jewish owners of domesticated animals must provide food and drink for their animals before partaking of their own meals (*Berachot* 40a). Rabbi Eleazar ha-Kapar extended this ruling and taught that a person was prohibited from buying a wild or domestic animal, or a bird, if they were not able to provide it with sustenance (Jerusalem Talmud, *Ketubot* 4:8).

There is a broad consensus among Jewish legal authorities that hunting for sport is prohibited. In some cases, this is based on the prohibition of *tza'ar ba'aley chayyim*, whereas other authorities justify the ban on hunting with reference to the general prohibition of *bal tashchit* (wanton destruction) (*AL*, 267). Other authorities, including the early modern Italian Rabbi Samson Morpurgo, forbade hunting, not just for sport, but also if the motive was for financial gain (e.g., selling the nonkosher carcasses of birds and animals to non-Jews for food) (*AL*, 267–69).

Jewish law does, however, permit the slaughter of animals for "legitimate" (*AL*, 267) human purposes, including for practical needs like food and clothing, for ritual reasons (such as animal sacrifices during the Temple period), and to safeguard human health and well-being in case of threats from animals. Maimonides explains that the rules of *shechita* (ritual slaughter) are designed to minimize the suffering of the animal.

> Since the desire of procuring good food necessitates the slaying of animals, the Torah commands that the death of the animal should be the easiest. It is not allowed to torment the animal by cutting the throat in a clumsy manner, by piercing it, or by cutting off a limb while the animal is still alive. (*Guide of the Perplexed* III: 48)

Although other explanations are offered by different authorities for these rules, Maimonides's statement has become well known and is often included in instruction manuals for *shochtim* (ritual slaughterers).

As noted above, not only humans but all animals were originally intended to be vegetarian, according to the creation narrative in Genesis. Divine sanction for meat-eating is granted, possibly reluctantly, to humanity only after the Flood (Genesis 9:2–3), and this permission is given together with restrictions (the blood must not be consumed, and, as mentioned above, flesh taken from an animal while it is still alive is prohibited). The laws of *kashrut*, the dietary laws which are understood to be incumbent specifically on Jews, involve additional restrictions, including distinctions between permitted and prohibited species of animals; specific instructions on the method of slaughter of animals; and the prohibition of cooking or consuming meat and dairy products together.

Contemporary advocates of vegetarianism as an authentic expression of Jewish values argue that these restrictions around the consumption of meat, together with the Edenic prehistory of harmony between humans and other animals, and the prohibition of *tza'ar ba'aley chayyim*, point toward vegetarianism as a morally and religiously preferable way of life. Although such authors are able to muster a number of other arguments, and to draw on numerous biblical and rabbinic texts, as well as philosophical and halakhic discussions of later Jewish thinkers, no leading Orthodox *poskim* (Jewish legal authorities) have ruled against the consumption of meat. However, Rabbi Joseph Soloveitchik, influential leader of American Modern Orthodoxy in the twentieth century, acknowledged that there are "definitive vegetarian tendencies in the Bible," and pointed out that "animal hunters and flesh-eaters are people that lust"; although such behavior is legalized in the Bible, it is also "classified [Numbers 11:34] as *ta'avah*, lust, repulsive and brutish."[15]

The debate over vegetarianism in Judaism has explored not just whether vegetarianism is preferable, but also the question whether it is halakhically permissible. Although this may seem like a surprising question, Jewish law does not simply forbid a range of prohibited foods, it also mandates the consumption of specific foods and beverages at specific times. For example, at the Passover Seder, every adult participant is mandated to consume four cups of wine (or grape juice), as well as a specified minimum quantity of unleavened bread and bitter herbs. (Prior to the destruction of the Temple and the consequent end of animal sacrifices, every adult would also have partaken of the Paschal lamb.) At Sabbath and festival meals, everyone adult is obliged to consume a specified minimum quantity of bread. In addition, there is a commandment to rejoice on the festivals, and according to some rabbinic opinions, the commandment includes eating meat and drinking wine. It would, of course, be troubling if vegetarians were compelled to eat meat out of a sense of religious obligation, particularly to "rejoice" on festivals. According to J. David Bleich's analysis of the relevant sources, if a person has no desire to eat meat, or "a fortiori, when it is found to be repugnant," there is no religious obligation to consume it.[16]

In addition to the various limitations and regulations surrounding the consumption of meat discussed above, there is an opinion in the Talmud that an ignoramus may not eat meat (*Pesachim* 49b). Although many scholars interpret this as relating to the risk of making a mistake in application of the dietary laws or the specifics of *shechita* (ritual slaughter), Hasidic writers, drawing on the kabbalistic teachings of Rabbi Isaac Luria, interpret this teaching in a more spiritualized way, and argue that a person should only eat meat if doing so will enable them to serve God with greater joy and passion than if they had eaten a vegetarian or vegan meal.[17]

Rabbi Joseph Albo's comments on the original prohibition of eating meat, and the subsequent, postdiluvium permission, reinforce the Torah's distinction between humans and other animals that we explored at the beginning of this section. Albo argued that meat was initially prohibited because killing animals involved "cruelty, rage, and the accustoming of oneself to the bad habit of shedding innocent blood." Nevertheless, Albo argues that by the time of Noah, humanity had degenerated to such an extent that the distinction between humans and other animals had been forgotten. Echoing the theme of the primacy of the distinction between humans and other animals that we see both in Levinas's thought and in the early stories in Genesis, Albo argues that permission to eat meat was given to emphasize the greater moral responsibility of humans.[18]

Although both vegetarianism and veganism are growing trends in Israel,[19] it is unlikely that the majority of Jews worldwide are going to abandon meat-eating any time soon. However, a greater understanding of and focus on the prohibition of *tza'ar ba'aley chayyim* could result in significant changes. As we have seen in the discussion above, this prohibition is subject to exceptions for human need. Although the possibility of exceptions seems to some critics to pave the way for people thinking they have carte blanche to deal with animals in any way they choose, this is clearly not the intention of the Jewish moral and legal system.

One of the strongest contemporary statements of a strict insistence on the primacy of *tza'ar ba'aley chayyim* was made by the leading twentieth-century halakhic authority, Rabbi Moshe Feinstein, in a responsum written in 1982.[20] Rabbi Feinstein was asked by his son-in-law, Rabbi Dr. Moshe Tendler, about "white veal"—the meat from calves taken from their mothers at birth, raised in tiny cages and fed a diet lacking iron so that their flesh remains pale rather than attaining a natural reddish color. The vehemence of Feinstein's response is remarkable. First, he prohibits the meat on technical grounds: the majority of these animals have defective internal organs that render them *terefa*, forbidden on the grounds that (without modern medical attention) they would be dead within a year.

Second, he states that the raising of calves in this way is itself prohibited because of *tza'ar ba'aley chayyim*. He explains that Jews are allowed to eat meat, so slaughter itself is permitted; and they are allowed to use animals for work such as plowing or carrying burdens. But they may not inflict pain for pleasure or profit. It is permitted to feed animals foods that will improve the quality of the meat, but not to feed them things that they don't enjoy, or that make them ill.

Most remarkable is the way in which Feinstein supports his case by citing a Talmudic passage that extends the prohibition from physical to psychological pain. The reference to *Bekhorot* 38b–39a is almost offhand, but, as is generally true of Feinstein's writing, the citation demands study. The Talmudic passage deals with a *bekhor*, a firstborn male calf, kid, or lamb (like the animals the responsum deals with), which the Torah treats as sacred. In Temple times, these firstlings were brought as offerings. In the absence of a Temple they retain their sacred status and cannot be set to work, nor may they be slaughtered for food, unless they develop some blemish that would have rendered them unfit for sacrificial use.

A *bekhor* is thus a financial liability, and in general one might expect the Talmudic authorities to recognize the economic pressure to declare an animal "blemished" whenever possible. The passage that Feinstein refers to deals with a condition that may be curable, and the rabbis insist that before determining that the animal is indeed disqualified, every attempt must be made to cure it. Not only must the appropriate medicine be given at the right time, with the right foods, but the animal must not be tethered, must not be isolated from other animals, and must not be kept in an unnatural, city habitat. The desire—and economic drive—to render the animal usable by declaring the blemish permanent is subordinate to the duty of attempting to cure the animal and, within that duty, of recognizing the influences not only of diet but also of environment and comfort on the efficacy of the medicine.

Feinstein invokes these criteria in his discussion of caged calves: in fact, the passage in *Bekhorot* is the only authority that he cites in objecting to the animals' treatment. He appears to assume that the prohibition of *tza'ar ba'aley chayyim* is well known and does not require explanation; he emphasizes instead the extent of the prohibition, and its priority over economic considerations. Although he does not explicitly extrapolate from the case in *Bekhorot* a duty to treat every domesticated animal with this level of care and concern, and presumably he would permit some animals to be tethered, kept in a city environment, or isolated from other animals for at least limited periods of time, the function of the reference to the case of the blemished calf seems to be to highlight the tradition's understanding of the physical, social, and psychological needs of animals, and to emphasize that these aspects need to be taken into account when considering the range of the prohibition.

Although a comprehensive discussion of *tza'ar ba'aley chayyim* and its application is beyond the scope of this essay, I have tried to show that Levinas's comment in "The Animal Interview"—that we don't want to cause an animal needless suffering—is consistent with an important traditional Jewish value. Given Levinas's familiarity with biblical and rabbinic texts, it would be surprising if the prohibition of *tza'ar ba'aley chayyim* did not inform his thoughts on the matter.

In "The Animal Interview," immediately after stating, "We do not want to make an animal suffer needlessly," Levinas argues that the prototype for this is human ethics.

> Clearly, one [animal] ethics is the transference of the idea of suffering to an animal, certainly. The animal suffers. It is because we as men know what suffering is that we can also have this obligation. (*AI*, 4)

There are two separate ideas that are worth noting in this passage. First, the definitive statement that animals suffer is unremarkable within the context of a discussion of Jewish approaches to animal ethics, as outlined above; however, within the history of Western philosophy, this idea is not taken for granted. Jonathan K. Crane introduced a recent collection of essays on animals as ethical agents with the following critique of Western philosophy (and theology):

> Long have we humans assumed non-human animals to be lowly creatures of scant intelligence whose sentience consists only in base and impulsive reactions. . . . In recent centuries Cartesian thought further severed any ties between the way humans think

about themselves and the way they consider non-human animals. Indeed, Descartes viewed animals primarily (if not completely) as automatons, flesh and viscera responding to stimuli with little if any cognitive activity. For him, bestial nature shared nothing meaningful with human nature beyond the organic.[21]

Maimonides, by contrast, argues that the commandment of *shiluach haken* (sending away the mother bird before taking chicks or eggs) and the prohibition of cooking a calf in its mother's milk, share the same rationale of prohibiting a person from "slaughtering the child in front of the mother's eyes." Maimonides explicitly states that "animals suffer extreme anguish because there is no difference between the anguish felt by a human or an animal; the love of a mother for its child does not come from the cognitive domain" (*Guide of the Perplexed* III: 48).

One potential critique of Jewish animal ethics is the tendency, among many thinkers, to see concern for the animal per se as subordinate not only to human needs, but to the development of specifically interpersonal virtues. Even Maimonides, who, as we have seen, argues that the rationale for specific commandments, such as sending away the mother bird or performing ritual slaughter in the least painful way, is to avoid causing unnecessary suffering to the animal,[22] ultimately sees this behavior in the context of developing human virtue. Schochet argues that, for Maimonides, "kindness toward animals is not an end in itself, but rather a training ground for the perfection of interpersonal relationships" (*AL*, 34).[23]

This leads us to the second idea in Levinas's statement above, namely, that the obligation to avoid causing unnecessary suffering to animals is based on the transference of the idea of suffering from humans to animals. Maimonides's assertion that there is "no difference" between the suffering of a human mother witnessing the slaughter of her child, and that of a cow witnessing the slaughter of her calf, requires the reader to transfer the idea of suffering in the way that Levinas suggests; understanding and empathizing with the predicament of the hypothetical human mother enables us to empathize with the cow. Maimonides also see this value of transference working in the opposite direction: through practicing compassion toward nonhuman animals, in accordance with the teachings of the Torah, a person will refine their own character, becoming less cruel and more compassionate in their treatment of other people.

The discussion in this section has, I hope, demonstrated that some of the key ideas about animal ethics that are expressed by Levinas in "The Animal Interview" are consistent with Jewish tradition in important ways. By way of conclusion, I would like now to return to the question of pedagogy, and consider how Jewish education can contribute to improvements to animal welfare.

Conclusion

Levinas's understanding of Jewish pedagogy—even arguably, of Judaism as a whole—is that it cultivates the development and expression of an ethical subjectivity, of a decentered self which, rather than being egoistic, experiences itself as responsible for the universe. Regardless of whether nonhuman animals are understood to have "faces" in the Levinasian, ethical sense, this responsibility includes compassionate treatment of animals and the prohibition of causing them unnecessary suffering.

Yet for Levinas, this awareness of responsibility for others is not in itself sufficient. One of the functions of the daily practice of Judaism's ritual law (inscribed within the system of texts, teachings and practices) is to discipline one's spontaneity, preparing oneself to set aside one's egoistic needs and desires for the sake of the other. My discussion of animal ethics in Judaism and in Levinas's thought suggests a further development of this understanding of the commandments: the disciplined observance of ritual law should lead to enhanced ethical sensitivity and awareness, both vis-à-vis interpersonal relations and with regard to our treatment of animals; and moral development within either of these spheres should positively impact the other domain. The more sensitive we become to the vulnerability and suffering of other human beings, the more able we should be to "transfer" these ideas of suffering to nonhuman animals; and our concerns for animal welfare should not distract us from, but rather enhance our sensitivity toward, the suffering of other people.[24]

Notes

1. The biblical text in Talmudic times was of course only the unvocalized, consonantal text. The wordplay in the Talmudic text rests on the multiplicity of possible vocalizations, and hence meanings, of a sequence of consonants.

2. Claire Elise Katz, *Levinas and the Crisis of Humanism* (Bloomington: Indiana University Press, 2013), 3. Hereafter cited as *LC*.

3. French original: "La loi rituelle du judaïsme constitue la sévère discipline qui tend vers cette justice. Celui-là seul peut reconnaître le visage d'autrui qui a su imposer une règle sévère à sa propre nature." This appears in the published translation as "The ritual law of Judaism constitutes the austere discipline that strives to achieve this justice. Only this law can recognize the face of the Other which has managed to impose an austere role on its true nature."

4. Levinas does not cite his source but it is a midrash that is quoted in the introduction to *Ein Yaakov*, a fifteenth-century compilation of *aggadic*, that is, nonlegal, material from the Talmud.

5. I have discussed this at greater length in *The Twilight of Jewish Philosophy: Emmanuel Levinas's Ethical Hermeneutics* (London: Routledge, 1999), 38–43.

6. Emmanuel Levinas, "Useless Suffering," translated by Richard Cohen in *The Provocation of Levinas: Re-thinking the Other*, edited by Robert Bernasconi and David Wood (London: Routledge, 1988), 164.

7. Tamra Wright, "Beyond the Eclipse of God: The Shoah in the Thought of Buber and Levinas," in *Levinas and Buber: Dialogue and Difference*, edited by Peter Atterton, Matthew Calarco, and Maurice Friedman (Pittsburgh, PA: Duquesne University Press, 2004).

8. Within rabbinic tradition, the translation of the Hebrew word *tzela* in this verse is contested, with some translating as *rib* and others translating as *face*. For a discussion of this biblical text and its rabbinic interpretations, see Levinas's Talmudic commentary, "And God Created Woman" (*NTR*, 161–77).

9. The discussion that follows, including the translation of the passage from Tanchuma to Genesis, is based on David Fohrman, "The Death of Cain: The World's First Murder," available at http://www.aish.com/jl/b/eb/ca/48950551.html. Excerpted from his *The Beast That Crouches at the Door* (HFBS Publishing, 2012).

10. Elijah Judah Schochet, *Animal Life in Jewish Tradition* (New York: Ktav, 1984), 24. Hereafter cited as *AL*.

11. See, for example, Marc Goldfeder, "Not All Dogs Go to Heaven," in *Beastly Morality: Animals as Ethical Agents*, edited by Jonathan Crane (New York: Columbia University Press, 2015), 73. Hereafter cited as *NAD*.

12. Rashi extends the idea of rest for the animal on the Sabbath; the owner must not only cease engaging the animal in physical labor, but must allow it to "pull up and eat grass from the ground as it pleases," thus, according to Schochet (*AL*, 263), enabling the animal to achieve a "state of inner satisfaction and contentment."

13. This prohibition will be discussed below.

14. Some scholars, however, understand this prohibition primarily within the context of concern about idolatrous practices. See David Novak, *The Image of the Non-Jew in Judaism: An Historical and Constructive Study of the Noahide Laws* (New York: E. Mellen Press, 1983).

15. Joseph B. Soloveitchik, *The Emergence of Ethical Man*, edited by Michael S. Berger (Jersey City, NJ: Ktav for the Toras HoRav Foundation, 2005), p. 36.

16. J. David Bleich, "Vegetarianism and Judaism," *Tradition*, 23, no. 1 (Summer 1987).

17. Schneur Zalman of Liadi, *Likkutei Torah*, *Behaalotecha* 31d, and *Vezot Haberachah* 97d. For an accessible discussion of this theme in Kabbalah and Hasidic thought, see Baruch S. Davidson, "Judaism and Vegetarianism," www.chabad.org/library/article_cdo/aid/858870/jewish/Judaism-and-Vegetarianism.htm.

18. Joseph Albo, *Sefer Ha-Ikkarim*, vol. III, chap. 15.

19. Sarah Toth Stub, "Life after Brisket," *Tablet Magazine*, February 2016; available online at www.tabletmag.com/jewish-life-and-religion/197361/life-after-brisket.

20. *Igrot Moshe, Even Ha'ezer* 4:92. I am grateful to Ian Gamse for pointing out this responsum to me and for his helpful insights.

21. Jonathan K. Crane, "Introduction," in *Beastly Morality: Animals as Ethical Agents* (New York: Columbia University Press, 2016), 4.

22. There is debate within the tradition not only as to the specific rationale for these, and other, commandments, but also whether one should investigate reasons for the commandments at all.

23. However, Maimonides also thought that interpersonal ethics itself was a means to an end; harmonious social existence would enable intellectual contemplation of God.

24. I am grateful to Peter Atterton for his helpful comments on an early version of this essay.

Contributors

Peter Atterton is professor of philosophy and associate dean of the College of Arts and Letters at San Diego State University.

Matthew Calarco is professor of philosophy at California State University, Fullerton.

Jonathan Crowe is professor of law at Bond University.

Sophia Efstathiou is a researcher at the Program for Applied Ethics, in the Department of Philosophy and Religious Studies, Norwegian University of Science and Technology.

Alphonso Lingis is professor emeritus of philosophy at Penn State University.

Katharine Loevy is associate professor of philosophy at Pacific University.

Michael L. Morgan is Chancellor's Professor Emeritus of Philosophy and Jewish Studies at Indiana University.

Bob Plant is an honorary lecturer in the School of Divinity, History and Philosophy at Aberdeen University and is also a psychotherapist.

Brian Shūdō Schroeder is professor and chair of philosophy and director of Religious Studies at Rochester Institute of Technology.

Tamra Wright is director of Academic Studies, London School of Jewish Studies and holds a visiting lectureship at King's College London.

Index

www.ingramcontent.com/pod-product-compliance
Lightning Source LLC
Chambersburg PA
CBHW030357270326
41926CB00009B/1154